The Ultimate Suburban Survivalist Guide

THE SMARTEST MONEY MOVES TO PREPARE FOR ANY CRISIS

Sean Brodrick

WILEY

John Wiley & Sons, Inc.

Published by John Wiley & Sons, Inc., Hoboken, New Jersey.
Published simultaneously in Canada.

For general information on our other products and services or for technical
support, please contact our Customer Care Department within the United States at
(800) 762-2974, outside the United States at (317) 572-3993 or fax (317) 572-4002.

Wiley also publishes its books in a variety of electronic formats. Some content that
appears in print may not be available in electronic books. For more information
about Wiley products, visit our web site at www.wiley.com.

Library of Congress Cataloging-in-Publication Data:

Brodrick, Sean.
    The ultimate suburban survivalist guide: the smartest money moves to prepare
for any crisis / Sean Brodrick.
        p. cm.
    Includes index.
    ISBN 978-0-470-46316-1 (hardback)
    1. Finance, Personal.   2. Saving and investment.   I. Title.
HG179.B7445 2010
332.024—dc22

                                                                2009029127

Printed in the United States of America

10 9 8 7 6 5 4 3 2 1

To my wife, Cindy,
my partner in all things.
And to my children, who,
along with other children,
are the last and best hope of this world.

Contents

Foreword

For many years, the author of this amazing book has been helping show investors how to protect themselves from financial harm and profit from opportunities around the world.

Along the way, he has traveled to far-flung locales from Guanajuato, Mexico, to Labrador, Canada. And he has kept us all informed and entertained with some of the wittiest research I've ever had the pleasure of reading.

In this book, Sean Brodrick takes several giant steps further, giving proactive prescriptions for steps you can take to make your life richer and *safer*. Only this time he's sticking a lot closer to home, by helping you prepare for threats that, in not-so-unlikely worst-case scenarios, could literally strike right in our own backyard.

If you read my book, *The Ultimate Depression Survival Guide*, you learned how to survive and thrive financially. Here, Sean will show you how to survive physically!

We all pray and hope that the scariest of future events will never come to pass. And even in a depression, which could return with a vengeance in years ahead, I remain optimistic that most will not come true! But suppose I'm wrong. Or suppose the forecasts of some of the most reasoned scientists—regarding an influenza pandemic or the impacts of global warming—come true sooner than most of us dream possible.

Then what? Sean will prepare you, and he'll do so *without* ever having to pack up and head for the hills. He's written each chapter like a stand-alone mini-book on each major challenge you face. Together, they form a complete guide for protecting yourself in even the wildest of crazy times.

You'll not only see more clearly the swords of Damocles hanging over our heads, but you'll also learn through the real-life stories of people who learned to cope under similar circumstances.

Worried about the real potential for a swine flu disaster and the resulting drug shortages? This book tells you how to prepare ahead of time and how to use drug alternatives in a pinch.

What would you do if gasoline became unavailable? Sean has multiple answers for you.

If a major disaster hit your neighborhood right now, would you have an emergency bag packed and ready to go? After you read this book, I guarantee you will! All without costing a small fortune or going to extremes!

Sean's book opened my eyes to a whole range of threats (and solutions!) that I had never before considered. I am certain he will do the same for you as well.

As Sean shows us, the solution is not getting rid of our creature comforts or living in caves. It's to take simple, logical, incremental steps towards self-sufficiency and better preparedness. This book tells you what to do, and how to do it. It's intelligent, engaging, and entertaining. Read it now and keep it by your side as a handy reference for years to come.

Martin D. Weiss, PhD
President, Weiss Research, Inc.
Author of the *New York Times* bestseller,
The Ultimate Depression Survival Guide
(published by John Wiley & Sons)

Acknowledgments

Thanks to Martin Weiss, for teaching me about keeping money safe, to Larry Edelson, for teaching me about gold, and to Eric Drawdy, for teaching me about guns. Also, to everyone who agreed to be interviewed for this book—thanks for being so kind with your time. Finally, thanks to caffeine, without which this book would not have been possible, and to wine, for celebrating when the book was finished!

Introduction

The shadow of what comes next looms over the world like a dark cloud of misery brought about by the madness of men.
— Jesse at Le Cafe American

D o you have a pervasive sense of anxiety, as if our modern world is on thin ice? Do you have an uneasy feeling that Wall Street seems to be collapsing under the weight of bad debts and bad decisions—and dragging your job along with it? Or, maybe you feel our society is coming apart at the seams, and that our civilization could actually break down and collapse.

You are not alone. A *lot* of people are worried. In fact, there is a growing movement of people who are preparing for the end of the world as we know it (*TEOTWAWKI*).

Serious survivalists use another acronym, *WTSHTF*, or *when the s**t hits the fan,* to reference the inevitable onslaught of disastrous events that is sure to befall our beloved nation in the near to semi-near future. Some people think after TSHTF, our civilized, cultivated selves will rapidly devolve to radioactive cannibals fighting each other over scraps of meat in the burned-out husks of our cities. These hard-core survivalists move to remote farms where they raise livestock, collect guns and ammo, and prepare for a global oil crisis/financial meltdown/zombie invasion/the end of the world (as we know it).

I want to be prepared, too. However, I'm comfortably ensconced in a twenty-first century lifestyle, and I don't want to give it up.

That said, I know the odds are increasing that my family and I will experience a disaster that will change our lifestyle and maybe even grind the gears of civilization. I'm not just talking about individual house fires or floods that affect neighborhoods. I'm talking about changes on a societal and national level—an economic crash, an energy crisis, terrorism, or even a plague.

A disaster could be any of a number of things, manmade or natural. I believe that yes, the U.S. empire is in decline, and may be on the brink of a catastrophic change. Now, I don't think it will happen all at once. I also don't think our civilization will go down without a fight. Even in the worst-case scenario, I expect there will probably be an initial panic, followed by an attempt at recovery and return to normalcy, and then a bumpy downward spiral. Rome didn't vanish overnight, and neither will today's Western world.

So what can you do if you want to maintain your modern lifestyle *and* you want to be a master of disaster?

The fact is, we *are* living in scary times, and changes are happening more rapidly than anyone would have imagined even six months ago.

Taking this into consideration, there are realistic goals you can set to prepare for dire situations. A few years ago, people who talked about these preparations might have been thought of as the wacky ones with foil hats; now, ordinary people are concerned. The ability to survive on your own for at least a few days after a storm blows through seems elementary, yet even in South Florida, where I live—an area that should be used to hurricanes by now—I've seen people out looking for ice and gallon jugs of water within hours after a storm has passed.

A little self-reliance and independence goes a long way. The scouts always say to *be prepared*—the problem is, we've had a generation or two that have outsourced nearly every single facet of their lives.

But *you* don't have to live that way—not anymore. This book you're now holding in your hands can be your checklist on how to start preparing and your roadmap to peace of mind when a crisis hits. And I'm not talking just storms and power outages—I mean the kind of world-changing crises that keep us awake for more than a night or two.

You can survive a world-threatening disaster, *and* live a healthier lifestyle and *save your money in the here and now*. Here's the best part—you don't have to move to a goat farm in the wilderness to do it.*

---

*This isn't meant as an insult to goat farmers. It's just that this particular lifestyle isn't for me—yet.

And I know it can be done, because my family and I have done much of it already. What we haven't done, friends and trusted sources have done. Preparing and protecting your family *is* possible. You can even prosper at the same time. It's up to you.

Reading this book will prepare you for the worst. So when the s**t hits the fan, you can not only survive but thrive. While you should never deceive yourself about the difficulties you face, neither should you allow yourself to become the prisoner of your own fears.

Being prepared for the bad times means a lot of things: reducing debt, living within your means, storing food, buying survival gear, and more.

This book is for people who are going to prepare as much as possible, but, for reasons of job, family, or social choice, *aren't* going to move to a safe house in a remote, undisclosed location (if you do, say hello to Dick Cheney for me).

The fact is, you can wait a long time for the world to end. You can also buy a ton of specialized gear that you won't use unless the world completely falls apart. Or, you could …

- Just buy the basics you're going to need anyway.
- Change your food shopping habits, building a necessary stockpile of food and saving money in the process.
- Start a garden and load up your table with the healthiest, freshest food you've ever eaten.
- Develop skills that will make you a more self-reliant, well-rounded, and interesting person.
- Develop plans for any kind of emergency that will put you three steps ahead of the general population—also known as *sheeple*—in a panic.
- Position yourself financially to coast through tough economic times and come out on top.

Some financial outlay is called for in this book. But unlike many stocks and bonds pushed by Wall Street, the things I recommend you buy won't see their value go to zero. Indeed, if history is any guide, some will greatly increase in value over time. And some could save your life.

Throughout the book, I'll explain three things:

1. The basics in each area of preparation
2. What my family has done, and what we've learned in the process
3. Where you can go to get more information on each of these topics

Major Disasters

Bad things are going to happen. You know it. You've probably been through temporary situations—blizzards, power grid down for days, water shortages—and are aware of looming worsening situations around us, both potential manmade calamities and natural disasters. Economically, our country slides into recessions now and again. The problem is, this time around, things seem to be much worse than average.

- **Economic Depressions**: The recession that started at the end of 2007 is the worst since World War II, and as bad as the Great Depression by some metrics. Car sales as measured by fleet turnover hit an *all-time low* in 2008. The number of Americans receiving food stamps hit a record. Stock market crash, bank failures, soaring unemployment—all compounded by worries that our economy is on a slippery slope.
- **Natural Disasters**: Whether it's fires raging in Southern California, tornadoes touching down across the Midwest, crippling ice storms in New England, or hurricanes blowing through the Southeast, natural disasters cause temporary cessation of services and life as you know it. And they seem to be becoming more frequent, thanks to global warming.
- **Oil Crisis**: Peak oil—when oil production peaks around the world, which is a prelude to much higher prices—is rushing at us like a runaway train. And we can have energy spikes and shortages long before peak oil really bites. Thanks to our just-in-time delivery system, a fuel shortage will very quickly lead to a food shortage.
- **Food Crisis**: In recent years, the populations of the world's developing countries have been growing about 7% a year, a rapid rate by historical standards. This means that hundreds

of millions more people are getting access to the basics of life, and many people—in China, India, and other emerging countries—are eating *more* food than they used to. That jump in demand is helping to drive up the prices of agricultural commodities and straining global food stockpiles. The 2007 to 2008 harvest-to-harvest year was the third in a row in which the world consumed more grain than it produced.[1] Soon, we could be just one bad harvest away from a global food crisis.

- **Climate Change:** The dramatic changes in our climate are real and are altering our world in unimaginable ways. Global warming has made storms stronger, hurt harvests, and could cause desertification across large swaths of the United States by making water shortages so severe that some cities will have to be evacuated. Sea levels will rise between one and three feet by the end of this century, and temperatures could rise an average of seven degrees Fahrenheit at the same time, making large sections of Africa and Asia uninhabitable. The subsequent mass migration could dump hundreds of millions of immigrants on our shores.[2]

- **Shutdown of large portions of the U.S. energy grid:** The U.S. electrical grid is actually three separate electric networks, covering the East, the West, and Texas. Each includes many thousands of miles of transmission lines, power plants, and substations—a 100-year-old amalgamation of local utilities. Much of it is out of date and prone to breakdowns anyway. More recently, the threat of cyber-attack has reared its ugly head. The growing reliance of utilities on Internet-based communication has increased the vulnerability of control systems to spies and hackers. According to national security experts, cyberspies have penetrated the U.S. electrical grid and left behind software programs that could be used to disrupt the system,[3] and perhaps shut down sections of the grid for a very long time.

- **Civil Unrest**: Rising unemployment is squeezing the working class hard, and strikes and protests could spark into riots. Beyond that, the Department of Homeland Security is warning of increased activity among right-wing domestic anti-government groups, ranging from militia movements to borderline terrorists. These aren't your average tax protestors. Some of them are hell-bent on secession. Others are dupes of the same moneyed interests they are supposedly rebelling against. Homeland Security warns that home foreclosures, unemployment, and other consequences of the economic recession "could create a fertile recruiting environment for right-wing extremists."[4] While the chances of civil war seem remote, it becomes more likely if the federal government runs out of money. There are many ties holding our country together, but the most important one is that the U.S. government can play sugar daddy to the states, dishing out fat federal subsidies every year. If that gravy train ends, some states may decide to unhitch and go their own way.

- **Pandemic**: Our world is increasingly interconnected, which means it's easier for germs to get around. Each and every human being on Earth is a living, breathing germ factory, and there are more people on this crowded planet every year. Compounding the problem, the equipment for genetic engineering has become so commonplace that backyard mad scientists called *biohackers* are tinkering with the building blocks of life, and could easily create new versions of old diseases. The swine flu that seemed to come from nowhere in early 2009 may be a harbinger of much worse to come.

- **Terrorism**: And of course, our favorite boogeyman of the twenty-first century: foreign-based terrorism—dirty bombs, chemical attacks, or some other form of terrorist attack. Think back to the days after 9/11 when many were afraid to leave their houses, people couldn't fly, and businesses closed temporarily. We don't want this to happen again, and we hope the government continues to stop potential terrorists in the fastest legal way they can, but we do have to face the fact that there are nasty people out there who would like to disrupt our lifestyle here in the United States.

Any of these disasters could be catastrophic for our highly complex society, but there's also the potential for a snowball effect: In other words, a global energy crisis could precipitate a financial crisis, which would lead to a food crisis, and perhaps a pandemic. The nightmare scenario is a societal collapse—when a nation or even a civilization breaks down. It's happened many, many times before in human history, and is almost certain to happen again.

The big-picture disasters can be so scary that people don't want to think about them. But by preparing for the smaller-scale disasters: floods, fires, severe storms, and the like—you can take the first steps toward being prepared for the big ones.

The Stages of Collapse

Change is the one constant of the universe. It's when change comes too fast that we see it as chaos. And when chaos engulfs a structured, ordered society, that society can come apart at the seams.

In his book *Reinventing Collapse: The Soviet Example and American Prospects*, which I highly recommend to anyone, Dmitry Orlov looks at the challenges facing the United States through a unique lens. Orlov was born in Leningrad and immigrated to the United States at the age 12. He grew up to become a computer engineer. As the Soviet Union fell apart, Orlov shuttled back and forth between his new home in the United States and his old home behind the fraying Iron Curtain. He came to the conclusion that Russia was in better shape to survive a collapse than the United States, but that their problems hold lessons for us.

Orlov also wrote an article, "The Five Stages of Collapse," which he explains as:

1. Financial collapse
2. Commercial collapse
3. Political collapse
4. Social collapse
5. Cultural ccollapse

Orlov believes the United States is undergoing a financial collapse right now. "Financial institutions become insolvent; savings are wiped out, and access to capital is lost," Orlov writes. Does that sound familiar?

After this comes a commercial collapse, when store shelves are stripped bare of necessities and remain that way for weeks at a time. Hoarding becomes popular.

Political collapse is a breakdown of public order, which Orlov sees as particularly dangerous for the United States because our population is so well armed.

Social collapse is when people lose faith that society will take care of them, and they only look out for themselves and their families and close friends. Finally, in a cultural collapse, even those bonds are shattered.

"If Stage 1 collapse can be observed by watching television, observing Stage 2 might require a hike or a bicycle ride to the nearest population center, while Stage 3 collapse is more than likely to be visible directly through one's own living-room window, which may or may not still have glass in it," Orlov writes.[5]

■ ■ ■

Human history is crowded with the ruins of civilizations that fell apart. And the track record so far is that all civilizations eventually fail; our own is probably not an exception.

What actually makes a society collapse depends on the place, time, and people. In his book, *Collapse: How Societies Choose to Fail or Succeed,* Jared Diamond talks about how, on Easter Island, the inhabitants literally used up their environment. The Vikings of Greenland got clobbered by climate change and their own refusal to adapt.[6]

And a bevy of historians have written about how the Roman Empire, probably the most successful long-running civilization in history, ran afoul of a number of things from changing weather and barbarian incursions to poor economic choices and incompetent rulers.

But apart from catastrophic events, what finally brings any society down? In his landmark book, *The Collapse of Complex Societies,* Joseph Tainter seems to say that a complex society gets more and more complicated until greater and greater investment produces less and less benefit. Finally, the point is reached where investment in complexity no longer brings any increase in benefits. Collapse becomes increasingly probable. At that point, a crisis the society easily weathered earlier in its history—a military loss, drought, resource depletion, and so on—is enough to cause collapse.

Our society is probably the most complex that has ever existed. Bigger and bigger investments in agriculture, medicine, energy, and government are bringing smaller marginal returns.

But all this is still not enough to bring about a civilization's collapse. In Tainter's view, a real collapse only happens in a power vacuum. That is the reason Europe did not collapse long ago—if one country fell, it was taken over by its neighbor—and, according to this line of reasoning, is why the next collapse will be global in scale. Because this time, if one of the leading powers of the world goes down, we're so interconnected that we all go down.

But the worst-case scenario isn't the only scenario. Even Orlov isn't completely pessimistic. In his book, he identifies three progressive stages of response to the looming crisis:

1. Mitigation—alleviating the impact of the coming upheaval
2. Adaptation—adjusting to the reality of changed conditions
3. Opportunity—flourishing after the collapse

In other words, after the collapse of what we've always known, something else can come along, and people can thrive.

Waves of Chaos Will Change the World Around You

Despite the scary scenarios I've outlined so far, I don't think societal collapse is a done deal. I believe we're going to see *waves of chaos* going forward. These chaos waves will trigger disasters and catastrophes that will plunge individuals, groups, and even large populations into situations of great stress—physically, economically, and mentally. These stresses will stretch the fabric of our society to the breaking point. But after a breakdown, the chaos wave will likely recede, and there will be some sort of recovery, perhaps even a return to *normal.*

As I said earlier, Rome didn't fall in a day. It took hundreds of years from when the first wave of barbarians crossed the frontier to when Rome itself was finally conquered. Even then, the Eastern Roman Empire, also known as Byzantium, hung on for hundreds of years more.

But if you were a Roman citizen unlucky enough to be in one of the areas that quickly descended into chaos, it was a world-changing and potentially fatal event.

Even if our civilization is on a slippery slope, I think we're still in the early stages. That means you will have to endure periods of chaos, but then government, law, society, and civilization will reassert themselves—eventually. Your goal—your *duty* if you have children—is to ride through the rough times and come out okay on the other side.

Survive, Thrive, and Discover a More Meaningful Life

The ability to adapt to change will make your life easier, no matter what lies ahead. There are qualities that will make you more successful at changing, and they're qualities for which you might want to strive—because if you're not in the right mental and emotional space, then preparing for potentially catastrophic change will be that much harder.

- You have to be adaptable.
- You have to know what's really important in your life and be prepared to give up or walk away from less important things.
- You have to realize that no person is an island, and you'll get through any emergency better if you work with your neighbors.

The times we are living in now are the richest, fattest days in human history. Life will probably *never* get easier. *This* is when you need to start preparing—right now—for the hard times coming.

Remember, luck favors the prepared, so be prepared and you're more likely to be able to make your own luck. This book you're holding in your hands is a guidebook to what could come next, and what you can do to better prepare for it. Stockpiling, self-sufficiency, and frugality, which I prefer to call *Spartaneity*, are three tools that will help you survive and thrive.

One more thing to keep in mind: The final collapse of the Roman Empire was not bad news for everyone concerned. Archeological evidence indicates that average nutrition actually improved after Rome's collapse in many parts of the former empire. Individuals may have benefited because they no longer had to invest (i.e., be taxed) to pay for the ever-increasing burden of the empire. If you can survive and thrive after a societal collapse, you may be able to find a more meaningful and fulfilling life.

Also, even Tainter doesn't believe collapse is inevitable at any given time. He wrote: "When some new input to an economic system is brought on line, whether a technical innovation or an energy subsidy, it will often have the potential at least temporarily to raise marginal productivity."[7]

If a new technology or energy source comes along, history's wheel can go around for another cycle. That can happen to us, too. The United States and Western civilization as we know it may appear to be coming to a close, but there's no rule written in stone that says calamity has to happen. And that's the great thing about the recommendations in this book. Even if society doesn't collapse, you can use this book to live more efficiently, build up more wealth, and become better prepared for just about any disaster—small- or large-scale.

By now, you are probably thoroughly depressed. Do not put down the book to pick up a drink. If you must, hold the book in one hand and your drink in the other because now is the time for us to review your options ...

So, What are Your Options?

If you are a couch potato sitting there worrying about the end of the world, you have my sympathies. I was once a lot like you. But, then I realized there were some choices I could make:

Option 1: Ignore the Problem. You can sit on that couch until you grow moss, playing Wii and eating take-out food, confident the government will rescue you when a bad thing happens. Good luck! In any of the situations I've now covered briefly, you can't count on the police to rescue you. In the event of a calamity, the odds are they'll find your desiccated corpse surrounded by empty fast-food bags.

Option 2: Move to the *Little House on the Prairie*. Give up the malls and your favorite coffee shop, buy a goat farm, learn to raise beets and cabbage, and surrender all your fun electronics because you don't have enough solar power for an Xbox and a man-sized freezer. More power to you if you can make it work; there are some folks going this route.

Option 3: Become Smarter—a Smart Suburban Survivalist. Stay where you are, enjoy your video games, eat out occasionally, and enjoy your life, while preparing for a variety of potentially disastrous situations. What's more—you can even get richer, happier, and healthier by preparing for these crises. My family is doing it. Some of our friends are doing it. So can you.

The great unknown is the future. We can't know what will happen. You have to look ahead, and prepare for what you can't see as well as what you can see.

Getting prepared costs money, and it's *easy* to overspend if you start getting overly scared. Luckily, this book is designed for people who want to learn how they can stretch a dollar and prepare as economically as possible.

Choosing to Plan Over Panic

To quote the late author Douglas Adams, *DON'T PANIC.* Brain and behavior studies clearly show that when information is scarce and threats seem imminent, people often stop listening to their own logic and look to see what others are doing.

That's why, in a panic, we have things like riots and ordinary citizens doing smash-and-grabs at the grocery store, pharmacy, and sporting goods store. And you'll hear about people who go out to get supplies for their family because the television tells them that everyone is doing it and then they get hurt, or worse.

This book is designed to separate you from the herd—from the mass of *sheeple* who are going to see their gooses cooked in a real collapse.

If you follow the tips in this book, you'll have a well-stocked pantry so you don't have to fight the mob for the last can of Spam at the grocery store. You'll have batteries and flashlights or an alternate power source if the grid goes out, and at least a week's worth of water tucked away so you don't even have to leave the house if the water supply is interrupted. Your home will be strengthened against the roving bands of thieves and thugs who tend to spring up in dire situations. You'll be able to *sit tight.* And that can make the difference between surviving and being a statistic.

What's more, you'll have plans in place to make a fast exit to a safer area if things get too dangerous.

But supposing you always find it tough to get organized, or to commit to long-term plans. Then you'll find a section at the end of each chapter called "The Least You Can Do," which will list, literally, the *least* you can do to store food, become a better shopper, have your house supplied with food and other essentials, get your finances in order, and more.

Let's start by looking at the disasters you are most likely to experience in this lifetime.

PART

I

THE END OF THE WORLD
AS WE KNOW IT

CHAPTER

The Most Likely Disasters You'll Face

This awful catastrophe is not the end but the beginning. History does not end so. It is the way its chapters open.

—St. Augustine

Sometimes we worry so much about the big disasters that could overtake us—an energy crisis, global financial meltdown, famine, or pandemic—that we don't prepare for smaller-scale disasters that can still be devastating on a personal or local level. Local disasters will turn your life upside down, but most Americans will watch them with only passing interest, and perhaps even indifference.

The two disasters you're most likely to face are fire and flood—it's as simple as that. And yet, most people are completely unprepared for them when they happen. If you do nothing else, skim over these next few pages and write down some notes on what you *should* do. Importantly, by preparing for fire and flood, you are also starting to prepare for the big, movie-of-the-week disasters that may be coming.

In this chapter, I'll give you some facts on fires and floods, how to prepare for them, what to do when they happen to you, and some useful web sites. Then we'll also look at two disasters that could have global impact—an energy crisis and a food crisis.

Two *Ordinary* Calamities

As mentioned previously, there are two ordinary disasters that we will likely face in our lifetime—fire and flood.

Fire

Deadly fires can start in anyone's home; in fact, there are about 400,000 residential fires in the United States annually. Modern building materials make homes *more flammable*, not less, so the risks of you having a serious fire are actually rising.

Common places where fires start are the kitchen, laundry room, or fireplace. From 1999 to 2002, 60,000 house fires started due to the improper cleaning or lack of cleaning of washers and dryers. As for fireplaces and chimneys, they cause more fires than oft-maligned space heaters.

Careless smoking causes 15,000 fires a year. And even Christmas trees get in on the action—200 residential fires each year are caused by Christmas trees. But the biggest single cause of *careless* house fires is candles. Candles alone cause 18,000 home fires every year.

There is good news. Deaths from home fires have decreased by 50% since the 1970s because of public education and the widespread use of smoke alarms. But the candle fire problem has been growing. Half of candle fires are caused by combustible materials coming too close to candles. A whopping 44% of candle fires begin in the bedroom.

How to Prepare.   Experts say 80% of all candle fires can be eliminated by four basic safety precautions:

1. Never leave a burning candle unattended.
2. Keep candles away from things that can catch fire.
3. Keep candles away from children and pets.
4. Place candles on secure, heat-resistant surfaces (like ceramic bowls), which will not transmit heat to the furniture on which they are placed.

You should always have a fire extinguisher in your bedroom. Also have at least one for every floor of the house, and the one in the kitchen should be able to put out grease fires.

Wildfires

Peak season for wildfires runs from April through October. Annually, wildfires claim hundreds of thousands of acres, resulting in the evacuation of millions of people. Thousands of homes go up in flames, causing damage estimated in the billions of dollars.

How to prepare: Remove dead branches and trim all trees and shrubs. Cut back trees near your home and roof. Clean gutters and remove debris from your roof. Store firewood at least 30 feet from your home.

A wildfire is a case when you want to plan and practice an *evacuation plan* from your home and neighborhood that includes primary and secondary routes. Ask someone out of state to be your *family contact* in case people are separated, and be sure everyone knows the contact's address and phone number.

Make sure every adult (and the bigger kids) in the house knows how to use the fire extinguisher; hold fire drills. Also, you need smoke detectors on every floor of the house and outside all sleeping areas.

Flood

Flooding is the United States' *most common natural disaster*, and caused more than $7.1 billion in property damage in the 10-year period leading up to Hurricane Katrina (Katrina alone caused more than $81 billion in damages). Flooding occurs in all 50 states, and not just in those areas considered to be at high risk for floods and other disasters. In fact, one in four flood insurance claims is submitted by someone who lives in a low or moderate flood risk zone.[1]

To find out if you live in a high-risk or a low-risk zone, go to http://www.floodsmart.gov and type in your address and zip code. This will tell you the general flood risk of your area.

How to Prepare.   Here's what you can do to prepare for the risk of flood:[2]

- Buy flood insurance coverage. Homeowners insurance doesn't cover flooding. It takes 30 days for a policy to go into effect, so don't wait. You can obtain flood insurance through the

National Flood Insurance Program, from your insurance agent. To find an agent near you call 1-800-427-2419.

- Stay alert during stormy weather. Listen and watch for thunder and lightning. Heavy rain upstream could send a flash flood your way without you even feeling a drop of rain.

- Know your local area. If you live near a dam, keep away from areas downstream of the dam when heavy rains hit. If the dam is breached, this can result in a flash flood. Also, know where the streams and rivers in your area run and locate safe zones of higher ground nearby.

- Take care of your property. Take photos or videos of important possessions. This documentation will help you in filing a flood insurance claim. You might want to store these photos on the Web or in a fire-and-flood proof container. Finally, make a list of items you might want to move as high as possible in the case of a flood, and move them.

- Avoid driving into water more than two feet deep. Nearly half of the deaths associated with flash floods involve vehicles. As little as two feet of moving water can easily carry away most cars and trucks. Abandon your car immediately if it stalls in water, and head for higher ground.

- Elevate your furnace, water heater, washer, and dryer. Admittedly, this involves a bit more effort than a couch potato is likely to exert, but if you're in a flood-prone area, consider it. It could save you a *lot* of money in the long run.

- As with fires, when dealing with floods it's good to plan and practice a flood evacuation route, and have an out-of-state person as your emergency family contact.

Lastly, if you live in an area like New Orleans that could be flooded by waters higher than your rooftop, consider doing two things:

1. Keep a crowbar, hammer, chisel, saw, and other heavy-duty tools, as well as a flashlight, up in your attic. If rising waters chase you up into the attic, you need some way to cut your way out.

2. This last tip isn't cheap, but you can also buy a life raft that stows in its own suitcase. You can buy a four-person emergency life raft that never needs recharging for $1,150 at http://tinyurl.com/c2gzo2, and you can Google for other options.

If I lived in a below-sea-level area like New Orleans, I might keep one of these in my garage.

Two Crises That Will Rock Your World

Now that we have looked at two ordinary disasters that can affect you regionally, let's explore two global crises you might face in more detail—energy and food. We'll also look at some smart ways you can prepare for them without moving to a goat farm.

Energy Crisis: America is Running on Empty

Our civilization runs on oil. If the oil stops flowing tomorrow morning, life as we know it starts to crumble tomorrow night. There is no economy without energy, no transportation besides your own two feet, and no communication beyond the sound of your voice.

Here are some facts that keep me awake at night:

- The United States only has 4.8% of the world's population, but consumes about 25% of the world's daily oil use.
- The United States has 3% of the world's known oil resources (there could be more in offshore fields or locked under ice in Alaska), but pumps about 7% of the world's production. In other words, we are depleting our resources faster than other parts of the world.
- Since the mid-1980s, oil companies have been finding less oil than Americans have been consuming.
- Of the 65 largest oil producing countries in the world, up to 54 have passed their peak of production and are now in decline, including the United States.
- The world uses a billion barrels of oil every 12 days. We don't find one-tenth of that. The peak of world oilfield discoveries already occurred way back in 1965.

We are on a collision course with an oil crisis, and would be in even worse shape than we are now if the recession of 2008 hadn't downshifted the world's oil use—for a while, anyway.

Bottom line: We don't have enough oil to meet our own needs and we cannot drill our way out of this. Pullbacks in oil prices are likely very temporary, and will also likely lead to even *higher* surges in oil prices—perhaps sharper than anything we've seen so far.

Lower oil prices in 2008 lead to droves of oil projects being shuttered in 2009. Non-OPEC oil production probably fell by 2.5 million barrels per day in 2009. A drop that steep, combined with OPEC cuts, could more than make up for the steep fall in global oil demand. In fact, experts say non-OPEC supply should continue to drop in 2010, losing an additional 460,000 barrels a day.

How the Next Oil Crisis Could Be Different—Supply. The high oil prices of 2008 deflated like a blown tire, and previous oil crises—in 1973 and 1979—also ended eventually. Maybe so, but things change.

U.S. oil production peaked in 1970 at about 9.6 million barrels a day. In 1973, we imported about 3.1 million barrels a day. So when the Arabs cut off our imported oil, it hurt, but we could adjust.

Today, the import to domestic production ratio has flipped; we import about two-thirds of our oil. So, when people say we're *addicted to oil*, that's only part of the problem. The real problem is we're addicted to *foreign* oil—much more so than in the past. (See Figure 1.1.)

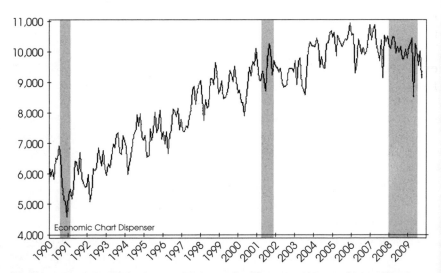

Figure 1.1   Total U.S. Crude Oil Imports (thousand barrels per day)
Source: Economagic.com.

We saw U.S. oil imports drop in 2008 and 2009 due to the recession. Oil imports have dropped every time we've had a recession. And every time the recession ends, oil imports go right back up.

In the 1970s, OPEC slapped an embargo on oil shipments as punishment for U.S. support of Israel (in 1973, Israel and Egypt fought the Yom Kippur War). The reason for oil stoppage was political and artificial. However, it caused real conservation in the United States. By 1979, virtually all the big *full-size* American cars were downsized. When the Iranians turned off the taps, it didn't hurt nearly as much as the first oil crisis.

And it went beyond cars. Conservation became the buzzword across the United States. President Jimmy Carter installed solar panels and a wood burning stove at the White House. Carter's energy saving measures were promptly trashed by Ronald Reagan when he took office, as the energy crisis receded in the rear-view mirror.

But America's conservation proved to be OPEC's undoing. When they wanted to sell oil again, we didn't need as much of it. And without U.S. demand, oil prices plummeted.

This time around, the demand growth isn't limited to the United States or even the Western world. There are 10 million new cars and trucks hitting the road this year in China alone, and millions more joining traffic jams in India and other emerging markets. OPEC is starting to realize that because of this new demand, they need us a lot less than we need them.

The stark differences between supply/demand then and now explain only part of the uncharted territory we are now navigating. Here are five other forces:

1. **Accelerating decline in net oil exports.** The *Export Land Model,* or ELM, is a theory proposed by Jeffrey Brown and others associated with TheOilDrum.com, an excellent site for information on the oil crisis. (See Figure 1.2.) Unfortunately for U.S. consumers, more and more evidence is showing the ELM oil prophecies to be painfully true.

   The ELM says that, after a country's oil production peaks, it will decline at a 5% annual rate at the same time that local consumption increases by 2.5%. Add the production decline and consumption increase together and the decline in a country's net exports will reach zero, nine years after peak

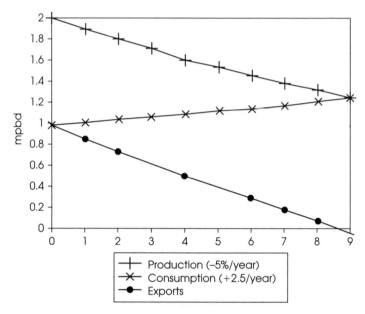

Figure 1.2   Export Land Model

Source: TheOilDrum.com.

production. After that, the former exporter becomes an importer.

We've seen this model hold true in the United States, China, Great Britain, and Indonesia. For example, China went from a net exporter in 1993 to importing four million barrels a day today—with those imports projected to rise another 50% over the next 10 years.

The real problem is that many of the world's exporters are now at their peaks. And that means much higher prices are on the horizon.

2. **Catastrophic decline in Mexico.** Mexican oil production is falling off a cliff. Crude oil production at Mexico's super-giant Cantarell oil field plunged 16.8% in 2008 from 2007. What's more, output at Cantarell was expected to decline by 28%—about 750,000 barrels of oil per day—by the end of 2009. Overall, Mexico's output should decline by 10% to 11% at the same time. Mexico produced 2.79 million barrels of oil a day in 2008.

Speaking to an energy conference in Houston, Pemex Chief Jesus Reyes Heroles said: "The decline of Cantarell and other mature fields will imply a loss of production with respect to today of 1.1 million barrels per day by 2012 and 1.8 million bpd by 2017."

Mexico is now the third-largest supplier of oil to the United States, according to the EIA, a drop from their prior spot at number two. We should really worry when one of our top suppliers goes into an oil crash.

Mexican President Felipe Calderon would like nothing better than to open up the Mexican energy sector to outside investment, but he faces stiff opposition in that country's legislature. Meanwhile, the Mexican government's battles with drug gangs are a civil war in all but name, so he's a bit distracted from pursuing energy initiatives.

Mexico does have a new field called Ku-Maloob-Zaap, but it is not enough to offset the failure at Cantarell. Importantly, the decline at Cantarell has been worse than the worst of the government estimates.

Mexico is a country in crisis. In the Joint Operating Environment 2008 report issued by the U.S. military's Joint Forces Command,[3] Mexico and Pakistan were listed the most likely states to collapse in the immediate future. One is our third-largest supplier of oil; the other has nukes. *Both* should be serious causes for concern. If Mexico implodes, it could destabilize our economy.

3. **Resource Nationalism will tighten the screws.** Americans sometimes act like other countries are sitting on *our* oil, and as such, they have a duty to provide it to us as quickly and cheaply as possible. But more and more countries are realizing *their* oil is a national treasure, and they're starting to sell as little of it as possible at the highest prices they can. It's called Resource Nationalism and it is bad news for U.S. consumers.

Here's why:
- In Venezuela, President Hugo Chavez's nationalization crusade has forced out two of the world's largest energy companies. In addition, the OPEC nation is preparing a *windfall* oil tax to boost its share of profits from its fields.
- In Russia, Vladimir Putin has used hook and crook to bring more than half of his country's oil industry under state control, grabbing properties and projects from large foreign oil companies in the process.

- Saudi oil executive Sadad Al-Husseini was quoted as saying: "There has been a paradigm shift in the energy world whereby oil producers are no longer inclined to rapidly exhaust their resource for the sake of accelerating the misuse of a precious and finite commodity. This sentiment prevails inside and outside of OPEC countries, but has yet to be appreciated among the major energy-consuming countries of the world."

The reality is that national oil companies control 94% of the world's conventional oil and gas reserves. And they'll want more control in the years to come.

When it comes to bargaining chips, the United States is sitting at the table with a pair of twos, and there are others at the table with full houses, aces high. And they *aren't* our friends.

4. **Oil demand is climbing with global population.** Everyone in the Third World wants to live and drive like big, fat Americans. The global recession may have slowed them down, but both India and China, to name two examples, are still adding drivers at a furious pace. In 2008, emerging markets combined (China, India, Russia, and their other *life in the fast lane* buddies) passed the United States in oil use. Going forward, global oil consumption is expected to keep climbing even as U.S. consumption eases. After all,

- Americans each use 25 barrels of oil per year.
- The Chinese each use 2 barrels of oil per year.
- And the folks in India each use just 1 barrel of oil per year.

Where do you think the growth is going to come from? The rest of the world wants to live and drive like Americans!

And there are simply more people all the time—6.7 billion of us at last count. And with a growth rate of 1.17%, the world's population in 2030 is expected to be double that of 1980, or 8 billion people.

I don't think we'll get to 8 billion, for the simple reason that we wouldn't have 6.7 billion if it weren't for how fossil fuels (oil and natural gas) have allowed our agricultural output to boom. And with oil production hitting a peak and about to decline, agricultural production won't be far behind.

Oil first entered general use around 1900 when the global population was about 1.6 billion. Since then, the population has quadrupled. That's not a coincidence.

5. **Peak Oil is going to hit like a ton of bricks.** Peak Oil doesn't mean *running out of oil*, but rather oil production *hitting a peak*. That's because we are rapidly running out of cheap and plentiful oil, and the oil we have left is harder to get and therefore much more expensive.

Inexpensive oil supports our very way of life, as we know it. It is crucial for our transportation, food production, economy, and basically everything that we use on a daily basis. Again, if we ran out of oil tomorrow morning, our civilization would end tomorrow night.

I don't think we're going to run out of oil. I think it will be used in some form in our grandchildren's day. But in the long run, it's going to get a lot more expensive—probably so expensive that we will have to seriously change our way of life, or have change forced on us.

All in all, it's a recipe for much higher prices. As long as the world's civilization runs on oil, we'll pay whatever it costs. There are alternatives to oil, but they aren't ready yet.

Oil prices went down in 2008—great! But when prices go lower, oil companies (1) stop their high-cost production and (2) stop looking for more oil. So, cheaper oil prices just lay the groundwork for the next oil shock.

And what does that mean? That means that sometime in your future . . .

Gasoline prices will go much higher. As in, high enough to cause a severe economic disruption and send the country sliding into a recession, or worse.

Get used to bumpy roads. Roads are paved with asphalt, and that requires oil. The last surge in oil prices sent paving bills soaring by about 25%, so cities and states are cutting back on needed roadwork. That means more potholes as you drive back and forth to work—that is, if you still have a job.

Your neighborhood will have a lot of empty homes. An oil crisis will bring an economic crisis, and that will be bad news for already strapped U.S. consumers and homeowners. Higher fuel prices are going to squeeze consumers mercilessly, worsening this problem, and perhaps even *doubling* the number of Americans kicked out of their homes.

Prepare for heating oil shock. Heating oil prices could double. If you heat with natural gas, you won't be spared—an energy crunch could send the price of nat-gas much higher as well.

Prepare for rolling blackouts. Our national power grid runs on natural gas and coal (and some nuclear power), so it might sound safe, but think again. Our natural gas supply is under threat, and it could be devastating for the American way of life.

Brace yourself for higher food prices. If oil and gas become more expensive, food costs will go along for the ride.

These are just *some* of the changes you may face as oil spirals higher. And the rise in oil prices might *not* be gradual. There are a number of triggers that could send oil prices skyrocketing overnight.

Four Forces That Could Cause the Next Oil Spike. Let's look at four wildcards that could cause an oil price spike—a sharp, sudden movement in oil prices. They include an Islamist takeover of Saudi Arabia, a confrontation with Iran, an al-Qaeda attack on U.S. oil facilities, and potential killer hurricanes in the Gulf of Mexico.

1. **Islamist takeover of Saudi Arabia:** The threat of militant Islamic attacks on Saudi oil facilities seems to have eased for now. But in recent years, the Saudis have had managing expectations of future capacity heading steadily downwards. All in all, Saudi Arabia is a mixed bag, and still has potential to have an explosive effect on oil prices.

2. **A confrontation with Iran:** The United Nations nuclear watchdog has warned that a military strike on Iran to prevent it from developing atomic weapons would turn the region into a *fireball.* Iran would probably use both the threat of blocking the flow of oil out of the Gulf and an actual sharp reduction

of its exports of oil to spike the price of oil. And that would almost certainly send prices spiking.

3. **An al-Qaeda attack on U.S. oil facilities:** Al-Qaeda seems disorganized, demoralized, and downright unpopular in much of the Muslim world. However, it remains very popular in so-called U.S. ally Pakistan, where a secret agreement between the Pakistani government and certain tribes allows al-Qaeda-linked militants to remain in North Waziristan. If al-Qaeda launches another attack on the United States, our energy infrastructure would be a likely target.

4. **Hurricanes:** The Gulf of Mexico is home to 40% of the United States' refining capacity, along with 20% of the natural gas and 30% of the oil produced in the United States. Hurricanes Katrina and Rita proved that the Gulf of Mexico is America's soft underbelly, vulnerable to a devastating punch from Mother Nature during hurricane season.

   Category 5 systems, such as Hurricane Katrina at its peak over the Gulf of Mexico, have winds greater than 155 mph. And while offshore platforms have been reinforced since hurricanes wreaked havoc in the Gulf of Mexico's *Energy Alley*, all it would take is one bad storm in the wrong place to still swamp refineries or even knock out the Louisiana Offshore Oil Port (LOOP), which is connected to 50% of U.S. refinery capacity.

How to Prepare. Basically, in a major energy crisis, you'll have to find alternative forms of transportation. Your job is at risk, food could become scarce, and civil unrest could break out in more urban areas. If you live in a northern climate, you could freeze to death. If you live in the Sunbelt, you run a higher risk of disease and heat stroke.

There are ways to prepare for these things:

- Stay plugged in to the local news. If you are on the Web and use Google, set news alerts for fuel shortages and gasoline shortages.
- If you're not the kind of complete idiot who could accidentally blow yourself up with a can of gasoline, get some jerry cans—cans specifically designed to store gasoline.

I recommend you only fill them when you hear that fuel shortages are beginning. *See Chapter 10 for more on storing gaso line and alternate transportation.*

What About a Long-Term Oil Collapse?

There is a nation that is living through Peak Oil right now. When the Soviet Union collapsed in 1990, Cuba's economy went into a tailspin—85% of its trade disappeared. Cuba's imports of oil were cut by more than half and its imports of food fell by 80%.*

Transportation ground to a halt. Without a substitute for fossil fuels used in large-scale farming, agricultural production plummeted. People went hungry—the average daily caloric intake in Cuba dropped by a third—and the average Cuban lost 30 pounds.

There were frequent blackouts in Cuba's oil-fed electric power grid, up to 16 hours per day. This went on for years! Without power, refrigeration didn't work. Without refrigeration, food spoiled and the food crisis became even more acute.

But it wasn't the end of the world. Cubans started to grow local organic produce out of necessity, developed biopesticides and bio-fertilizers as petrochemical substitutes, and incorporated more fruits and vegetables into their diets. Today an estimated 50% of Havana's vegetables come from inside the city, while in other Cuban towns and cities, urban gardens produce from 80% to more than 100% of their food.

Since they had no fuel for their cars, they walked, biked, rode buses, and carpooled. Cubans are also replacing petroleum-fed machinery with oxen, and their urban agriculture reduces food transportation distances.

Today, Cuba's life expectancy is the same as in the United States, and infant mortality is below that in the United States. The literacy rate in Cuba is the same as in the United States.

Despite the peak oil crisis, Cuba maintained its free medical system, one of the major factors that helped them to survive.

The Cubans showed an amazing ability to adapt, had a government that was willing to try anything in pursuit of long-term goals, and the people pulled together as a nation and in local communities to take care of each other. Will the United States, a much more car-focused, *me*-oriented society, be able to make that transition? Without violence? Maybe.

*Megan Quinn, "The Power of Community: How Cuba Survived Peak Oil, "Global Public Media, Feb. 25, 2006, http://globalpublicmedia.com/articles/657.

But Cuba's adaptation still doesn't make it a place you'd want to live. Along with a repressive government, it still has plenty of problems, many of which have been worsened by the fuel crisis.

And Cuba isn't immune from the global economic crisis, either. Lines are getting longer in Cuba, electricity is being cut back, and food rations are getting smaller.

The Cubans are to be congratulated for not letting their fuel crisis spiral into a severe food crisis. In contrast, the United States—a nation that is designed around the automobile—is almost guaranteed to see a fuel crisis turn into a food crisis.

A University of Michigan study in 2000 states that every calorie of food energy consumed in the United States embodies over seven calories of non-food energy. Other studies place the ratio at 10 calories of energy for 1 calorie of food.

What's more, the food on your dining table travels an average 1,200 miles to get there. Along with wheat from Iowa and potatoes from Idaho, we eat Granny Smith apples from South Africa, bananas from Honduras, and grapes from Chile.

Now, we give the world back much more than we get. Agriculture in Europe, America, and Australia produces 80% of the world's wheat exports, and 86% of corn exports. If oil and gasoline prices continue to climb, those exports will start to fall. And that could be the difference between life and death for two billion chronically malnourished people in the world.

- Look into alternatives to heat or cool your house. Depending on your locale, climate, and financial situation, a woodstove or solar backup might be a worthy investment.
- Have a month's worth of food on hand. I can't emphasize enough that if we have an extreme fuel shortage, your local supermarket is probably going to run out of food *very* quickly.

Now for the good news: I don't think we're going to run out of gasoline overnight, and I think we'll see a lot of mini-shortages before a major fuel emergency starts. Our energy supply lines are more resilient than you might think. But a mini-shortage can happen after any natural disaster. So it's best to be prepared.

Food Crisis—The Era of Cheap Food Is Over

Over the past eight years, the price of food worldwide has increased 75%; the price of wheat has gone up a dramatic 200%.[4]

And the rate of inflation is accelerating. In a recent report, the United Nations predicted that food prices are likely to remain high for a decade.

Here are some facts:

- As of December 2008, 37 countries faced food crises, and 20 had imposed some sort of food-price controls.
- The prices of the world's three main grains—rice, wheat, and corn—have more than doubled in the past year.
- Part of rising food prices is due to rising fuel prices—as the Saudis raise the price of the oil they sell us, we're going to be raising the price of wheat we sell them.
- Another part of the equation is weather. Extreme weather shifts over the past two years have reduced the worldwide wheat harvest by nearly 10%. And it's not just wheat. Since 1971, in the United States, droughts or floods have wiped out up to a third of the Midwest corn crop four times.
- Wheat production in South America and Western Europe has been cut from 5% to 20% in each of the past two growing seasons.
- Australia was once the second-largest exporter of grain, harvesting about 25 million tonnes in a good year. But the worst drought in a century reduced the crop to only 9.8 million tonnes in 2006 and 13.1 million tonnes in 2007.

Now, this year could be different. If good weather holds, we could see record crops that would send prices tumbling.

On the other hand, people in China and India are changing their diets, eating more and better food.

- The Chinese ate just 44 pounds of meat per capita in 1985. They now eat over 110 pounds a year. Each pound of beef takes about seven to 10 pounds of grain to produce, which puts even more pressure on grain prices.
- In fact, over the next decade, according to tentative U.N. and OECD forecasts made in February, the price of corn could rise 27%, oilseeds like soybeans by 23%, and rice by 9%.

- U.S. consumers know that food prices are already rising. The Bureau of Labor Statistics reports that ground beef, milk, chicken, apples, tomatoes, lettuce, coffee, and orange juice are among the staples that cost more these days.

Overall, food prices rose nearly 5% a year in 2007 and 2008. And this is already having an effect. A survey by the Food Marketing Institute showed the average number of weekly shopping trips falling below two per household for the first time.[5] Food banks are seeing increases in their overall client loads.

If things worsen, we'll probably see food riots. Americans rioted over food in the Great Depression,[6] with the former middle class smashing the windows of grocery stores and grabbing everything they could lay their hands on.

Could that happen again? Yes! The U.S. food supply is more vulnerable than ever, due partly (or mostly, depending on your point of view) to the Green revolution—the advances in agriculture that allowed more and more food to be grown by less and less people, usually at a cost of more and more energy.

Energy consumption by agriculture has increased 100 times, or more. According to 1994 data, 400 gallons of oil equivalents are expended annually to feed each American. The energy consumption breaks down as follows:

30%   for the manufacture of inorganic fertilizer
18%   for the operation of field machinery
15%   for transportation
12%   for irrigation
 7%   for raising livestock (not including animal feed)
 5%   for crop drying
 5%   for pesticide production
 8%   miscellaneous[7]

These estimates don't include the energy used in packaging, refrigeration, transportation to retail outlets, and cooking.

At the same time, the vast majority of Americans have gotten further and further away from their food sources. Many Americans have never been to a real farm. End result of all this—some depressing facts about Americans and food:

- 1% of the U.S. population grows all of the food for all Americans.[8]
- Most Americans know essentially nothing about where the food they eat every day comes from, and they don't want to know. All they know is it's cheap, it's as close as their local store, and it's there in enormous quantities.
- Nothing is stored for very long in a supermarket, but then, with just-in-time inventory, nobody stores anything. Grain is produced and stored in the Midwest and shipped daily to the rest of the United States.
- Again, the lion's share of grain produced in the United States comes from a concentrated part of the Midwest—Missouri, Illinois, Iowa, and Kansas—and moved to the coasts, where two-thirds of Americans live, by only two railroads. The bulk of the food we eat comes from grain. Half of what a meat animal is raised on is grain so when you eat meat you are really eating grain, primarily corn. The grain our food animals eat is not produced where the cows and pigs are located.
- The system we have now is a huge contrast to what the United States did up until the 1980s. At one time, up to a year's worth of grain was stored in elevators around the country. But now, very little is stored. We produce what we consume each year. So what's plan B if something goes wrong? *There is no plan B.*

This disconnect between modern American life and our food source will likely prove deadly in a real energy crisis or another emergency that disrupts our national transportation system or food supply.

Heck, in order for riots to break out the whole food supply doesn't have to be wiped out. It just has to be threatened sufficiently. And if heavily armed Americans start to panic about food, there won't be enough police and National Guard to hold the line between order and chaos.

How to Prepare.   The devastating potential of a food shortage is why having your own food storage is so important. For more on that, see Chapter 4. Long-term food storage is daunting, so start with building up just a week's supply of food and water for everyone in your household. If even a week is too big of a task for you to tackle, just work on gathering three days' supply of food. If you have three days' worth of food in emergency storage, plus whatever you have in your cupboard, you'll be way ahead of most of the semi-conscious land mammals on your block.

I also recommend you grow a garden; we'll cover that in Chapter 8. Most U.S. gardens are only 100 square feet in size. That's not enough to feed your family, but it is plenty enough to make your emergency rations palatable as you wait for normal life—or whatever comes next—to be restored.

These disasters that I've outlined here may still seem a little esoteric. You might be thinking, civilized people don't *really* have to worry about living through a societal collapse, do they? In the next chapter, we'll look at a couple of real-life stories of people who did just that—in the societal chaos of post-Katrina New Orleans and the economic and civil chaos of Argentina.

The Least You Can Do

- Learn and follow the basic fire safety precautions explained in this chapter.
- Keep fire extinguishers in your bedroom and kitchen.
- Make sure you have working smoke detectors for every floor of the house.
- Buy flood insurance coverage and stay alert during stormy weather.
- Stock up on extra food now, before an emergency strikes.

CHAPTER 2

The Quick and the Dead—
and the Survivors

*If you have a major disaster involving hundreds of thousands, or
in this case millions of people, whether it be a natural disaster or an
act of terrorism, the first 72 hours are going to be totally chaotic no
matter what you plan to do.*
—Senator Warren Rudman, on Hurricane Katrina

You can learn a lot from people who have been through
WTSHTF. And yes, it *can* happen to *you*! In this chapter, you'll
read about how a man saw society fall apart in New Orleans after
Hurricane Katrina—and had to struggle to save his dogs *and* escape
from a government-run detention camp. His experience has valuable lessons for all of us. Also, we'll take a look at how a journalist
in Argentina coped with that country's snowballing economic, currency, and social crisis, and what he learned from it all.

Hurricane Katrina—*Then Everything Went to Hell*

"During Katrina, I saw the total breakdown of civilization," Katrina
survivor Michael Homan told me. "I've seen it before in war zones
in my travels, but never here—it was terrifying."

In 2005, a hurricane named Katrina sideswiped Florida, killing nine
people, before heading on to the Gulf of Mexico. I live in Florida but
can barely remember Katrina, because her impact in Florida didn't

hold a candle to the storms in 2004 that shook us from floor to rafters: storms including Ivan, Charlie, Frances, and Jean.

By the time Katrina got through with New Orleans and the surrounding areas, it wasn't just the story of a storm. It became a story of government breakdown, detention camps, food shortages, looters, vigilantes, and more.

On Saturday, August 27th, 2005, the citizens of Louisiana knew that Katrina would stomp their way. The low-lying parishes south of New Orleans ordered mandatory evacuations. But even though she was a Category 3, New Orleans Mayor Ray Nagin only called for a voluntary evacuation.

By Sunday, Katrina strengthened into a Category 5, and Mayor Nagin made the evacuation mandatory. Still, many people in New Orleans didn't evacuate.

For many, staying put was a matter of money—they barely scraped by as it was and didn't have the cash to get out of the way. Others flat-out refused to evacuate because of what happened a year earlier, when they fled the path of Hurricane Ivan. The roads from New Orleans to Baton Rouge became clogged; a trip that normally takes 90 minutes took as long as 10 to 12 hours. People went hungry, ran out of gas, and worse just trying to get out of town. And then Ivan didn't live up to the fears. So, for many, the evacuation process had proved to be worse than the storm.

In the wee hours of Monday, August 29, 2005, as Katrina approached, strong winds were lashing New Orleans. The storm made its landfall at 6:10 A.M. as a Category 3 storm.

By 8:14 A.M., officials knew the city was in trouble—a levee breached at the Industrial Canal. By 9 A.M., there were six to eight feet of water in the lower ninth ward. By 11 A.M., the water was more than 10 feet deep in many places. At the same time, more levee breaches were confirmed. And by then, people were already drowning by the hundreds.

And That Brings Us to Michael Homan's Story . . .

Mr. Homan still lives in New Orleans about 20 miles from the Louisiana coast. At the time of the storm, his family was in Mississippi, but he decided to ride out the storm with his dogs. His house took some damage—the high wind blew so hard that the first-floor walls ended up permanently askew. In the morning, he walked around outside and talked to his neighbors, and it seemed the worst was over. Five hours later, foot-deep flood waters had invaded his home. Over the next 36 hours, the water kept rising. By Tuesday evening there was eight feet of water in the street, and the ground floor of Mr. Homan's house was under three feet of water.

Faced with a flood and lacking a boat, Homan swam around the neighborhood, splashing through water containing God knows what, to his office at the nearby university. After a few days, he and his dogs hitched a ride with some rescuers in an airboat.

"I was very worried because I had heard that they were not letting people evacuate with their animals. But these guys said that had changed," Homan told me. So, he put his computer in his backpack and headed off with his dogs on an airboat.

"Towards dusk on Friday I arrived at I-10 and Banks Street, not far from my house," Homan says. "There they packed all of us pet owners from Mid City into a cargo truck and drove us away. They promised they would take us to Baton Rouge, and from there it would be relatively easy for me to get a cab or bus and meet the family in Jackson [Mississippi]. But then everything went to hell."

Rather than going to Baton Rouge, Homan's rescuers locked the truck and drove the evacuees to the refugee camp on I-10 and Causeway. There, the truck was unlocked, and the evacuees were ordered out. Anyone who refused to get out of the truck was forced off. The van drove away quickly and the driver appeared to be "terrified," according to Mr. Homan.

So now, Mr. Homan and his dogs were in the midst of 20,000 people. And they weren't *refugees*—they were detainees. He estimated that 98% of them were African Americans and some of the most impoverished people in the state. Nobody knew how to get out of the camp. There were supposed to be hundreds of buses picking them up to get them out of the area, but people told Mr. Homan they had been there five days, and that on that day only three buses had shown up.

"I saw murdered bodies, and elderly people who had died because they had been left in the sun with no water for such a long time. I've traveled quite a bit, and I have never seen the despair and tragedy that I saw at this refugee camp. It was the saddest thing I have ever seen in my life."

Officials were going around the camp, confiscating people's pets. That's when Mr. Homan knew he had to try to escape. "I could never have told my children that I gave up the dogs to save myself," he said.

Mr. Homan knew that the closest anyone was allowed to come to the camp was the town of LaPlace, 30 miles away. He knew a girl in the camp from his neighborhood, Robin, was trying to save her cat. They met up with an oil-rig worker named Carlos who also wanted to try to get to LaPlace. In the wee hours of the morning, the band of three humans, two dogs, and one cat snuck out of the perimeter.

Mr. Homan's next big worry was the armed looters he knew were operating outside the camp. But he said that his group was so bizarre that they weren't stopped by police or the looters *or* shot by the vigilantes trying to stop the looters. They found a shopping cart in which to carry the cat, and walked and walked until, Homan recalls, his feet were bloody, the dogs were exhausted, and he was ready to give up.

But then—*finally*—something went right. The travelers found a neighborhood that still had power. A gas station there was closed, but Robin found a broken window to climb through. She charged her cell phone enough to call her uncle. He was retired from the Mississippi government and so able to talk his way through one checkpoint after another and pick up the three people, two dogs, and even the darned cat. Within a few hours, Mr. Homan was reunited with his wife and children, who were waiting for him at the Jackson Airport.

Mr. Homan writes that he saw acts of heroism and compassion after the storm:

> The world clearly has plenty of empathy and compassion left. I saw people slide down ropes out of helicopters to rescue people from rooftops. I saw my neighbors break into grocery stores, fill up their boats with supplies, and row through neighborhoods distributing food and water to those in need. And as I drove 1,000 miles north to escape the carnage, I saw convoy after convoy of people and supplies heading south to help. They are their brother's keeper, and I am so thankful for their support. Maybe there is hope for the world after all.

But he also writes:

> I also learned that catastrophes such as this bring out not only the very best in people, but also the worst. I have witnessed and experienced some pretty awful things . . . I saw dozens

of dead bodies floating in toxic waters. I heard about invalid elderly humans dying in attics and hospitals believing that the world did not care as they gradually ran out of medication and oxygen while the politicians gave press conferences about how well Democrats and Republicans were cooperating. I saw sick babies and paraplegics living for five days outside in 100 degree weather, while gangs of armed youths roamed, raped, and terrorized in filthy refugee camps of 20,000 of society's most afflicted and abandoned. These poor people were placed in massive outdoor "security" pens for as many as 6 days, and many of them died. This incredibly large group of people desperately needed food, water and transportation out of New Orleans. The immediate federal response for relief was so incredibly inept it left many of us to wonder if the lack of support was deliberate. This gross inaction while so many people suffered and died occurred in the world's richest country, and it makes me so angry with the government . . . families grieved over death and misery and desperately searched for missing loved ones. I saw drug addicts take over parts of the city and terrorize, and heard that they shot nurses in the back of the head to steal pharmaceuticals to ease their drug withdrawals. And despite what you might read in the news, this wasn't a case of everyone working together to save lives. Officials from neighboring more affluent parishes [counties] than Orleans said that citizens of New Orleans were not welcome in their parishes because they only had enough supplies for their own.[1]

The Themes We'll Explore

I excerpt Mr. Homan's gripping narrative because it shows many areas that we're going to cover in this book:

1. **Large groups of people need food and water.** In New Orleans, the storm blew through on Monday. On Tuesday, the looting began, and on Wednesday, it started in earnest. The TV cameras focused on idiots and opportunists stealing clothing and television sets from waterlogged stores, but according to Mr. Homan, "I saw my neighbors break into grocery stores, fill up their boats with supplies, and row through neighborhoods distributing food and water to those in need."

There were also many people like those interviewed in an Associated Press story:

"A man walked down Canal Street with a pallet of food on his head. His wife, who refused to give her name, insisted they weren't stealing from the nearby Winn-Dixie supermarket. "It's about survival right now," she said as she held a plastic bag full of purloined items. "We got to feed our children. I've got eight grandchildren to feed."[2]

Some of the salvaging/looting took place in full view of National Guard trucks and police cruisers. But in other instances, people were shot while trying to take food out of stores. You know, it would really suck to live through one of the nation's worst disasters and then get toe-tagged for trying to feed your family.

Examples like this are why you need to have your own food stockpile. (See Chapter 7.)

2. **Medication runs out.** It's illegal to give more than a 30-day supply of many drugs (basically, because neither our government nor our doctors want you to be in charge of your own health). In this book, we'll look at alternatives if your quality of life—or maybe your life itself—depends on getting a prescription filled. (See Chapter 10.)

3. **You may have to live for days in 100-degree weather.** Or you may have to encounter dire straits in weather so cold that pipes are bursting around you. Your air conditioning and heating shouldn't have to depend on a power grid. Solar can keep you cool while others swelter and wood can keep you warm while others freeze. (See Chapter 11.)

4. **Gangs of armed youths roamed, raped, and terrorized.** The nightmare of those who are poor and helpless came true in New Orleans. In this book, we'll cover home defense and personal defense, too. (See Chapter 11.)

5. **The immediate government response can be inept.** The Republicans hate government, so it shouldn't surprise anyone that they bungled the response to Katrina. In the Bush administration, the Federal Emergency Management Agency (FEMA) became a place for political appointees and lucky idlers. And sure, FEMA Director Michael Brown urged local

fire and rescue departments outside Louisiana, Alabama, and Mississippi *not* to send trucks or emergency workers into disaster areas without an explicit request for help from state or local governments. To be fair, though, it's likely that the aftermath of a disaster like Katrina could overwhelm any government response, at least for a while. Therefore, you shouldn't relax just because Bush is out of office. There are still risks, and you'll do much better if you are prepared.

6. **Governments may become the enemy.** Here's another interesting fact: The New Orleans suburb of Gretna sealed the Crescent City Connection bridge across the Mississippi River, turning back fleeing flood victims at gunpoint.[3] If you take away nothing else from this book, understand that you can't count on the government—any government—to save your lazy butt in an emergency. *I believe that in the immediate aftermath of a disaster, the amount of government help will be inverse to the scale of the crisis.*

That's because a real disaster knocks the government for a loop, and it's busy trying to find its feet in the first few days; saving *you* becomes secondary. So you need to be prepared to take care of yourself and your loved ones first.

How Long Does a Short Emergency Last?

New Orleans descended into chaos, and the anarchy got worse after darkness. After a few days, the stench of urine, excrement, and garbage was overpowering across the city.[4] People were actually forced

---

The Survival Rule of Threes

- It takes about three minutes to die without air.
- It takes about three days to die without water.
- It takes about three weeks to die without food.
- It takes about three months to die without hope.

A smart suburban survivalist doesn't want to get into a situation that threatens any of the above. Try and think your way out of tough situations. Your brain is your best weapon.

out of evacuation shelters because of fears of dysentery (which you get from bad or *fouled* water). Another thing we'll cover in this book is the importance of a stored water supply and—even better—water purifiers that won't cost you an arm and a leg. (See Chapter 6.)

A week went by before law and order was restored. That was a very long week for anyone who wasn't prepared for the worst.

Mr. Homan may have gotten off to a rough start—no supplies and no boat. But put in a tight spot—a detention camp—he did some things very right. He made allies. He and his group came up with a plan to sneak out of camp and get to a town where their families could meet them. They stuck together, and utilized things they found (a grocery cart and a gas station with electric power).

As awful as Mr. Homan's experience was, it could have been worse. At least 1,836 people lost their lives in the actual hurricane and in the subsequent floods. Some people were never found. Another two million people, like Mr. Homan, were displaced due to the disaster.[5]

Mr. Homan believes that his city and state are much better prepared to withstand another major disaster. As for preparations he's making in case of another storm, he says:

> . . . it's about information. Before Katrina, I didn't know who my neighbors were. Now, I know them very well and we'll look out for each other. Most will evacuate, but not all, and those of us who stay behind will know very well about the people who might need assistance.
>
> Before every hurricane we've always had plenty of food. First, acknowledging power will go out, everyone in the neighborhood donates their perishables. Then, we all have stockpiles of canned goods. Shopping before a hurricane is an amazing adventure. Stores sell out quickly, so you have to plan ahead. These storms and potential disasters certainly are kinder to those with the mental capacity and resources to plan ahead.

For Mr. Homan's sake, I sure hope so. Even now, after Katrina, many people are dead-set against bugging out. In 2006, a research team from the Harvard School of Public Health interviewed more than 2,000 people living in high-risk hurricane zones in eight states. One fourth of them said they would not leave even if evacuation became mandatory.

Of those surveyed, 68% said they thought their homes were built well enough to ride out a storm. It didn't matter if the respondents lived in mobile homes, which goes to show that people generally feel safer at home.

The real crisis of law and order lasted about two weeks. The curfews were lifted after about six weeks. It took up to a year for many of the Katrina survivors to get back to some semblance of normalcy, and it took Mr. Homan and his family three years to rebuild their home.

But the bottom line is if you could live through that first two weeks in the city, you probably survived. To me, that's the encouraging thing about Katrina—civilization melted away, but then it came back.

Of course during that period of anarchy, if you were in Katrina's flood zone, your home, your job, and the life you knew could all have been swept away or changed forever—by a short-term crisis.

What about when the crisis isn't short-term? What if, say, your country is the next Argentina?

Argentina—The Crashed Society

Argentina has suffered through a series of military dictatorships and short-lived democratic governments, but economically speaking, for much of the twentieth century, the people had lives similar to first-world countries. Argentina in the nineteenth century attracted a flood of British capital and European immigrants. By 1913, it was one of the world's ten richest countries, ahead of France and Germany. But the country's economic cycle peaked after World War II, and between 1976 and 1989, income per person shrank by more than 1% per year.[6]

Things turned around in 1991, as the government embarked on free-market reforms and restricted the money supply to the level of hard-currency reserves. Between 1991 and 1997, Argentina's economy grew at an annual average rate of 6.1%, the highest in the region.

But then the country suffered a series of economic shocks and slipped into a grinding recession, which deepened in 1999. Competitive currency devaluation by neighbor and trading partner Brazil kneecapped Argentina's exports. In 2001, the government lost the elections. The International Monetary Fund came in to fix things. Its policies only made things worse. Millions of Argentineans became unemployed and poverty-stricken.

As the economy collapsed, the emergency was used as an excuse to implement policies that allowed billions of dollars to be swindled by foreign banks and corporations. Many of Argentina's assets and resources were plundered, and its financial system was used for laundering of drug money through Citibank, Credit Suisse, and J.P. Morgan, according to a report by the U.S. Senate Permanent Subcommittee on Investigations.[7]

If all this starts to sound eerily familiar to you, you're not alone in your thoughts. Many survivors of the Argentinean collapse note striking similarities between that country's early stages of trouble and the United States right now.

In 2001, it seemed that Argentinean society simply broke down. Wholesale looting started. A run on banks ended when the government froze bank deposits. Finally, spontaneous uprisings began, as people demanded the government resign. This wasn't just leftists and troublemakers; this was the middle class and professionals on the march. The marches led to crackdowns including tear-gas, skull-cracking, and mounted policemen riding through crowds.

The people fought back. Chaos ensued. And all the while, Argentina's debt spiraled out of control. Hundreds of thousands of people lost their life's savings and half the population dropped below the poverty line.

In the countryside, an already hard life became tough. In the cities, it became a nightmare. Food ran out, the water wasn't safe, and a large number of people were kidnapped off the streets or shot dead over money or food. The police were overwhelmed by the rising tide of crime. Argentina couldn't afford fuel and the country was gripped by blackouts.

An Argentinean blogger, Fernando Aguirre, who writes under the pseudonym *ferfal*, relates his experience on his blog:

> Being in a city without light turned out to be depressing after a while. I spent my share of nights, alone, listening to the radio, eating canned food and cleaning my guns under the light of my LED head lamp. Then I got married, had a son, and found out that when you have loved ones around you, blackouts are not as bad. The point is that family helps morale in these situations.

A note on flashlights. Have two or three head LED lights. They are not expensive and are worth their weight in gold. A powerful flashlight is necessary, something like a big Maglite or better yet a SureFire, especially when you have to check your property for intruders. But for more mundane stuff like preparing food, going to the toilet or doing stuff around the house, the LED headlamp is priceless. Try washing the dishes on the dark while holding a 60 lumen flashlight on one hand and you'll know what I mean. LEDs also have the advantage of lasting for almost an entire week of continuous use and the light bulb lasts forever.

Rechargeable batteries are a must (get a solar powered battery charger) or else you'll end up broke if lights go out often. Have a healthy amount of spare quality batteries and try to standardize as much as you can.[8]

When the middle class is scrounging for enough batteries to clean its guns by flashlight, you know things have gone to hell in a handcart. We'll talk more about flashlights in Chapter 11.

For those Argentineans who stayed, life became a gamble. Many decided to get out. One expatriate, Willy Tovar, sat down with me to discuss his experiences.

Willy had been a journalist in Argentina. Newspapers were early victims of the economic troubles, and Willy counted himself lucky to land a job working in a think tank, writing an analysis of each day's events for private clients.

Willy had political contacts, and thanks to his job he was privy to more information than the average Argentinean. He came to the conclusion that the monetary peg of the Argentinean peso—one-to-one to the U.S. dollar—was unsustainable. "I realized that sooner or later, this would explode," he told me. "They just didn't have the money. I told my wife to go exchange all our pesos for dollars at the 1-to-1 exchange rate."

At the time, in 2001, Argentina was trapped in a downward economic spiral. President Fernando de la Rúa tried one extraordinary measure after another, only to see them all fail. The derivatives markets saw his desperation as weakness and a massive shorting of Argentine bonds ensued, followed by at least $40 billion in U.S. domestic capital flight.

Willy and his wife had a daughter, so he decided to get out. "I didn't want my daughter to live in what was coming," he says.

He and his family moved to Miami. His only major asset was his apartment, which he left a banking friend in charge of selling. "There were delays—but finally the sale went through for the equivalent of $32,000," Willy remembers. "My friend put the money in the bank, but there was a wait to transfer the money out of the country.

"Two days later, everything blew up. Our bank account—all bank accounts—were frozen. The President ran away," Willy says, and the government collapsed.

President de la Rúa was actually forced to resign. Had the bank withdrawls continued, Argentina's entire banking system would have collapsed. As it was, massive queues at every bank and a growing political crisis tipped Argentina into a state of panic. Food riots spread across the country and devolved into general looting. de la Rúa tried to work with the army to hand out food, but the plan failed after it was blocked by his political enemies. The president tried one last time to form a coalition government and that failed, too.

He resigned, and because of widespread violence, he fled onboard an air force helicopter. The images of de la Rúa's escape by helicopter were broadcast throughout the country.

The equivalent would be seeing Barack Obama flee Washington, an angry mob nipping at his heels. But that couldn't happen here . . . or could it?

Argentina's crisis eased when the country devalued its currency by 30% and defaulted on (and then renegotiated) its enormous foreign debts. The peso settled at about four to the U.S. dollar (it has since risen to about three to the dollar). Willy's $32,000 nest egg quickly turned into $8,000, which was how much he was able to get out of the country.

However, Willy's experience offers some important lessons:

- He paid attention to economic and political developments, soaking up information like a sponge. He also questioned everything the government told him, and made his own informed decisions.
- When he realized that life in his country was going to change for the worse, perhaps forever, he developed an escape plan. The only thing of real importance to him was his family—he wasn't sentimental about physical things.

- The financial loss was devastating, but Willy didn't cry in his beer. He got on with life and got back on his feet.

Now, the former Argentinean journalist cleans pools in Florida. But he's okay with that. "My daughter will have a better life here," he says. "If I go back to Argentina it will be for vacation, and I'll be sure to have a return ticket in my pocket."

A warning (maybe) for Americans is that Argentina's foreign debts at the time of the crisis, $141 billion, seem like child's play compared to the massive debts that the United States has been racking up lately.

Argentina did recover. By 2003, four years after the deep recession started and two years after the breakdown in social order, the economy was growing again.

Argentina's economy grew at least 7% a year starting in 2003 through 2008, but slowed sharply in the last three months of 2008. And there are some parts of Argentinean life that have changed forever. Crime is epidemic, as is drug use and corruption.

"Corruption is so bad in Argentina, if you have money, you can commit murder and not go to jail," Willy says. "Whereas someone who steals a chicken goes to jail for life."

Lessons Learned from New Orleans and Argentina

Disasters and emergencies bring out the best and the worst in people. The more you prepare ahead of time, the better your chances of coming out with a rep as one of the best. The less you prepare, the more likely you are to fall prey to one of the worst. There is no time to buy supplies after disaster strikes.

The police will be good for directing traffic and enforcing the law in the early stages of a disaster. But when the s**t really hits the fan, they'll be looking to protect their own families. Police lines will stretch thin and even disappear, leaving you to fall prey to looters and vigilantes.

We, all of us, stereotype people based on looks. The troublemakers in New Orleans came from many races, and from both the lower class and the middle class. Just because someone doesn't fit your profile of a bad guy doesn't mean they're safe—after all, Mr. Homan was lied to and locked up by the supposed good guys. Also, you may find fast friends and allies if you can look past skin color and find common ground.

(Continued)

(Continued)

The police can't tell the good guys from the bad guys, either. In the aftermath of Hurricane Katrina, New Orleans Chief of Police Eddie Compass ordered police and National Guard units to confiscate firearms from citizens who remained in the area. The Disaster Recovery Personal Protection Act of 2006, which prohibits the confiscation of legally possessed firearms during a disaster, has supposedly rectified this, but it has yet to be tested.

The vast majority of the violence in a crisis occurs inside cities. If you aren't hunkered down for the long term, get out of town!

Getting your finances in order is a priority and something you can do *before* disaster strikes. It's too late to do it afterward. You can start by spending less than you make, but there are many other things you can do. You'll find some ideas in this book.

We Are All One Bad Turn Away from a Crisis

The way things are going—what with floods, fires, global warming making both summer and winter storms more severe, economic crises, crazies with nukes, you name it—I think it's likely that you'll be caught up in your own crisis or disaster in your lifetime. And if you can't avoid disasters, the important thing is how you cope when they occur.

The real danger is that, as our government creaks under the weight of insurmountable debt, the U.S. empire crumbles, and society totters on the brink, we may see law and social services disappear for extended periods of time. I don't want to live through that, but the odds are increasing. For that reason alone, you *must* become resilient and self-reliant.

In my own life, I've experienced a string of hurricanes that rattled the shutters like an oncoming freight train, sent tree limbs tumbling into my house, and knocked power out for weeks at a time. Getting through those times would have been much easier if I knew better then and was prepared the way I am now.

The Least You Can Do

- Keep working flashlights and plenty of batteries handy.
- Know what's really important in your life and be prepared to walk away from material things in a crisis.
- Stay tuned in to the news—it's tough to know when the government is lying to you, but you've got to try and figure it out.

PART

II

MONEY—PERSONAL FINANCE, CASH, AND PRECIOUS METALS

CHAPTER

Personal Finance

How did you go bankrupt?
Two Ways. Gradually, and then suddenly.
                    —Ernest Hemingway, *The Sun Also Rises*

In this chapter, we'll look at personal finance—how you can improve your finances to improve your odds in a regular economic downturn, a full-blown recession, and an economic collapse. I'll also show you what we can learn from financial crises of the past. I'll give you tips to get your financial house in order, including a 401(k) survival guide. And, I'll look at what careers may thrive in a post-collapse society.

But in order to learn how to move forward, it's important to know how we got to where we are today.

A Big-Picture Look at the U.S. Economy— We're So Screwed

You know about the housing bubble, and how its bursting has knee-capped the U.S. economy. And yes, the banks blew all our money on exotic derivatives that few people could understand (I sometimes wish they blew the money on exotic *dancers*—it would cost tax-payers a lot less dough, because you can't leverage strippers).

There's also the problem of state budgets—from Maine to California, states have seen their revenues dry up with the economy.

According to the Center on Budget and Policy Priorities (CBPP), at least 48 states from Maine to California faced or are facing short-falls in their budgets at least through 2010, and severe fiscal prob-lems are highly likely to continue into the following year.

The CBPP posted this dire warning on its web site: "Combined budget gaps for the remainder of this fiscal year and state fiscal years 2010 and 2011 are estimated to total more than $350 billion."

Unlike the federal government, states cannot run deficits when the economy turns down; they must cut expenditures, raise taxes, or draw down reserve funds to balance their budgets. Reducing services and payrolls becomes urgently necessary. This, in turn, adds another twist to the vicious downward spiral in the fourth fac-tor in a worsening economy: consumer spending.

Consumer spending accounts for about 70% of total economic activity, so it's bad news that 2008 and 2009 saw consumer spending con-tract. This trend is probably going to become more pronounced mov-ing forward because consumers have a lot of debt to unwind. An *average* unwinding of debt would suck about $300 billion out of the economy.

The debt of households has climbed much faster than their net worth in the last 50 years, according to data compiled by the Federal Reserve.

Four rounds of debt reduction took place during that period, and they lasted for about 10 quarters on average. That means we have a long, long way to go.

Americans are becoming savers just at the time when the govern-ment wants them to go out and spend. While I applaud the return to individual responsibility, this is really going to put the brakes on any government-led scheme to jump-start the economy.

Keep in mind that the personal savings rate dropped from 9% in the 1980s to just 0.6% from 2005 to 2007. By May of 2009 the personal savings rate had rebounded to 6.9%—a huge increase in a short period of time. That was a *gigantic hit* to consumer spending.

I think we have a long way to go in our economic downturn. In fact, the global economy in early 2009 was worse by some metrics than the global economy in 1930.

That's not to say we couldn't see a recovery—one that may last for months. In the Great Depression, it looked like the worst was over in 1933, as the plunge paused and the economy improved. Many people breathed a sigh of relief, only to see the Depression continue in this country until around 1939 (in some countries, it lasted longer). (See Figure 3.1).

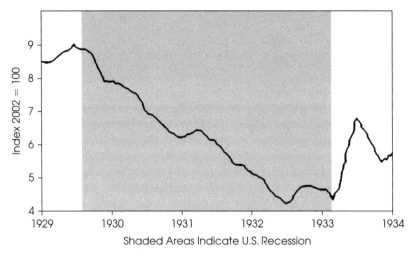

Figure 3.1   Industrial Production Index
Source: St. Louis Fed.

That's not to say we're in another economic event that will play out just like the Great Depression. While that seems to be the furthest that most Americans' memories can reach back, there have been financial panics that were just as bad. Two of them—in 1837 and 1873—were worse than the Great Depression by some metrics.

In fact, there are some eerie similarities between today's downturn and the panic of 1873—real estate speculation causes a massive market collapse, the failure of leading bankers, and a currency crisis—that make me think it may be more of a blueprint for the coming decade than the Great Depression.

It Was Bad in the United States, But in Europe . . .

Here in the United States, the Panic of 1873 actually started in 1869; it just took a few years to get to the really bad part. It was a combination of railroad speculation, a run on physical gold, and brand-name bank and brokerage houses failing.

Across the pond, in Europe, it was much worse. And it gave one of the world's most legendary capitalists the chance to make a fortune for himself and his friends.

I'm talking about Baron Nathan Mayer Rothschild. Rothschild was a respected French investor who became the stuff of legend during the financial crisis.

It was a terrible time. A building boom ended with a mortgage bubble bursting. This was followed by a swoon in the prices of many industrial commodities. There was even an energy crisis of sorts—an outbreak of equine influenza (horse flu) saw many forms of transportation temporarily grind to a halt.

Europe fought the Franco-Prussian War, which ended in defeat for France. Emperor Napoleon III was captured, and the French government collapsed. The economic woes combined with military defeat allowed socialists to seize control of the French capital. Paris was turned upside down, and mobs ruled.

And that's when Rothschild told his clients it was *time to buy*. The story goes that a panic-stricken investor turned up at Rothschild's office and exclaimed, "You advise me to buy securities now? *NOW?!* The streets of Paris run with blood."

Rothschild, calm as ever, answered, "My dear friend, if the streets of Paris were not running with blood, do you think you would be able to buy at the present prices?"

There is a second part to Rothschild's quote—one that is perhaps even more impressive: Buy when there's blood in the streets, *even if the blood is your own.*

Rothschild proved to be quite prescient. French bankers were able to fund a counter-revolution. And the investments that Rothschild and his friends made doubled in value, and then went higher!

While many U.S. banks failed in the Panic of 1873, we got off lightly compared to Europe. The global depression lasted until 1879. And the end result was that the center of gravity for the world's credit shifted from Europe to the United States.

Rothschild's lesson for us is that investors can do very well in a panic, but only if they have a strong stomach for pain and a very long (many-years-long) time frame.

And this time around, the world's financial center of gravity may be shifting again—to Asia. Yes, our economy is huge compared to China's. I'm not saying this shift will happen overnight. I'm saying that we may be at the start of a process that will see the sun dim on the U.S. economy and the U.S. dollar.

Are Things Bad? Yes!

Fast-forward to today, and, just as in Rothschild's day, we've seen a building boom end with a mortgage bubble burst. There are parades of bad news up and down Wall Street and Main Street.

On Wall Street, the easiest way to get your hands on truckloads of government bailout dollars is to own a bank. Heck, you won't even have to tell the Treasury what you do with the money!

And if you don't own a bank, you could go from being chairman of the Nasdaq to setting up a hedge fund so secretive that your closest friends don't know you're ripping them off for tens of billions of dollars.

On Main Street, manufacturing, employment, and retail sales all got shredded like they went through a wood chipper. Problems are rippling around the world, too. The question now is: Are we close to *blood in the streets*—the time when Rothschild would advise buying?

I'll give you my opinion on that in a bit. First, an important difference between now and the panic of 1873 . . .

The Loosest Money Policy Possible.   In 1873, the United States moved to the gold standard, which meant it stopped minting silver dollars altogether. This reduced the domestic money supply, which hurt farmers and anyone else who carried heavy debt loads.

In 2008 and 2009, by contrast, we embarked on the loosest money policy possible. In addition, the Treasury and Federal Reserve have been handing out cash by the hundreds of billions to every Tom, Dick, and Citibank who drives by with a sob story.

Through the first quarter of 2009, Washington had already spent or pledged $12.8 *trillion*.[1] As a result of all the bailouts for banks, automakers and other new federal outlays, our nation's budget deficit is expected to come close to $2 *trillion* in 2009, and the national debt stood at a staggering $11.5 trillion. The long-term effects of that free and easy money policy are horrific!

And that's just the tip of the iceberg.

In 2009, the Grandfather Economic Report series calculated that the United States owed a total debt (including government, household, business, financial sector, etc.) of $57 trillion.[2] That's $186,717 for every man, woman, and child in the country, an increase of $32,104 per family of four over the previous year.

However, that's the longer-term consequences. In the short term, that easy-money policy could be just what the doctor ordered for an ailing economy. I agree with critics of the administration that if you're going to try to stimulate the economy by building roads, railroads, and bridges, do a *lot* of it. Unfortunately, the Obama Administration's wishy-washy, middle-of-the-road approach seems like it will load us up with more debt without being big enough to have the desired stimulative effect.

Also, in the short term, there's a simple reason why the government has an easy money policy: They're deathly afraid of deflation. Deflation makes the huge debts of the government insurmountable, while inflation makes those debts smaller over time. If the policy makers in Washington can get the United States back to 2% inflation and hold it there, that would cut the real value of debts in half in a generation. Of course, the money you hold would also lose half its value in the same amount of time.

Why Deflation Is Bad.   In 2008, U.S. commodity prices, wholesale prices, and consumer prices plunged; mortgage debts, corporate debts, and other forms of debt were liquidated at the fastest pace since the 1930s; and the U.S. dollar enjoyed the most rapid surge overseas since the mid-1980s.[3] That is deflation in a nutshell—the value of a currency strengthens while the value of everything else (relatively speaking) goes down. These trends continued in 2009.

Many people would think that prices going down would be a good thing. But when we're in deflation, even nominally low interest rates become punishing. That is because the real interest rate is the nominal rate minus inflation, which can be positive or negative. When we experience deflation, the real interest rate is brutally positive—higher than the nominal interest rate. When we are experiencing inflation, the real rate of interest is lower than the nominal rate. We saw a period of negative real interest rates begin just a few years ago when Alan Greenspan slashed interest rates and goosed the rate of inflation to juice up the economy.

This comes with consequences: When real interest rates are negative, consumers take on huge amounts of debt—in the short term, they'd be fools not to, because they're effectively being paid to borrow money!

The problem with the short term is it's followed by the long term, and real interest rates usually aren't negative for long. But they last long enough to sucker people into taking on more debt than they can service if interest rates go up or incomes go down. Many people find themselves in that trap today.

This is why some people believe there is no safe level of debt to hold, including home mortgages. I disagree with that point of view, and I'll explain why in just a bit.

If you are going to own a home, remember that real estate can become illiquid (you won't be able to sell it) in a severe financial downturn. So own only what you're going to live in—speculative real estate is for suckers. By the time you realize that you need to sell a property because you can no longer pay the mortgage, it may be too late.

More importantly for the broad economy, deflation makes it nearly impossible for governments to pay off the kind of huge debts that Uncle Sam is racking up. Right now, international investors are willing to ignore that as they buy into the big lie. But if and when they start demanding the United States act like a fiscally responsible adult and *not* run up more debts than we can ever hope to pay off, the economic adjustment—and hit to the U.S. dollar—could be huge.

How would they punish us? They'd slow down their purchases of our Treasuries.

In March of 2009, China's premier, Wen Jiabao, expressed concern about the safety of China's $1 trillion investment in U.S. government debt, the world's largest such holding, and urged the Obama administration to provide assurances that its investment would keep its value in the face of a global financial crisis.

"We have lent a huge amount of money to the United States. Of course we are concerned about the safety of our assets," Wen told reporters. "To be honest, I am definitely a little worried."

Does that sound to you like a guy who might shift some of his country's foreign reserves out of Treasuries? It sure does to me.

After Deflation, Brace for Surging Inflation.   Everything goes in cycles—that's why it's dangerous to say "you should always invest in Investment A," as if the markets and the global economy—and their effect on Investment A—will never change.

For decades, the U.S. dollar has been the reserve currency of the world. Many people think this will never change. Roughly 65% of the world's foreign exchange reserves were in U.S. dollars at the end of 2008.

However, the winds of change are blowing. China and Russia have expressed a desire for a new global reserve currency based on a mix of currencies and gold, and in the form of IMF special drawing rights (SDRs). Zhou Xiaochuan, the governor of China's central bank, is calling the new currency a "super-sovereign reserve currency."

Russia, India, and Brazil, along with China—the emerging powers of the world—also back the idea of a new reserve super-currency. Such a transition would take time. But once it starts, the U.S. dollar will be on a very slippery slope.

And in 2009, Chinese premier Wen Jiabao threw down the gauntlet, calling for more surveillance of countries that issue major reserve currencies. Without mentioning the United States by name, he ripped us a new one.

"We should advance reform of the international financial system, increase the representation and voice of emerging markets and developing countries, strengthen surveillance of the macro-economic policies of major reserve currency issuing economies, and develop a more diversified international monetary system," Wen said.[4]

More Problems for the U.S. Dollar

China's desire for a new international super-currency isn't the only problem facing the U.S. dollar.

> **Soaring deficit could get bigger!** Because of the economic slow-down, the stimulus package, and the various financial-relief measures, the federal deficit for 2009 could come in close to $2 trillion. If things go wrong—and they haven't exactly been going right—the deficit could be even larger.

> **We have to borrow more to fill the gap.** Usually, federal tax receipts provide 80% to 90% of the money needed to fund the U.S. budget. In 2009, Uncle Sam will need to borrow 45% of the money the government will spend. Not since World War II has the government borrowed anything close to what it is borrowing now.

> In a March 2009 forecast, Goldman Sachs estimated average annual deficits of $940 billion through 2019. If this proves true, deficits would remain above 4% of GDP through the next decade, and the national debt—now at $11.5 trillion—would reach a whopping 83% of GDP, a level not seen since World War II.

> **Reserve balances ballooning.** When we say the Fed is *running its printing presses* to create money, that's only partly true. The Fed creates money mostly by crediting banks with deposits at the Fed.

Those deposits are called reserve balances. Reserve balances are the key component—along with currency—of base money or central bank money, which ultimately brings about changes in broader money supply measures.

These deposits or reserves have been exploding as the Fed has made loans and purchased securities. In the third quarter of 2008, reserves were $8 billion. As of March 2009, reserves had soared to $778 billion—an increase of 9,625%!

The reserve balances are soaring as the Fed creates money to finance loans in an attempt to unwind the mess created by AIG and other banks. Just to keep up with what it plans in 2009, the Fed will likely have to increase reserves by another $1.15 trillion to $3.37 trillion!

Here's my point: In the short term, it is prudent to hold a lot of U.S. dollars and Treasuries, and to have as little debt as possible. In the long term, we are probably going to see inflation return, and it could be particularly vicious this time around. When that happens, the U.S dollar will tank and longer-term Treasuries will come under pressure—hammering two investments that many investors see as safe havens.

In an inflationary period, stocks can be a good investment. Heck, the Zimbabwe Stock Exchange grew by a record 322,111% in 2007,[5] mainly because the Zimbabwe currency turned into toilet paper.

When paper currency turns to toilet paper, where do you hide? Gold can also protect you from inflation. *Gold provides protection against a currency collapse or government collapse—both of which we could experience in the next decade.*

Gold works in a variety of economic circumstances. It did very well during the inflationary heyday of the 1970s *and* it held its value very well through the ups and downs of the Great Depression. I'll talk more about gold in the next chapter.

One last important point . . .

The Economy is NEVER Going Back to the Old Normal

From 1995 through 2009, America's central bank, the Federal Reserve, flooded the economy with trillions of dollars through increased money supply and easy credit. This triggered a massive consumption boom along with several bubbles such as the stock and housing bubbles. All of this created artificial *stimulated demand* as consumers bought and bought and grew more and more indebted as they spent beyond their means.

- The tumble in interest rates—from 18% to 1%—fueled a shopping boom as consumers spent like there was no tomorrow.
- That sparked a surge in spending on new technology—and when the tech bubble burst, the financial froth flowed into real estate.
- Lending standards declined, allowing people who never should have gotten loans to each borrow hundreds of thousands of dollars.
- Many of those *liar loans* were spent on homes. The housing boom provided millions of jobs.
- And since so many people were buying homes, everybody's home values went up—allowing people to borrow more equity against their homes, and start the cycle all over again.

In other words, the lifestyle we enjoyed for 15 years was *based on a lie.* It was like living a high-falutin' lifestyle paid for with bad checks. Eventually, those bills come due. A *sustainable* lifestyle—the new normal—is actually at a much lower level.

Another reason why we won't see the old normal any time soon is because many of the actions taken by both the Bush and Obama administrations in the name of *stimulus* are not stimulus at all. The bank bailout is a pass-through of taxpayer dollars to well-heeled con artists on Wall Street. Another name for it would be legalized fraud. It is the mass looting of national wealth to enrich a well-connected few.

Sure, these ruinous bank bailouts may have helped reinflate the bubble, but they may also worsen the coming crash, as the bill for trillions of dollars in debt and derivatives comes due. As Martin Weiss wrote on MoneyandMarkets.com:

> The Treasury's plan primarily shifts the burden of toxic assets from the private banking sector to the public. This can only (a) bloat an already-ballooning federal deficit, (b) damage the credit of the U.S. government, and (c) raise the risk that borrowing costs will surge for nearly everyone.[6]

I'm not saying the fault lies entirely with President Obama. Former President George W. Bush presided over a 33% increase in total government spending in his first term alone. Not content with the level of spending in which he already was engaged, he declared a war against a country that hadn't attacked us—the Iraq War alone will cost us about $3 trillion.[7] And that war with its big-ticket price tag was rubber-stamped by both parties in Congress. Heck, that's just part of the problem. The big spenders in Washington are bipartisan.

Rearranging the Deck Chairs on the Hindenburg

Even though President Obama is doing the bidding of the worst special interests on Wall Street, I sincerely hope he succeeds in pulling our collective fat out of the fire. So far, it seems Obama's economic team is enacting policies as if they're hell-bent on reinflating a doomed zeppelin, and we all know how the Hindenburg story ended.[8]

Throwing more money at banksters in the hopes that they'll loan out some of it is, at best, hoping to artificially boost demand. Keeping every insolvent bank and delinquent mortgage afloat is not a strategy—it's just putting off necessary pain. Probably one of the better potential outcomes is that we just give up trying to reinflate the Hindenburg, discover and implement a new sustainable lifestyle, and pay down our debts as quickly as possible so we don't burden our great-grandchildren with them.

Many U.S. families are going to be way ahead of the government on this one. If you haven't joined this trend already, you really might want to start.

Get Your Financial House in Order

Are you in debt up to your eyeballs? That's not a good place to be—it's stressful, and it may become untenable in a time of rising unemployment and falling incomes. The common-sense thing to do is pay off your highest interest-rate debt first. I don't advocate cutting up credit cards—you might need them in a real emergency—but I'm all in favor of burying them in a waterproof container in the backyard to keep you from using plastic unnecessarily.

One thing many survivalists recommend is to pay off your mortgage. The best reason to pay off a mortgage is to have emotional peace of mind. But I can also think of a couple of reasons *not* to pay off your mortgage:

1. **You might need that money**—especially if you're preparing for the end of the world as we know it. I'm much happier with a fat cash cushion. In fact, if you can pay off your house, one option would be to *not* pay it off and put the money in an interest-bearing account. As long as mortgages stay tax deductible, you'll come out ahead of the game.
2. **The value of your home may go down**. In fact, it may go down a lot. So how will you feel if you've sunk all your money into your home and it is worth less every month?
3. **It's much more important to pay off credit card debt** and other high-interest debts. As long as you have a low rate of interest on your home loan, that's the last debt you want to pay off.
4. **The next person to get bailed out may be you.** Honestly, the way they're throwing money at problems in Washington, I wish I could walk into the White House, perch on the edge of Barack Obama's desk, and confess to every bad financial decision made by Wall Street in the previous eight years. I'd probably get off with a stern look and be sent on my way with a billion dollars in my pocket. That seems to be what's happening to the other financial miscreants and banksters.

    Seriously, we've already seen the Obama administration roll out one mortgage bailout plan that costs hundreds of billions of dollars. Who knows what they'll do next? What if they devise a mortgage forgiveness plan or something else of which you can take advantage?

So for all these reasons, I don't think your goal should be to become completely debt-free. However, prudence dictates you . . .

1. **Pay one extra payment a year on your mortgage.** This can save you hundreds of thousands of dollars in interest and years on your mortgage. You can save even more time and money when you make payments to reduce your principal balance earlier in the year—for example, instead of increasing your monthly mortgage payment by one-twelfth, you are better off increasing your monthly mortgage payment by one-sixth for the first six months of every year.

By the way, if you're struggling to pay your mortgage, see if your lender is participating in the HOPE for Homeowners Act. Passed by Congress in July of 2008, this government-run program encourages lenders to refinance mortgages for borrowers who are at risk of losing their homes. The program will refinance mortgages for borrowers who are having difficulty making their payments, but can afford a new loan insured by the Federal Housing Administration. Call (800) 225-5342 for more information.

2. **Pay off your credit cards every month.** Credit cards are one of the most expensive kinds of debt. Interest rates can run as high as 25% for credit-card holders who are late with a payment or have low credit scores. If you have multiple credit card balances—*ouch.* Focus on paying off high-interest-rate cards first. But don't do a balance transfer without reading the fine print. Credit card companies got wise to the fact that consumers were switching debt around, so now they charge to let you do it. As of this writing, the average fee for a balance transfer is 3% or a minimum of $5 to $10 and a maximum of $50 to $75. And these costs are on the rise.

  Also, try to aim not to have more than two credit cards. The theory goes that two cards with a $10,000 limit each is better than 20 cards with a $1,000 limit each. It's too easy to use a card without thinking (and forget to pay it—therefore putting yourself in line to get spanked with higher interest rates and late fees), and it's far too easy to lose a card or have one stolen—and not realize it—when you have a wallet stuffed with them.

3. **Get rid of auto loan debt.** Next to credit cards, auto loans often carry the highest interest rates that many consumers pay. But you can refinance a car loan as long as you improve your credit score since you bought the car. That way, you can turn a 10% loan into a 6% loan.

4. **Double-check the figures on any medical debt.** One of the worst disasters any U.S. citizen can face is a serious medical problem—both physically and financially, it can wipe you out. Medical debt is responsible for nearly half of personal bankruptcy filings, according to Health Affairs, a policy journal.

  But many things can end up on your medical bill that shouldn't be there. For example, an insurance company will use a code for a procedure and your doctor incorrectly inputs the code—this gets kicked out by the insurers' computer and you get stuck with the bill. The insurer *won't* pay unless you bring it to their attention.

If you're really underwater, speak to the medical provider. Many hospitals have government funds to help patients who can't afford their medical care, and independent nonprofits also provide financial assistance. Finally, unlike the soulless junkyard dogs who seem to populate credit card companies, medical providers are often open to working out payment plans with patients.

5. **Take a good hard look at your current spending.** It's tough to change spending habits, even wasteful ones. One method that works—but that can blow up in your face if you do it wrong—is for a husband and wife to keep track of *all* their expenses in a week or a month and then go over each other's list of personal expenses. Studies have shown that couples have more fights over money than sex, so try to keep the emotion out of it when you question each other's spending. Cut back all expenses wherever you can. Streamline for more efficiency and *stop wasting money on frivolous or impulsive items.* Shop like you're preparing for the end of the world, because you are.

One you have your personal debt and spending in hand, develop a budget for your survival purchases. How much money are you going to spend on stockpiling food every month? How much are you going to spend on new tools? Gardening equipment? Are you buying a bicycle? Remember to purchase things you will absolutely need (a three-month food supply) before things you may or may not use (an expensive gun and 1,000 rounds of ammunition). Make a monthly budget, stick to it, and remember to include something—even a small amount—for building up cash.

Once you're gotten your personal spending and debt under control, it's time to look at your investments. If you don't have any investments outside of Ruger, Smith, and Wesson, then you're probably feeling pretty smart right now. Don't get cocky, kid! You can skip ahead. But if you have a 401(k), this next part is for you.

Your 401(k) Survival Guide

If you're like Baron Rothschild, with an eye on the really long term, a strong stomach for losses and the luxury to wait things out, you can try to do just that. But if you're going to need your money in the next decade, be aware that (1) we probably haven't seen the real bottom in stocks yet; (2) we don't how far stocks will go down; and (3) we don't know how long they'll stay down. And by the time stocks *do* come back, resurgent inflation might have destroyed all your gains anyway.

With these things in mind, you might want to consider doing the following:

1. Get a list of the investment options available in your 401(k).
2. Look for the safest investments. The safest is a Treasury-only money market fund. The next safest is a government-only money market fund. Third is a standard money market fund. Fourth is a fund that invests mostly in U.S government notes and bonds and as little as possible in corporate bonds.

    What you're trying to do is choose government paper over corporate or bank paper and short-term instruments over long-term.

3. Put at least 50% of your money in the safest fund. If you're doing this *after* the market has plunged, and you worry you are selling at the wrong time, cut the amount you were going to put in the safe fund in half again. When you get a rally, sell the rest into that.

    So now half of your total 401(k) money should be in very safe investments.

4. The rest can be invested in a mix of precious metals, bonds, ETFs that track sectors or commodities, and U.S. and foreign stocks. The hard truth is that the market changes constantly— there is no one investment to fit all people all the time. And depending on market conditions and business and market cycles, there may be times when you want to put money to work.

The mix of these other investments will vary depending on your financial situation and market conditions, but one investment I keep coming back to again and again is precious metals. Just to talk about gold (we'll talk about silver later), it has eternal value, it will never go to zero, it's a hedge against inflation, and I sleep better having a substantial portion (10% or so) of my wealth in it.

I've been at financial conferences where speakers have advised people to put 100% of their money in gold. That's absolutely insane,

What to Do in a Bank Holiday

When a bank fails, the FDIC steps in, finds a merger partner or takes the failing bank over. This usually happens quickly and with a minimum of panicking.

And it really helps that the FDIC has raised its banking insurance coverage to $250,000 worth of deposits in an individual account.

However, in a bank holiday, a broad-based banking crisis, we may see some of the rules bend or break.

If the FDIC is overwhelmed by the number of failures, or if the banks are shut down by Federal order, you may have to wait a while before you can access your funds. *That's why it's important to have a stash of cash that is not in the bank.*

And importantly, even in the best of times, do not count on the government to cover uninsured bank deposits, debentures, or other bank obligations.

For the latest list of the weakest and strongest banks in the United States, visit www.moneyandmarkets.com/banks.

and if anyone tries to tell you that, run away! You wouldn't have wanted to have all your wealth in gold during its 20-year bear market. But it definitely has a place in your portfolio. In the next chapter, I'll explain some of the reasons why I think it could outperform going forward.

The fates of empires are often sealed by snowballing debts, compounded by expensive wars. We saw it happen to the Soviet Union and to the British Empire before them. If the United States continues on the road it is on now, it may very well happen to us.

Heck, we're seeing major banks fail week after week—a parade of pain down Wall Street. That's not supposed to happen in the United States! It hasn't happened for decades, and it may be a prelude to the worst hard times to hit this country in generations.

How Bad Could It Get? Pretty Bad!

I once heard a story told by a 90-year-old man who lived through the Great Depression. He was from a large farming family. During the Depression they couldn't feed all the kids so the older boys drew straws to see who would leave the farm.

He and another brother drew short straws and left the next morning with a loaf of bread each. He slept in culverts and nearly starved to death (he started to cry as he recalled a woman who saw he was hungry and gave him cornbread), but he kept walking because to go back would only add to his family's almost unendurable hardship.

He walked more than 80 miles before he found a farmer who took him in to milk a herd of cows. He worked for two years for room and food and one pair of coveralls.

Now, looking around at the financial sinkhole our country is in, this man said: "Things are going to be worse in our future than *anything* I've lived through."

Wall Street is just waking up to the bad times. Main Street's hard times started seven or eight years ago. You can see it in the faces of mothers as they cut back on grocery purchases, people whose dream homes are sliding into foreclosure, and owners of small businesses who have to fire their longtime workers, who are often their friends as well, as business dries up in a withering economic climate.

I don't know if we're going to have a depression, or even a severe recession. It depends on if Washington can save Wall Street's bacon. I *do* know that a recessionary environment is usually deflationary. But gold can hold its value quite well because investors are scared to the point of panic.

And no government is going to sit around and let deflation strangle a nation. An easy way out is to start printing money, and that's highly inflationary!

I hope that Washington can fix the problem. But there's a real possibility they can't.

And if we see a Great Depression II, just remember that *the sequel is usually worse than the original.*

New Careers for a Brave New World

Even if the economy and/or society collapses, you'll still have to earn a living. You may know some skills now that you can translate into a vocation for the future. Some tips would be to:

- Think simple
- Think necessities
- Think stress

Everyone is going to be stressed after a collapse. As long as you're willing to take at least part of your payments in alternative currencies, you might be able to make a good living thinking outside the box on how you can relieve stress from other people's lives.

Here are some ideas on new careers:

- **Bike mechanic.** If we have an energy crisis, bikes are going to become a lot more popular, as will people who can fix them.
- **Seamstress/Tailor.** People won't have money for new clothes and will probably line up to have them repaired on the cheap.
- **Cobbler.** The shoes Americans wear today are made to wear out in a matter of months. Resoling shoes—with rubber cut from old tires or other materials—could be a booming business
- **Making beer.** There's that relieving stress angle. If the government goes away, you might want to be the guy who already knows how to make beer at home. If the government is still around, making a lot of beer could be legally dubious.
- **Acoustic musician.** When was the last time anyone had to live without iTunes? Playing music can score a bed and a meal for a traveler trying to get from one place to another.
- **Tool maker.** If you have the equipment—a mini-mill, and the power to run it—you might be able to write your own ticket.

These are just examples. We don't know exactly what crises will strike, so we don't know what kind of world will be coming. I think it's very likely that one part of the population sinks into desperate poverty while another part continues on just fine, oblivious. In that case, private security will probably be a booming profession.

The point is, you have to be flexible, willing to adapt (to go from, say, being a journalist to being a pool cleaner), and remember that you can't eat pride. If you don't have any secondary skills, skills that can be done in the absence of electricity, now would be a great time to learn how to do something new.

Having a new skill is *cool.* You'll be showing it off to all your friends. Stocking up on necessities (potential barter items) has very few downsides. If disaster never comes, then you'll have learned some new skills, and stocked up on necessities, which ultimately saves you money.

The Least You Can Do

- Pay one extra mortgage payment a year—but don't pay off your whole mortgage if you have other uses for the money.
- Pay off credit-card debt and other high-interest debt as fast as possible.
- Get your 401(k) in order.

C H A P T E R

Gold, Hard Assets, and Alternative Currencies

Give me control over a nation's currency and I care not who makes its laws.

—Baron M.A. Rothschild

In this chapter, I'll tell you why I believe gold and silver are great places to put some of your money. I'll give you reasons why the long-term trend in gold and silver should be higher, and the dos and don'ts of bullion buying. I'll also talk about foreign currencies as a potential investment, and alternatives to cash currencies that we could be using if the economy really goes belly up.

With the stock market's tumultuous ups and downs, many people are getting the feeling that gold, guns, and Spam are much better investments. Gold and silver, precious metals, have long been the standbys of survivalists and people who don't hold out much hope for the U.S. dollar or other investments. Gold will always be worth something 20 years from now no matter what the economy is like—you can't say the same for any stock. But cash still has its place, even though we may eventually experience a currency meltdown.

That said, there's something you have to realize, and it's best understood when looking at a U.S. one-dollar bill. Go ahead and take one out—I'll wait.

You see that picture of George Washington on the front? He knows what a nightmare a fiat currency can be. The paper currency (Continental dollar) issued by the Continental Congress declined in value by 97% in three years. Runaway inflation and the collapse of the Continental dollar prompted delegates to the Constitutional Convention to include the gold and silver clause in Article 1 of the United States Constitution. I'm pretty sure Washington would say hard experience shows it is ludicrous for a government could print as much paper money as it felt like with nothing to back it up but promises and confidence. Today, it is only due to agreements worked out between shadowy and powerful men that a dollar is worth anything at all.

The Eternal Store of Value

Gold has enjoyed a great run over the past few years, but it hasn't been a straight path. There have been enough dips and outright plunges to make gold traders feel like they're riding the Devil's own roller coaster.

On the other hand, gold is doing a lot better than the broad commodity indices, and certainly a heck of a lot better than domestic or international stocks.

"The real dynamic in gold right now is fear," according to Charles Nedoss, Senior Account Manager at Peak Trading in Chicago. "Gold is a proxy for fear. Gold is the vehicle that people use as a hedge against the volatility in currencies and other markets."

Why is that? It's simple. Gold is the hardest of hard assets. And as paper assets go up in smoke—a trillion dollars in stock market equity disappearing overnight, and trillions more in arcane debt instruments not worth the paper they're printed on—gold starts to look better and better.

The new rush into gold isn't taking place in a vacuum. It's happening in the context of a meltdown in the global credit markets, massive shifts in the global economy, and the declining value of the money in your wallet.

So, again, do I think it's a good time to own gold? I think it's a *great* time to own gold. I don't know if the manure is about to hit the fan, but if it is, gold is a nice hedge to have.

Of course, gold doesn't have to go higher. I think its long-term trend is up but in the shorter term, it could go lower due to the tremendous stress on the global economy.

What Can Drive Gold Lower in the Short Term?

I don't know if we're going to have a depression, or even a severe recession. It depends on if Washington can save Wall Street's bacon. I *do* know that a severe recession is usually deflationary. But gold can hold its value quite well because investors are scared to the point of panic. In fact, a financial panic is the kind of environment where investors and ordinary citizens snap up gold bullion and coins by the fistful.

At the same time, we can have steep corrections because investors the world over are simply terrified that we are facing a severe global recession, along with deflation. While I wouldn't be surprised to see deflation in the short term, especially since the credit market has frozen up, I think longer term we're going to see strong inflation.

Sure, we have economic weakness, but at the same time, the United States is paying for a war that is ruinously expensive in both blood and money. In many ways, it's a repeat of what we had in the 1970s. If you'll refer to Figure 4.1, you can see I've charted the year-over-year change in inflation with gray areas showing U.S. recessions. On top of that, I've added the U.S. gold price.

You can see that in the 1970s, the United States went into recession, yet inflation kept going higher, and so did the price of gold. Now, more recently, inflation was red-hot, and gold went higher.

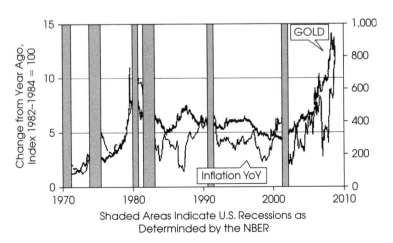

Figure 4.1   Consumer Price Index for Urban Consumers
Source: St. Louis Fed.

Meanwhile, the U.S. government is pouring liquidity into the market in an attempt to break the corporate credit logjam and keep the economy from stalling. Eventually, that logjam will break and liquidity will flood into the system.

Here's what I think:

- It is not too late to profit from rising gold prices—not by a long shot.
- You will want to have gold and the right gold stocks in your portfolio.
- Gold could move farther and faster than many people on Wall Street believe possible.

Five Forces That Will Push Gold Prices Higher

There are many forces lining up to push gold higher. Let's look at just five of them:

1. Lack of new supply
2. Gold ETFs
3. A flood of red ink in Washington
4. Central banks
5. The rise in China's gold reserves

Any one of these forces is bullish for the yellow metal—together, they could send gold smashing through overhead resistance to soar.

Force #1: Lack of New Supply

Gold comes from a bunch of sources—mines are just one of them. There's also central bank selling and sales of gold scrap. Another source is hedging, or forward selling of gold production by miners, which isdifferent from regular production in that it locks in future sales of mine production at a set price and helps price stability.

However, mines are *the* source of new gold supply. And despite higher and higher prices, gold mine output fell in 2008 to a 12-year low! (See Figure 4.2.)

Looking ahead, GFMS consultancy—a London-based research group that serves gold mining companies and supplies the World Gold Council with its data—says that gold production will fall *again* this year.

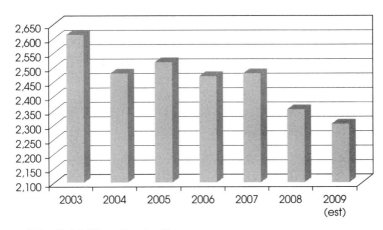

Figure 4.2   Gold Mine Production
Sources: GFMS, World Gold Council.

And the production decline certainly isn't due to lower prices. Prices more than *tripled* from $271 an ounce in 2001 to touch $1,000 an ounce in 2008 and again in 2009.

The *easy* gold has been dug up. New projects can take as long as 10 years to bring on line, compared with just three to five years in the past.

Why is this happening, with gold prices so high? The easy gold has been found; that's why. Many new deposits are smaller and lower-grade, and not worth investigating after the initial find.

In 2001, the production costs of gold were roughly $160 per ounce as prices dipped to $270. Then in early-2008, production costs rose to $400 to $500 an ounce as prices briefly hit $1,000.

Companies *were* ramping up exploration budgets—right up until 2008, when the global economy ran off the rails.

Industry nonferrous (non-iron) metal exploration spending budgeted for 2008 was in the vicinity of $13.2 billion, according to Nova Scotia-based Metals Economics Group. That was a 26% increase over 2007, and the sixth consecutive yearly increase since 2002.

But then the bottom fell out of the market. Difficulties in raising financing—including an outright disappearance of credit for junior miners—and ballooning capital costs forced many projects to be delayed, and others outright canceled. Even big miners like Rio Tinto and Freeport McMoRan Copper & Gold slashed explorations budgets.

This puts a serious kink in the supply chain of projects coming online, and means there will be less gold coming out of mines in the future.

Another reason why production isn't ramping up with gold prices is there are fewer mining companies. The 20-year bear market in gold forced many marginal mines to close. And over the past 15 years, a wave of mergers has created a bunch of mega-sized gold miners. While the top five each produce between 3.5 and 7 million ounces out of the ground every year, they're likely to concentrate more on working their existing mines and buying up other mines, and focus less on new exploration.

Force #2: Gold ETFs Can Boost Demand

Investors poured money into gold ETFs through mid-2009. The gold holdings of the world's largest gold-backed exchange-traded fund, the SPDR Gold Trust (GLD), surged to over 1,125 metric tonnes in June of 2009. Other ETFs around the world are also buying gold. The more ETFs stock up on gold, the higher the price of gold goes. (See Table 4.1.)

I'm thinking that the smart money is betting on a big rise in gold.

As the banks melt down, and as other investments turn to dust, investors will likely turn more and more to gold. And the GLD, XAU, and other gold ETFs and funds make buying gold easier than ever.

Table 4.1   Official Gold Holdings by Country

Country	Metric Tonnes	Percent of Reserves
USA	8,133.5	78.3
Germany	3,412.6	69.5
Italy	2,451.8	66.1
France	2,450.7	73.0
GLD (Gold ETF)	**1,125.7**	**N/A**
China	1,054.0	1.8
Switzerland	1,040.1	37.1
Japan	765.2	2.1
Netherlands	612.5	61.4
ECB	501.4	18.3
Russia	536.9	4.0

Source: World Gold Council, June 2009.

Indeed, the SPDR Gold Trust, the biggest of the gold ETFs, now holds more gold than many countries.

Is this investment demand sustainable? Well, nothing lasts forever, and we saw ETF gold holdings dip in 2009. At some point, gold ETFs will start selling gold, and that will weigh on the market. But it's impossible to tell when the peak will be. I do think investment demand will get *more* urgent in 2010.

Meanwhile, silver investment demand lagged gold, but now seems to be playing catch-up. Implied net silver investment more than doubled to 50.2 million ounces in 2008, largely due to record inflows into ETFs and a surge in Indian investment.

Force #3: A Flood of Red Ink from Washington

As I told you in Chapter 3, fundamentally speaking, the U.S. government is issuing far too many dollars, eating away at its value. This has been going on for quite some time, but it accelerated when the government started throwing money at the financial crisis in 2008.

The U.S. fiscal deficit could top $2 trillion in 2009—a whopping 15% of gross domestic product. That would increase by one-third the total stock of federal government debt outstanding. What's more, the deficit will probably be even larger 2010.

A $2 trillion deficit means that, if the economy produces $14 trillion in goods and services in 2009, the government's deficit is more than 14% of the economy.

Supporting all the debt eats away at our nation's productivity. That's just the deficit. That does not count the rollover of the existing federal debt, which is at least another $2.5 trillion in 2009.

So then, where will capital come from to finance the recovery? Answer: It won't.

Instead, we'll keep borrowing. We'll borrow from U.S. citizens and foreign investors. We'll borrow from foreign central banks (Hello-o-o-o, China!).

Heck, our government is even buying its own debt. Our government buying its own debt is like a snake eating its own tail! How can Uncle Sam possibly repay these mountains of debt? The only way to do it—that I can see, anyway—is to make those mountains into comparative molehills by devaluing the U.S. dollar lower—perhaps much lower.

Since gold is priced in dollars, as one goes down, the other tends to go up. It's what I call *The Seesaw of Pain.*

Force #4: Are Central Banks Catching Gold Fever?

Sales of gold by the world's central banks are typically a bearish force for gold prices. In September of 2004, a new five-year agreement limited sales to 500 tons per year.

However, bank sales did not reach their limit in 2008 and some are guessing that banks are no longer eager to sell their gold.

In a recent Gold Demand Trends, the World Gold Council pointed out an interesting fact: Central banks are selling a lot less gold.

"Muted central bank sales contributed just 35 tonnes to total first quarter supply, less than half the level of net sales in Q1 2008," the WGC wrote.

The WGC also noted that China revealed after the end of the period under review that it had added 454 tonnes, purchased since 2003, to its reserves.

And that brings us to Force #5.

Force #5: China's Gold Reserves Are Probably Going Much Higher

In fact, from 2002 to 2008, China stealthily increased its holding of gold to 1,054 metric tonnes from just 600 tonnes.

That put China's gold holdings at 1.8% of its foreign exchange reserves—much lower than the share of gold in the foreign exchange reserves of the United States, Italy, and Germany. Some would argue that not only is this way too low, but that China is going to correct it, using some of its huge worth of foreign exchange reserves.

The problem is the sheer size of China's foreign reserves—$2 *trillion* worth. If China decided to hold 5% of its current reserves in gold (the international average is 10%), it would need to buy more than 3,000 tonnes of gold—or about one full year of global production.

What do you think that would do to the gold price? It would send it through the roof!

What would China sell to buy gold? Probably U.S. Treasuries. China is the largest single holder of U.S. Treasuries, with $763.5 billion at the end of April, according to U.S. Treasury data.

Of course, if China sells Treasuries, that would weaken an already troubled U.S. dollar.

This would have a double-barrel effect on the price of gold—pushing gold prices up as China buys gold and pushing the value

Could Gold Prices Go Lower?

Sure, gold prices could go lower. And I think that would be a heck of a buying opportunity. While I expect that deflation will be short-circuited by the Fed's reflation efforts, these might fail and the country might slide into deflation and depression, and bring the world along with it. And while gold did well during the last Great Depression, that doesn't mean it will do well in the next one.

Also, if the recession continues, it could really dampen worldwide demand for gold jewelry, which is 68% of all demand.

On the other hand, investment demand for gold is growing by leaps and bounds. Also, consumer demand for gold in newly wealthy countries like China and other emerging markets is ramping up; many of these countries have a cultural affinity for gold.

Add it all up, and while nothing is certain, I think the easy path for gold is much higher over the long term.

of the dollar lower, which, in turn, would push gold even higher, because gold is priced in dollars!

These are just five of the forces coming together to drive gold and silver prices higher.

Buying Gold—Let's Get Physical

Now let's talk about ways you might want to buy gold—and ways you might want to avoid.

How do you want to own gold? Some people say that to be really safe, you have to own gold bullion. And I won't argue against it—heck, I own gold bullion. Nonetheless. . . .

Here are some arguments against buying gold bullion.

Just remember that:

- If you buy gold through a dealer, you'll have to pay his markup.
- If you buy your gold in the form of gold coins, they will usually carry a bigger markup than gold bars.
- Once you own it, you'll have to store it securely, whether it's paying for a safe deposit box or burying it in the backyard.
- Once you decide to sell it, the dealer will want his cut on the other end, as well. The exception is when demand is high, and a dealer may pay you the spot price.

All these things aside, there are great reasons to buy and own gold bullion.

Gold can't be destroyed by fire, flood, or plague. It *can* survive the complete collapse of a financial system. I'm not saying that's what's going to happen; I'm saying gold has a well-earned reputation as the ultimate safe harbor. Gold will never go to zero. If you want to play it safe, own gold.

Let's talk about some of the physical ways to buy gold. I talked to some experts about this: One is Patrick A. Heller, owner of Liberty Coin Service (http://www.libertycoinservice.com) in Lansing, Michigan. Another is Dan Rosenthal, the founder of the widely respected *The Silver and Gold Report*, and now a consultant for Natural Resource Hunter. Both of these gentlemen have forgotten more about buying gold bullion than I'll ever know, so I've included their comments where appropriate.

Bullion Bars and Coins

Both experts favored coins over bars, Rosenthal strongly so. Bullion coins—American Eagles, Buffaloes, Canadian Maple Leafs, and so on—allow you to own investment grade gold (between 0.90 and 0.9999 fineness) in a quantity that will be recognized at any gold dealer in the Western world.

Most bullion coins are minted in ¹⁄₁₀-ounce, ¼-ounce, ½-ounce and 1-ounce form (some can be larger). However, one-ounce gold bullion coins such as Eagles or Krugerrands are by far the most popular for small investors.

So what's wrong with bars? They're much easier to counterfeit than a coin. "If you go to Asia with a bar of gold, or to another country, they won't know a particular bar from a hole in the wall," Rosenthal said. "Coins have much, much wider recognition."

Not everyone agrees with Rosenthal on this. One dealer told me: "Engelhard gold bars (made by Englehard Australia) are very widely accepted, and they are numbered as well. And I have seen more phony Kruggerands and $20 U.S. pieces than fake ingots."

The point is to be very careful.

Rosenthal especially warned against buying gold bars on eBay, craigslist, or some other online site. "If you do buy a bar, the only place to do it is on a reputable commodity exchange," he added, like the COMEX. "You can take delivery of the bar and leave it in storage on the exchange."

Futures trader Charles Nedoss of Peak Trading Group in Chicago confirms that he has clients who do this from time to time. "You take delivery and hold the receipt. The storage fee is nominal."

"If you take delivery of the bar from the COMEX, it loses all liquidity," Rosenthal says. In other words, it's much harder to sell. "The person who buys it is going to insist on drilling it if they have any brains," to make sure the bar isn't counterfeit or hollowed out and refilled with some other metal.

Back when he was running his newsletter, Rosenthal saw one of the reputable mutual funds get stuck with 500 counterfeit bars of gold.

"There are lots of ways to counterfeit bars, it's infinitely harder to counterfeit coins," he says. "Tungsten has the same approximate weight as gold down to several decimal places. A counterfeiter can make a tungsten bar, coat it with gold, and stamp it. Then it looks, weighs, and feels real."

Now for the bad news—COMEX gold futures contracts are for 100 troy ounces. That's a lot of gold, especially when the price of gold is going up and down like a yo-yo. Nedoss says his clients usually buy a futures put option to protect themselves against violent price swings.

There are still bargains to be had in coins, and if you work with a reputable dealer, he can steer you to them.

On the other hand, Heller recommends avoiding "obscure" gold coins. "Dow Chemical used to give retiring employees a 1-ounce gold medal," he explains. "That is not something I would recommend for people to purchase as a way to own an ounce of gold. That's what we sell to jewelers to melt down."

One fairly common source of silver coins is ordinary U.S. pre-1965 coins. The amount of silver in pre-1965 coins is commonly 90%.

Here is the silver content of various earlier silver coins:

- Silver dollars contain 0.77344 troy oz. silver content.
- Half dollars contain 0.36169 troy oz silver content.
- Quarters contain 0.18084 troy oz silver content.
- Dimes contain 0.0723 troy oz silver content.

Precious metals are usually sold by the troy ounce, which weighs more than the typical ounce we use in everyday life. But just to add further confusion, there are 12 (not 16) troy ounces in a troy pound.

So, if you want to pick up silver on the cheap, you can look for the big bags of pre-1965 coins sold by some dealers and online. However, be aware of a few things.

While many silver bugs and survivalists are stocking up on pre-1965 coins for their silver content, that may not be a fact that is generally known. Heck, nearly half of the U.S. population doesn't know that it takes Earth a year to orbit the sun![1] And 18% of Americans think the sun revolves around Earth.

What I'm saying is that, after a crash, if silver shoots up in value, you may have some difficulty convincing Bubba at the corner store that your pre-1965 coins contain 90% silver.

Calculating the Premium on Gold Coins or Bars

To calculate the premium you're paying for a gold bar or coin, use this formula:

Divide the cost of the coin by its gold content to get your cost per ounce. Call this "*x*"

Divide *x* by the spot price to get your cost over spot. Call this number "*y*"

y minus 1 × 100 equals your percentage premium.

Here's an example. Let's say you're buying a U.S. Gold Eagle.

A U.S. Gold Eagle has a gold content of one ounce. That means each Gold Eagle coin has a fineness of 1.000—it contains its specified weight in pure 24-karat gold. An alloy is added to make it more durable, so a one-ounce American Gold Eagle, for example, actually weighs 1.0909 troy ounces.

So, when the spot price of gold was $935, you could buy a U.S. Gold Eagle for $1,020.

$$\frac{935}{1} = 935 \text{ per ounce}$$

$$\frac{1,020}{935} = 1.09$$

$$1.09 - 1 = 0.09. \text{ Then, } 0.09 \times 100$$

$$= 9\%. \text{ This is your percentage premium.}$$

If you want the dollar premium rather than the percentage premium, take the cost per ounce and subtract the spot price. In this case, $1,020 − $935 = $85.

This formula works for all coins, and the cost of gold doesn't matter.

Here's another example. Let's say you want to buy an Austria 1 Ducat. It's a small coin with a gold content of 0.1107 ounces. And let's say you buy that coin for $115.80 when the spot gold price is $935.

$$\frac{115.8}{0.1107} = 1,046.07 \text{ per ounce}$$

$$\frac{1,046.07}{935} = 1.11879$$

$$1.11879 - 1 = 0.11879. \text{ Then, multiply your}$$
answer times 100 to get a
percentage premium of 11.9%.

It doesn't matter what the price of gold is when you read this book. The same formula will work.

Be sure to check the fineness of the gold coin or bar you are buying, and you can calculate the premium you are paying over the spot price of gold.

What You Should Buy and What You Shouldn't

Now that you know how to buy gold, below are two types of gold products—one you should buy and the other you should run away from.

Semi-Numismatic and Numismatic Gold Coins. Numismatic or older and rare coins are bought not solely for their precious metal content but also for their rarity and their historical, aesthetic appeal. They are leveraged to the gold price, which means that the price of these coins can increase faster than the gold price in a bull market (due to their historical and aesthetic value and to their rarity) and can decrease by more when gold is in a bear market.

Many investors opt for high-quality pre-1933 gold coins graded MS-60 or better by either the Professional Coin Grading Service or the Numismatic Guaranty Corporation.

These can be great investments. On the other hand, if you're one of the people worried about a money panic and a potential breakdown in society, you have to wonder how well numismatic value will hold in such a situation.

Physical Alternatives to Coins and Bars.   Most people buy gold bars or coins. But gold buyers and sellers also traffic in gold dust, nuggets, wire, and even gold chips used by dentists to fill teeth. But none of these are as fungible as coins or bars and coins are the most fungible of all. The more a gold piece is a fabricated product of known weight and purity, the better off you usually are. Gold dust in particular can be diluted or even counterfeited.

Non-Physical Ways to Own Gold

There are ways to buy gold without taking physical delivery. It's not my choice, but if it suits you, here's some information.

Allocated Accounts

Let's say you want to buy some gold, but don't have a safe place to keep it. Major bullion banks and specialist depositories offer to buy the gold and store it for you. The gold can be in a pooled account or a segregated account. In a segregated account, your gold is kept separately. A segregated account has higher fees.

For more information, you can check out the pooled and holding accounts description on Everbank's web site (http://www .everbank.com/001Metals.aspx).

Dan Rosenthal is not a big fan of allocated accounts. For one thing, there's the potential for fraud (see sidebar). For Dan, it's also the principle of the thing. He says:

> The whole point of gold, to me, is that you don't trust the government. It's the government's (fiat) money versus gold. You buy gold because you don't trust the government's money. If you don't trust the government's money, why the hell are you going to trust some stranger who could easily be as unreliable as the government?
>
> So, you buy and you take delivery. That's the only good way.

Buyer Beware—A Cautionary Tale

When Dan Rosenthal ran *The Silver and Gold Report*, he once blew the lid off a gold storage scheme that ripped people off to the tune of $59 million.

The company was called Bullion Reserve of North America, run by a flashy Los Angeles gold and silver dealer named Alan Saxon. He claimed to be holding $60 million worth of customers' gold in allocated accounts that were locked away, 200 feet deep in underground vaults managed by Perpetual Storage, Inc., near Salt Lake City.

Saxon asked Rosenthal for an endorsement to his newsletter subscribers. Rosenthal gave a temporary endorsement on the promise that Saxon would send him a certified audit of the gold in storage.

The audit never arrived. After some back-and-forth, Rosenthal arranged to visit Perpetual Storage and check it out for himself.

Within five minutes he knew it was a sham. There wasn't nearly enough gold in the vaults to back up Saxon's claims.

"They should have had between 60 and 100 million dollars worth of metal," Rosenthal said. "I looked and said: 'This is a real problem.' I saw maybe $3 million worth of gold."

After close physical inspection, with laborious inspection and logging of the bars, Rosenthal went to Los Angeles to confront Saxon. "I expected him to be jumping to give me answers and he just bulls__ed me," Rosenthal remembers. " I left, and I wrote him up according to my Mommy Rosenthal test. And that is: If this was my mother's money, would I tell her to store her money there? In this case, the answer was no."

The way he put it to his readers was that if Mommy Rosenthal had any money in Bullion Reserve of North America, he would tell her to get it the hell out.

After his report hit the press, all hell broke loose, Rosenthal remembers. Other dealers rallied around Saxon. Rosenthal received death threats and thugs tailed him.

But six weeks later, Alan Saxon was dead. He had run a hose from the exhaust pipe of his motorcycle into the sauna of his luxury condo in Venice, California. He apparently started the engine, and then sat in jeans and socks while the sauna filled with carbon monoxide. When his body was found, so was a tape recording—naming Rosenthal's expose and Saxon's mounting business losses as the problems that drove him to kill himself.

(Continued)

(Continued)

When accountants examined the books of the company, every word Dan Rosenthal had said was proved true. The FBI came in later, but too late to save the customers who had been hoodwinked by Saxon.

Digital Gold or e-Gold.   My personal view on e-gold, e-bullion, or whatever you want to call it is simply: *Don't.* There are a couple of reputable firms in this business: GoldMoney.com and BullionVault. com, for example. But the lax operating procedures of the Internet make this business attractive to financial predators.

There are no specific financial regulations governing digital gold currency (DGC) providers, so they operate under self-regulation. DGC providers are not banks and therefore do not need to comply with bank regulations and there are concerns that unscrupulous operators are operating in this emerging sector.

Gold Exchange-Traded Funds (ETFs).   Trading in precious metals got a whole lot easier when Exchange-Traded Funds (ETFs) and Exchange-Traded Notes (ETNs) came along.

As seen in Table 4.2, there are a bunch of gold and silver ETFs. The iShares and SPDR funds hold physical metal. The GLD and the Barclays iShares Comex Gold Trust (IAU) are fixed at one-tenth the price of gold, minus a small amount to account for fees. That is, if

Table 4.2   Gold, Silver, and Metals ETFs and ETNs

Fund Name	Symbol	Total Expense Ratio
iShares COMEX Gold Trust	IAU	0.40
iShares Silver Trust	SLV	0.50
SPDR Gold Shares	GLD	0.40
PowerShares DB Gold Fund	DGL	0.50
DB Gold Shares Double Long	DGP	0.75
DB Gold Short	DGZ	0.75
DB Gold Double Short	DZZ	0.75
PowerShares DB Silver Fund ETF	DBS	0.50
PowerShares DB Precious Metals Fund ETF	DBP	0.75

gold is trading at $800 an ounce, you can buy the GLD or the IAU for about $80. They are backed up by gold bullion in a vault.

There are fees associated with gold ETFs, but they're small, and you can't beat the convenience. On the other hand, if you're a stickler for physical gold, these funds aren't for you.

And some funds, like the PowerShares gold funds, don't hold physical gold. Instead, they track the performance of a fully collateralized futures position, meaning they capture changes in the spot price of the underlying metal plus any *roll yield* and interest income.

If a fund's holdings of physical gold are not important to you, you might just go with the fund that has the lowest total expense ratio. However, I highly recommend a fund that is liquid (has plenty of volume). Just as important as getting into a gold ETF is being able to get out when you want to.

And then there are the leveraged Gold ETNs—DGP and DZZ. DGP targets twice the movement in gold, while DZZ targets twice the *inverse* of the *daily* movement in gold.

If the metals do well, long gold ETFs will likely outperform. If the metals do poorly, they will likely under perform. And visa versa for the short and double-short gold funds.

Importantly, I wouldn't use the leveraged gold ETFs as ways to be positioned in gold for the long term. They're trading vehicles—you move in, hold them for a while, and get out. Hopefully, the short-term trend is in your favor. And the safest way to invest in gold is by buying and holding physical gold.

One More Idea—Central Fund of Canada. The Central Fund of Canada (CEF on the AMEX) is a great closed-end fund that invests 90% of its holdings in gold and silver bullion (the rest is in cash).

As a closed-end fund, CEF is a bit different from the traditional open-ended mutual fund that you might be used to. An open-ended mutual fund or exchange-traded fund creates new shares every time an investor buys the fund and redeems the shares every time an investor sells the fund.

A closed-end fund limits its amount of shares. It is a publicly traded entity that raises capital through an initial public offering and invests the proceeds according to the fund's objectives.

Because closed-end funds limit their shares, they can trade at a premium or discount to their net asset value (NAV). It carries a premium because its limited amount of shares means CEF's price is leveraged to the price of gold. And as a plus, if silver outperforms gold, CEF will let you participate in that, as well.

Gold Investing—Keep It Simple

In a nutshell, below are my recommendations for investing in gold. Depending on your personal situation, your investment advisor may have other ideas, but this is a great starting point:

> **Investment #1—Buy gold.** And I mean physical gold, the kind you put in a safe. You don't buy physical gold to get rich; you buy it to preserve wealth. If Treasuries implode, gold will make a mighty fine insurance policy. Also, you might want to pick up gold in forms that you can easily barter if paper money becomes worthless—simple gold rings, for example. Wedding bands are good for this. I know of a guy who has hundreds of wedding bands stored on clothes hangers in his closet.

Five Tips for Gold Bullion Buyers

Here is a collection of five tips from expert sources.

1. Call at least three dealers for a price. The difference between a good price and an almost good price can be the difference between getting 100 ounces of gold and 90 ounces of gold.
2. Make sure you include shipping costs in your calculation of the price of the coin—shipping costs vary wildly from dealer to dealer.
3. You need to be explicit on what you are locking in, including price, merchandise, and terms of payment. If there seems to be any waffling on the part of the dealer, this is a warning sign to steer clear.
4. Look for a dealer who has been in business for a number of years. Ideally, if you go to someone who was in business in the 1970-to-1980 boom, they've seen enough ups and downs in the market to handle the challenges of price fluctuations and coin availability.
5. Get to know a local dealer. The advantage is he can call you when he gets new inventory and there will be no shipping involved.

The worst time to buy gold is when it's going higher. Nothing travels in a straight line, so wait for a pullback and pick up simple gold coins or gold bars.

Investment #2—Silver. Again, I mean physical silver. If our economy, financial system, and paper money go south, you'll want gold *and* silver. Flashing around too much gold could make you a target. Silver doesn't attract as much attention and it's still a precious metal. In fact, silver is undervalued compared to gold by some metrics.

What to Use as Money If the Dollar Loses Its Value

I think you can see why gold should be in your portfolio, and why you might want to have some at home: If the value of the U.S. dollar collapses, gold will more than hold its value; it will soar in value. The same goes for silver. And I like silver a lot—its lower value means you can use it for smaller purchases, it doesn't attract as much attention as gold, and silver is also an industrial metal, which means it can do well in the good times as well as the bad times.

What could drive the value of the U.S. dollar much, much lower? Well, if the economy is bad enough, long enough, and the government continues to try and inflate its way out of its problems, there is the potential for hyperinflation. The difference between hyperinflation and inflation is the difference between lightning and a lightning bug, to twist a phrase from Mark Twain.[2]

Inflation takes place during credit expansion—a virtuous cycle causes GDP to expand. This is what the government and the Fed are trying to revive. Hyperinflation is when inflation spins out of control—prices increase rapidly as a currency loses its value. The breeding ground for hyperinflation is when money velocity increases rapidly while economic output declines at the same time.

Hyperinflation is a horrible time to live through, but it doesn't last forever. It usually ends with drastic remedies, such as imposing the shock therapy of slashing government expenditures or *altering the currency basis.*

During a tumultuous time of hyperinflation, alternative currencies usually come into play, and they can also be used in other times of economic distress. I think we'll see some of them used in the next 10 years. Those alternative currencies can include. . . .

Local Paper Currencies: These were widely used in the early 1900s up until the early days of the Great Depression, when they were used to organize trade of services and products when there was a shortage of national currency. In 1933, there were three- or four-hundred different scrips circulating in the United States, Canada, and Mexico. A top economist urged Roosevelt to encourage local currencies as a way to stimulate local economies. However, F.D.R opted for The New Deal, which flooded the nation with Federal Reserve Notes, put an end to the currency experiments, and effectively centralized power.[3]

Today, local currencies are making a comeback in different parts of the United States and Canada. Sometimes they are backed by things like food, and sometimes they are exchangeable for local services.

For example, a farmer who needs to build a grain silo can issue credits to local workmen and suppliers redeemable in his harvest.

This system is how *paper* currencies originally started. In ancient Egypt, people had to store their grain at government granaries, and when they brought it in they were given a receipt. Whenever they were hungry they could bring in the receipt and get the grain back. Thus, the receipt came to act as a currency, with people accepting it in exchange for non-food goods.

However, rats would eat the grain in the granaries, so the receipts lost value over time. Result: Everyone hurried to spend them as soon as possible. This may seem like a problem, but it's actually an advantage when towns are trying to stimulate their local economies, and *time value* is being incorporated into some local currencies today.

Showing there's nothing new under the sun, in California's Mendocino County, some local businesses are using a currency called Mendo Credits that is backed by locally grown grain.[4] The paper used for the currency is the same kind used by printers of banking checks and pharmaceutical prescription pads. The special paper is one line of defense; another is that each note gets a unique serial number. Each Mendo credit expires after a year.

Another local currency is BerkShares, which are used in the Berkshire region of Massachusetts. You can exchange 95 U.S. dollars for 100 BerkShares. You get a 5% discount, and in return the money is all spent locally.

If you want to find out how *you* could set up an alternative currency for your locality, you can get a kit from Paul Glover, who started the most successful local currency in the United States, *Ithaca HOURs.* Paul sells a "Hometown Money Book and Starter Kit" for $25. The Ithaca HOURs system equates one hour of work with a $10 denomination. For more information, you can contact Paul at paul5glover@yahoo.com or (215) 805-8330, and his web site is http://www.ithacahours.com.

Pros: Local businesses have a vested interest in seeing the currencies circulate and succeed. Money and services circulate in the community, boosting the local economy.

Cons: Limited area of acceptance; easier to counterfeit than U.S. currency, though limited circulation limits the appeal for counterfeiters. Also, local currencies can fall out of circulation.

Local mutual credit currencies. This is known as Local Exchange Trading Systems (LETS). Each transaction is recorded as a corresponding credit and debit in the two participants' accounts. No fiat money is involved.

LETS systems are already in place in some Canadian cities—Vancouver and Edmonton are two examples. In Seattle, the system is called *dibits* and can be found on Dibspace.com. Basically, it's a barter system. Reminder: The IRS taxes barter.

Pros: Can't be counterfeited, and scammers are foiled by letting users dispute a charge or nonpayment.

Cons: Really, really not liquid.

Candy bars, gum, deodorant, razors, and other small items: Russian emigrant Dmitry Orlov draws some eerie parallels between the collapsing Soviet Union and the United States in his book *Reinventing Collapse.* It's a fascinating read. One really interesting part describes how people function when paper money becomes worthless.

A Man, a Plan, and a Printing Press

Local currencies resurfaced in the United States in 1991 in Ithaca, New York, with the *Ithaca HOUR*. One Ithaca HOUR is valued at U.S. $10. It is generally used as payment for one hour's work, although the rate is negotiable. It can be exchanged for U.S. dollars at participating businesses, including a credit union, in Ithaca.

This local currency was created by Paul Glover, a graphic designer.

"I had a longstanding interest in local initiatives," Glover told me. "And it seemed natural, during the Great Recession of the early 90s, to design money. We didn't have gold for backing—neither does the dollar—but we had extra hours of time for extra income. As a journalist and graphic artist, it was easy to make the leap from idea to design to launch."

Thanks to the recession, many of Glover's neighbors were unemployed or short of cash. Glover hoped that the HOURs would encourage local spending and stimulate the economy. The first printing was 2,250 HOURS, but now 10,000 HOURS have been printed, with denominations ranging from one-tenth of an HOUR to two HOURS.

"HOURS bring new skills into the market, reinforce small local business and farms, strengthen community capacity to meet needs with least reliance on distant board rooms and bureaucracies," Glover explains. "And they introduce us to one another as resources for assistance, rather than as competitors for scarce dollars."

Glover says interest in local currencies is steady, and increasing "as the formal economy stumbles. I've been contacted by many people interested in creating their own cash."

When he talks to potential currency printers, Glover emphasizes that successful currencies will have at least one full-time employee. That's because, just as dollars have armies of brokers moving money, each local currency needs a regular Networker to promote, facilitate, and troubleshoot circulation.

Does Glover think the U.S. dollar is in trouble? In a word, "yes."

"All national currencies will lose value, some faster than others," Glover says. "U.S. dollars are particularly vulnerable since we've relied on cheap imported fossil fuels to warm our homes and move our cars."

Glover believes the future is bright for local currencies. "They'll move in to take up slack as dollars fade. The more they prove stable and useful, the more they'll contribute to rebuilding America's economy."

For example, certain stores would take payment in Snickers bars and make change in chewing gum. If you needed a driver's license, you'd bring along some nice women's hygiene products to pay the clerk.

Pros: Easy to stock up on these small items now.

Cons: As long as these are things you'll use yourself, there aren't many cons.

Black Market Currencies. Alternative economies are typical of decaying societies. Orlov relates that in the Soviet Union, people would engage in *asset stripping*—pulling the copper out of the wires of abandoned homes, carrying off the vinyl siding and the fiberglass insulation. In a functioning society, this would be called *stealing*. In a collapsed society, this is *raising capital*. This *junk* was a treasure trove of currency for future transactions over food, water, or medicines.

Black market drugs became a premier currency in the New Russia, and there was plenty of value in drugs, alcohol, and cigarettes. Doctors and nurses traded their services side by side with carpenters and electricians. And since licensed professional currency carried a premium, some consumers chose discounts from back-ally medical practitioners and Crazy Ivan's Cut-Rate Carpentry.

Much to my lawyer's relief, I am not going to recommend anyone engage in the illegal drug trade or unlicensed electrical work. However, you can see how a medicinal herb garden could become a secondary source of income if TSHTF.

Indeed, the black market already exists all around you. *Social prostitution* is the name sociologists give to the practice of women, mostly single moms, trading sex for getting a broken car fixed, plumbing patched up, etc. We'll probably see a lot more of it in a collapsed society.

Pros: Just using medicinal herbs as an example, you'll be able to grow your own money.

Cons: Getting arrested. Also, it's easy to get scammed by a bum passing himself off as a carpenter or electrician.

Note: The police will probably stop arresting people for growing weed about the time they stop answering 911 calls. As with everything else, there are trade-offs in a collapse.

Even more alternative currencies: Copper wire, salt, sugar, choc-olate, tobacco, alcohol, bread, and bullets could all become currencies in a real hyperinflation/currency collapse.

Just keep this in mind: As of this writing, we are in a deflationary environment. Inflation is probably a ways down the road, and hyperin-flation, if it comes, probably won't be soon. You have other things to worry about, because *your* next big disaster could be around the corner.

Could we see hyperinflation? It's always possible. Widespread hyperinflation would eliminate current debts but it would probably also end future borrowing. And trading with other countries becomes problematic when the currency you use loses its value every day.

This is a real problem for the United States, because we are a consumer-oriented society and we import so many of our consumer goods. But this also represents opportunity for a savvy survivalist.

Inflation takes place, causes, and is caused by credit expansion. A virtuous cycle causes GDP to expand. This is what the govern-ment and the Fed are trying to revive.

Hyperinflation takes place when money velocity increases and GDP declines. In a hyperinflationary environment, trading with other countries probably will not work very well either.

Should You Put Your Money in Foreign Currencies?

I think gold, silver, and other investments can insulate you against a potential dollar collapse, but investing in foreign currencies works for some people, especially if their escape plan involves fleeing to another country. Swiss francs used to be held in high regard until it turned out that Swiss banks bought more than their fair share of the toxic debt issued by the banksters in the United States.

I like commodity currencies—currencies where commodities make up a large share of a country's gross domestic product, partic-ularly the New Zealand and Australian dollars. The Canadian dol-lar is also a commodity currency, but the United States is Canada's largest trading partner. Therefore, if the U.S. economy goes south, it's probably going to drag the Canadian dollar (called the *loonie*) along with it. Here are three ideas:

1. You can buy travelers' checks in foreign currencies. You can do this right now online. American Express will sell you trav-elers' checks in just about any currency.

2. A foreign bank may open an account in a foreign currency for you. This is prudent if you're planning on fleeing to that country when TSHTF here in the United States.
3. You can also buy an international bond fund that invests in high-quality, non-dollar denominated government debt securities outside the United States. One example is the American Century International Bond Fund (ticker symbol: BEGBX). Another is the PIMCO Foreign Bond Fund U.S. Dollar-hedged (ticker symbol: PFBPX). Either of these funds could have a place in a diversified portfolio.

You can also trade the FX, or foreign exchange markets. But you have to be a pro (or at least get professional recommendations) to do it well—it's very easy to lose your shirt *and* your shorts in the FX markets.

Welcome to Barter-Town

Variations of a list of "First 100 Things to Disappear in a National Emergency/Crisis/Power-down" have been around the Web for a while. These lists are quite well thought-out. I find them useful for ideas on things we could barter if the U.S. dollar goes belly up.

A barter economy is not the worst thing that can happen. It may only be short-term, while a new government and/or new currency gets on its feet. If you're a good haggler—and even if you not—this list will give you some ideas of things you might stockpile to use as trading items. Even better, most of the items on this list are things you'll use anyway.

1. Generators (Good ones cost dearly. Gas storage, risky. These are also noisy, a target of thieves, and they require maintenance, etc.)
2. Water Filters/Purifiers
3. Portable Toilets
4. Seasoned Firewood (Wood takes about six to 12 months to become dried, for home uses.)
5. Lamp Oil, Wicks, Lamps (First Choice: Buy *clear* oil. If scarce, stockpile *any!*)
6. Coleman Fuel (Impossible to stockpile too much)
7. Guns, Ammunition, Pepper Spray, Knives, Clubs, Bats, Slingshots
8. Hand-operated Can Openers and Egg Beaters, Whisks
9. Honey, Syrups, White and Brown Sugar

(Continued)

(Continued)

10. Rice, Beans, Wheat
11. Vegetable Oil (For cooking: Without it, food burns and must be boiled, etc.)
12. Charcoal, Lighter Fluid (Will become scarce suddenly)
13. Water Containers (Any size. If small: *hard clear plastic only*–Note: Use food grade if for drinking.)
14. Mini Heater Head, Propane (Without this item, propane won't heat a room.)
15. Grain Grinder (Non-electric)
16. Propane Cylinders
17. Survival Guide Book
18. Electric Lanterns (Aladdin, Coleman, etc.)
19. Baby Supplies (Diapers, formula, ointments, aspirin, etc.)
20. Washboards, Mop Bucket (With wringer; for laundry)
21. Cookstoves (Propane and Kerosene)
22. Vitamins
23. Propane Cylinder Handle-Holder (Urgent: Small canister use is dangerous without this item.)
24. Feminine Hygiene (Hair-care, skin products, etc.)
25. Thermal Underwear (Tops and bottoms)
26. Bow saws, Axes and Hatchets, Wedges (Also, honing oil)
27. Aluminum Foil (Regular and Heavy Duty; Great cooking and barter item)
28. Gasoline Containers (Plastic and metal)
29. Garbage Bags (Impossible to have too many)
30. Toilet Paper, Tissues, Paper Towels
31. Milk (Powdered and Condensed)
32. Garden Seeds (Non-Hybrid)
33. Clothes Pins/Line/Hangers
34. Coleman's Pump Repair Kit
35. Tuna Fish (in oil)
36. Fire Extinguishers
37. First-Aid Kits
38. Batteries (all sizes)
39. Garlic, Spices and Vinegar, Baking Supplies
40. Dog Food
41. Flour, Yeast, Salt
42. Matches (Boxed, wooden matches will go first.)
43. Writing Paper/Pads/Pencils, Solar Calculators
44. Insulated Ice Chests (Good for keeping items from freezing in wintertime.)
45. Work Boots, Belts, Blue Jeans, Durable Shirts
46. Flashlights, Lightsticks, Lanterns
47. Journals, Diaries, Scrapbooks
48. Garbage Cans (Plastic: great for storage, water, and transporting—if with wheels)
49. Men's Hygiene (Shampoo, toothbrush/paste, mouthwash, dental floss, nail clippers, etc.)

50. Cast Iron Cookware
51. Fishing Supplies/Tools
52. Mosquito Coils, Bug Repellent (Sprays and creams)
53. Duct Tape
54. Tarps, Stakes, Twine, Nails, Rope, Spikes
55. Candles
56. Laundry Detergent
57. Backpacks, Duffel Bags
58. Garden Tools and Supplies
59. Scissors, Fabrics, Sewing Supplies
60. Canned Fruits, Veggies, Soups, Stews
61. Bleach
62. Canning Supplies (Jars, lids, wax, etc.)
63. Knives, Sharpening Tools (Files, stones, steel)
64. Bicycles, Bicycle Parts (Tires, tubes, pumps, chains, etc.)
65. Sleeping Bags, Blankets, Pillows, Mats
66. Carbon Monoxide Alarm (battery powered)
67. Board Games, Cards, Dice
68. d-con Rat Poison, MOUSE PRUFE II, Roach Killer
69. Mousetraps, Ant Traps, Cockroach Magnets
70. Paper Plates/Cups/Utensils
71. Baby Wipes, Oils, Waterless and Antibacterial Soap
72. Rain Gear, Rubberized Boots.
73. Shaving Supplies (Razors, creams, talc, aftershave)
74. Hand Pumps and Siphons (for water and for fuels)
75. Soy Sauce, Vinegar, Bullions, Gravy, Soupbase
76. Reading Glasses
77. Chocolate, Cocoa, Tang, Punch (water enhancers)
78. Spam (or other canned meat)
79. Woolen Clothing (sweaters, scarves, earmuffs, mittens, etc.)
80. Roll-on Window Insulation Kit (MANCO)
81. Graham Crackers, Saltines, Pretzels, Trail Mix/Jerky
82. Popcorn, Peanut Butter, Nuts
83. Socks, Underwear, T-shirts (extras)
84. Lumber (all types)
85. Wagons, Carts
86. Cots, Inflatable Mattresses
87. Gloves (for work, warming, gardening, etc.)
88. Lantern Hangers
89. Screen Patches
90. Teas
91. Coffee
92. Cigarettes
93. Wine, Liquors
94. Paraffin Wax
95. Glue, Nails, Nuts, Bolts, Screws
96. Chewing Gum, Candies
97. Atomizers (for cooling/bathing)
98. Hats, Cotton Neckerchiefs
99. Large Livestock (including big dogs)
100. Goats/Chickens

The Least You Can Do

- Have some cash on hand—imagine a world with no ATMs or credit cards
- When gold prices dip, stock up on gold. And I mean physical gold—the kind you put in a safe. Also, you might want to pick up gold in forms that you can easily barter if paper money becomes worthless—simple gold rings, for example.
- When silver prices pull back, stock up on physical silver. If our economy, financial system, and paper money go south, you'll want gold *and* silver. Flashing around too much gold could make you a target. Silver doesn't attract as much attention and it's still a precious metal.
- Stock up on potential barter items—tools, wire, toothbrushes, toilet paper, and the like.

CHAPTER 5

Investing for the Five Emergencies

It sounds very easy to say that all you have to do is to watch the tape, establish your resistance points and be ready to trade along the line of least resistance as soon as you have determined it. But in actual practice a man has to guard against many things, and most of all against himself—that is, against human nature.

—Edwin Lefevre
in *Reminiscences of a Stock Operator*

There are four intersecting emergencies that will probably exert a great deal of influence on the stock and bond markets over the next five years and beyond:

1. Energy
2. Water
3. Food
4. Climate

These sorts of headlines and alerts are now part of our everyday world. Hang on; it will be a very bumpy ride.

These four crises will likely be compounded by a fifth emergency: indebtedness. Debt will make society a lot less likely to adapt peacefully to the other crises, and there is less money capacity to invest in mitigating alternatives. And our national indebtedness threatens the very value of our currency. But it's not easy getting off debt—the U.S. economy is hooked on it, and a potential transition from a society of borrowers to a society of savers would be brutal.

The good news is that, if you have the stomach for risk and volatility, there are investments that can make the most of these emergencies—protecting you by insulating your portfolio, and potentially dishing up nice profits.

We've got a lot of ground to cover in this chapter. We'll look at how the five emergencies will shape our world, and probably Wall Street, too. We'll look at three dangers that could shake the market to its foundations, as well as three potential profit bonanzas. We'll look at the three levels of investment risk, six every investor must know about the stock market, whether you should invest in stocks or funds, six stock investor *dos*, asset allocation, and the pros and cons of exchange-traded funds.

Whew!

Finally, we'll look at potential investments you can make to protect your portfolio and even profit in the brave new world.

The Five Emergencies

Without energy, there is no economy, and precious little food. Without water, life as we know it can't exist. When the climate goes to hell, the world as you know it could be turned upside down. Now, it's possible to adapt to change, but in the middle of a debt crisis it becomes a heck of a lot harder. The intersection of all these crises can be a very tricky time for your portfolio. In order to save your money *and* profit, you must first understand these crises.

Energy Crisis

Worldwide demand for energy will grow 44% by 2030, according to the U.S. Energy Information Administration.[1] While I think that energy demand will be capped by soaring prices, the fact is that demand from awakening giants including China and India is relentless, and the world will start using oil at a rate of 1,000 barrels per second within the next couple years. (See Figure 5.1.)

The United States is the world's largest consumer of oil, guzzling more than 7.5 billion barrels per year. We import more than half the oil we use, and that amount is rising, which is why the United States is described as *addicted to oil.*

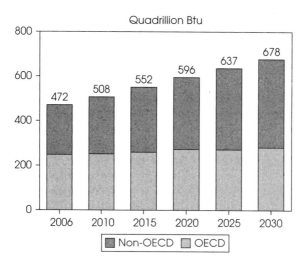

Figure 5.1   World Market Energy Consumption
Source: Department of Energy.

More than 81% of the world's discovered and useable oil reserves come from just 10 countries. Most of them don't like us much. And 30% of the world's oil is in three countries—Iraq, Kuwait, and Saudi Arabia. Saudi Arabia, home to 15 of the 19 September 11th hijackers and a major source of funds for Islamic terrorists, is the world's *Central Bank of Oil.*

The drop in oil prices in 2008 caused the shelving of many important oil projects—projects that won't be there to fill the pipeline when they're needed in three to five years. The cheap oil has been found, and new oil fields are both smaller and hideously expensive. The supply chain to your gas tank has never been tighter. Electric cars and trains are nice, but they can't bridge the gap for a nation built around automobiles and cheap, plentiful gasoline to run them.

Bottom line: The United States (and the world) is headlong on a collision course with a new energy crisis that will make the price spike of 2008 look like a bump in the road. And companies that depend on cheap transportation are going to get crushed. Oil companies that can find oil for a thirsty world should prosper.

Water Crisis

Americans who think cheap, clean water is an inalienable right are in for a rude awakening sometime in the next decade, and probably sooner than you think. Water upheavals are intensifying thanks to global warming. Dry areas are becoming drier and wet areas wetter as the oceans and atmosphere warm. Meanwhile, the population is growing fastest in places where fresh water is either scarce or polluted. Result: The World Bank famously declared, "The wars of the twenty-first century will be fought over water."[2]

In 2002, 8% of the world suffered chronic shortages. More than 80 countries, with 40% of the world's population, are already facing water shortages. This century, the world's population is forecast to double, though I believe we may hit Malthusian limits. The UN forecasts that by 2050, 4 billion people will lack adequate water as entire regions turn dry.

During the droughts of the Dust Bowl in the 1930s, technology advanced so U.S. farmers could pump water from underground aquifers to save their fields through irrigation. Much of that water is now gone. The Ogallala Aquifer, the giant aquifer that runs under eight U.S. states, will likely be gone in 25 years or less. Other problems are more immediate. Here in the United States, seven states that depend on the Colorado River face potential cutoffs as water levels trend increasingly lower.

Towns and cities across the country with decades-out-of-date municipal water systems are finding it difficult in the current credit environment to raise money to do urgently needed work. If water systems fail, or if the outdated power grids that provide electricity to their pumps fail, people will start going thirsty in a hurry.

To see if your area is in danger of a serious drought, check out the U.S. drought monitor map at http://drought.unl.edu/DM/MONITOR.html.

This will impact localities; whole cities may have to be evacuated if droughts get too severe. We see this on a small scale as fires rage across dry landscapes—imagine if a city the size of Los Angeles had to be evacuated because it simply ran out of water.

Bottom line: Bad for localities, but potentially good for water companies.

Food Crisis

Global agriculture entered a new bull market in 2003, and it shows signs of accelerating. Global warming is worsening droughts in countries that are normally breadbaskets (Australia), aggravating stormy weather and flooding in low-lying countries like Bangladesh, and causing crop-eating pests to flourish around the world. All these endanger the global food supply. In addition, a World-Bank-funded study in 2008 noted that rising energy and fertilizer prices and the depreciation of the U.S. dollar have contributed to about 35% of the rise in food prices.

Finally, the world's population has grown annually at a rate of 1.14% since 1997, and consumers in awakening giants like India and China are starting to eat more and more like big, fat Americans—more people with bigger appetites means the world needs more food.

The world has been consuming more grain than it produces for years now. The trend in global stockpiles has been lower—hitting 31-year-lows in 2008—as once-mighty surpluses were used up.

And this has to be taken in the context of an expanding global population of 78 million more people every year, who need at least 31 million more tons of grain every year. Is that a long-term boost for prices? I sure think so!

Thanks to a bumper crop in 2008 to 2009, global grain stocks are expected to go up—briefly, anyway. (See Table 5.1.) However, production is then expected to fall again in the 2009 to 2010 growing season.[3]

Table 5.1   World Grain Production, Consumption, and Balance

Year	Million Metric Tonnes		
	Production	Consumption	Balance
1997	1,879	1,821	58
1998	1,876	1,835	41
1999	1,872	1,855	17
2000	1,843	1,857	−15
2001	1,875	1,902	−28
2002	1,822	1,909	−88
2003	1,862	1,934	−72
2004	2,043	1,990	53
2005	2,017	2,019	−2
2006	1,992	2,043	−51
2007	2,075	2,098	−22

Source: Compiled by Earth Policy Institute from U.S. Department of Agriculture, Production, Supply & Distribution, electronic database, www.fas.usda.gov, updated 11 January 2008.

The good news is that if there were an OPEC of grain, the United States would be the Saudi Arabia! The bad news is that the average U.S. meal travels about 1,500 miles to get from farm to plate.[4] Like the rest of our civilization, our food supply depends on tenuous long-distance relationships between supplier and user—relationships that run on fossil fuels.

What's more, you'll have plans in place to make a fast exit to a safer area if things get too dangerous. If there is a real oil crisis, people will start going hungry pretty quickly. The average supermarket only has about three to four days worth of food stocks on its shelves. In an emergency situation or real disaster, this food is going to disappear in a matter of hours as people stock up. While large-scale shortages in the United States will likely be short term, this will incentivize people to store food—worsening a supply squeeze longer term.

Bottom line: The bull market in food should continue. A decline in the U.S. dollar would add extra oomph to grain prices, because grains priced in dollars are relatively cheaper for foreigners to buy with their currencies. Investors can play along with some exchange-traded funds that focus on agriculture and farm equipment stocks.

Climate Crisis

Severe weather already costs North America tens of billions of dollars annually in productivity and damaged property, and those costs are expected to rise, according to a UN report.[5]

Droughts will also occur more often in the U.S. Midwest and Southwest as warmer temperatures evaporate soil moisture. Droughts will worsen the depletion of underground aquifers—not only the huge Ogallala aquifer but also ones like the Edwards Aquifer in Texas, which supplies two million people with water.

Our use of fossil fuels gets blamed for much of global warming. But part of it is a cyclical pattern in Earth's weather. And a much bigger contributing factor than fossil fuels is modern industrial agriculture, which is responsible for an estimated one-third of emissions that contribute to global warming and climate change, according to a report from the International Forum on Globalization.[6]

Pesticides and chemicals used in agriculture, as well as deforestation and the burning of biomass, contribute about 25% of a greenhouse gas, carbon dioxide, which is raising global temperatures.

Paradoxically, one of the biggest victims of climate change is agriculture. Some scientists say that for each temperature rise of

1.8 degrees Fahrenheit (1 degree Celsius) above the historical average during the growing season, there is about a 10% decline in grain yields.

Looking ahead, global warming could lay waste to a wide arc of fertile, wheat-growing farmland stretching from Pakistan through Northern India and Nepal to Bangladesh.

But agriculture isn't the only victim of global warming. Global warming makes storms more severe, and intense hurricanes and other mega-storms will likely hammer countries around the world. And we could see the global icecaps melt much faster than scientists have predicted so far—the melting outpaces all models. As a result, sea levels could rise as much as three feet by the end of this century—or worse.

If the American people really start to worry about global warming, we could see money pour into *green* stocks—stocks that help the environment or work in alternative energy. That, in turn, should be good for exchange-traded funds that hold baskets of these stocks.

Four Plus One Equals Potential Catastrophe

It's plain that these four crises I've described—in energy, water, food, and climate—can all feed on each other. Fixing these problems will take the ability to make tough choices even when they aren't popular, as well as a willingness to embrace change, ingenuity, and money. And it's that last one—money—that can be so critical. It's hard to have expensive new government initiatives or spark new private investment when credit is tight or even unavailable.

That brings us to the fifth emergency: Indebtedness. The synchronized collapse of credit bubbles around the world raises the risk of sovereign defaults. At the same time, the credit crunch is making it more difficult to borrow money. Municipalities that want to put in a new water treatment plant or augment their power with a solar array, for example, find it nearly impossible to raise money.

Meanwhile, the debt of households has climbed much faster than their net worth in the last 50 years, according to data compiled by the Federal Reserve. Finally, enough's enough—in late 2008 and into 2009, consumers started unwinding their debt. But this raises a couple of problems.

First, we've seen periods where consumers reduce debts before. These unwindings last for about 10 quarters on average. And an average unwinding of debt would suck about $300 billion out of the economy.

Second, consumer spending, which accounts for 70% of total economic activity, tends to go down along with consumer debt. This batters the economy and kneecaps attempts at recovery.

This, in turn, means states and cities have less revenue, so they need to borrow more money—but when credit is tight, this becomes difficult. As a result, spending priorities get skewed to absolute necessities, and projects that would alleviate future crises in energy, food, water, and climate just don't get done.

The Many Other Dangers.   In addition to these five emergencies, there are numerous dangers associated with a weakening economy and failing currency. Here are three examples:

Danger #1—Government intervention in the markets. The market bubble could continue to deflate, with the S&P 500 heading to 500, 400 or lower. In response, the government may activate its *plunge protection team* to bid up stock prices. This is a danger because (1) this prolongs whatever pain the market was going to go through anyway, (2) you can only artificially hold up stocks for so long, and (3) it will spark false hopes and bring more investor money into the market at the wrong time.

Danger #2—Devaluation. If the government continues to paper over its problems with fiat currency, there is a danger that China and other nations that underwrite Uncle Sam's profligate spending will balk at buying more U.S. Treasuries. This could send bond prices crashing, bond yields soaring, and the U.S. dollar slumping lower. This would be bad for all Americans, but especially bond investors.

Danger #3—Hyperinflation. Following hot on the heels of a U.S. government bond default and devaluation would likely be hyperinflation—the collapse of the U.S. dollar against hard assets like gold. While people who own gold will be able to preserve some of their wealth, the cost of imported goods will soar for everyone. Since the United States has exported many of its factories to Mexico and China, this would be terrible news for consumers. The economic carnage would likely devastate the stock market.

Even if these dangers don't rear their heads, we're going to be in one of the trickiest investing environments in living memory. However, the important thing is not to let your fears get the best of you, because even in the worst of times, there are areas where you can do well.

Three Potential Profit Bonanzas

Now that I've scared you out of the market forever, let's take a deep breath and talk about things that could go very right for investors. These three potential areas for profits may give you a reason to get in, if you're comfortable with the risk in the market.

Potential #1: A New Industrial Renaissance

If the government and banks can work out the debt problem, then we can see spending on new projects. And new technology exists that could revolutionize the way we live and are just waiting to be financed.

Renewable forms of energy—solar, wind, geothermal, hydropower, biomass, and even ocean waves and currents are all within reach. Some, like solar, have seen amazing breakthroughs in just the past couple years.

Research and Development.   We're already seeing billions invested in renewable energy research; for the cost of what we've spent on the Iraq War—probably less—it could become a doable reality.

One of the biggest developments is reimagining buildings not just as places to work but as power plants, with independent solar power systems. This is already happening in parts of Europe, and it could take place in the United States, too.

Back to work!   To bridge the gap between the murky now and a bright future, we'd need an industrial effort like the United States hasn't seen since World War II. The nation's industrial muscle turned into the *rust belt* over decades, but if we enact a moon-shot level renewable energy push, there will be a new use for those old factories—building the power systems of the future. Cities like Pittsburgh, Buffalo, Youngstown, Cleveland, Detroit, and more were built at their locations *before* cars came around. That means they have excellent access to waterborne transport and existing railways—exactly the kind of industrial centers we'll need in a post-oil age.

Power Up!   One project those factories will be working on is a new power grid—our old one is falling apart. The new grid can be a smart grid—a self-monitoring, automated grid that can provide power to where it is needed the most with vastly improved efficiency.

President Obama already announced plans to modernize 3,000 miles of transmission lines and install smart meters in 40 million homes.[7] A real smart grid will do the same on a much bigger scale. According to some reports, utilities will need to add an aggregate of nearly 40 gigawatts of clean energy generation by 2030, and to get all that power to customers, a total investment of as much as $2 trillion into transmission and distribution networks will be required.

The power-up could be enhanced by a build-out of new power lines using new superconductors;[8] materials that transmit electricity with zero resistance. A set of cables carrying five gigawatts of power can fit into a pipe just one meter across, and it can be buried underground. Part of the pipe will be taken up with a cooling system; these superconductors work only when kept at the temperature of liquid nitrogen. The cooling equipment draws some energy from the cable, but still far less than the losses in today's cable.

None of these three pillars of the new industrial renaissance are cheap. But they would be a brilliant investment for our country.

Potential #2—A Transportation Revolution

A transportation revolution will use some of the same industrial platform as potential profit area #1, but since the United States is car-centric, it deserves its own discussion.

Electric cars are only part of the solution. And they'll have their own limits; if everyone switches to electric cars, we're going to run up against the limits on how much lithium the world has to offer. But a vibrant electric car market is only one step down the road to a new transportation future.

Reimagined fossil fuel vehicles are another. We'll see vastly more efficient gasoline and diesel engines, as well as cars and trucks that run on natural gas.

Finally, we'll see a lot more rail. And if we follow the examples of Russia and China—two countries that know a thing or two about how to build railroads—we'll build electrified rail. Most European and Japanese railroads are electrified, too. At theoildrum.com, Alan Drake has laid out the case for why the United States cannot afford to get onboard electrified rail before that train leaves the station.

We'll probably be using more rail transport in the future anyway. Today's diesel railroads are roughly eight times more energy-efficient than heavy diesel trucks. Trucks get subsidies that railroads don't; that's probably going to change. At the same time, Alan writes:

> USA railroads have pointed to property taxes as the reason that they have not electrified (no taxes on their diesel, property taxes on electrification infrastructure). Exempting any rail line that electrifies from property taxes under the Interstate Commerce clause would promote the rapid electrification of many rail lines.
>
> The United States once built 500 electric streetcar systems in 20 years. Most towns of 25,000 and larger built a non-oil electrical transportation system. The USA did this with a population of less than one-third of today's, approximately 3% of today's GNP, and simple technology. We did it once; we can do it again![9]

As for my view, I know that politicians love big projects they can show off. Nothing shows off nice and pretty like a brand spankin' new railroad engine. And, frankly, if we took just some of the money we now spend building ever-more-horrific bombs and spent some of it subsidizing railroads, we'd probably get along better with our neighbors.

Potential #3—Asia Transitions from Producer to Consumer

Potential profit area #3 builds on the other two points—*if* we can jumpstart an industrial renaissance and *if* we can proactively work on solving the next energy crisis before it begins, then the United States will be positioned to get a piece of the biggest action in the twenty-first century—the transition of Asia (led by China and India) from the world's backroom factory and call center to 2.4 billion consumers.

The United States' industrial revolution reshaped it into a world-class economic and political power; it created titans of industry and wealth like the world had never seen, it rewrote the rules of the global economy, and it created America's middle class. These things are already starting to happen in China. And if China leads the world out of the recession, we could see a lot more of it.

Energy: Chinese citizens are transitioning from bicycles to mopeds to cars—and using more energy all the time. While China's oil imports flattened out in early 2009, that's probably just temporary—and we'll see demand grow enormously in the future.

Metal: Chinese consumers are buying more finished products—boosting China's demand for aluminum, lead, zinc, nickel, iron, copper, and all types of metals.

Grains and Meat: As the Chinese get more money, they still eat noodles but they eat a lot more meat. In 2008, pork consumption in China rose 25%.

Drugs: China is the world's seventh-largest market for pharmaceuticals. And as China's consumers get more cash, they're buying more western drugs. China's pharmaceutical sales are projected to rise 20% annually. After some embarrassing deaths due to counterfeit drugs, the government is cracking down on the counterfeit drug trade, which opens the door to potentially big profits for legitimate firms.

Each of these profit areas could be an exciting place to invest in the years ahead. There is peril in this market, but also the potential for a big payoff if the global economy shifts into higher gear.

So should you invest? That depends on how comfortable you are with risk.

Three Levels of Risk and Reward

So far I've told you about five intersecting emergencies that could shake the world and Wall Street. I've also told you about three dangers facing investors, as well as three potential areas of profit. I could write a lot more about each one. But by now, you might be asking: Which of these dangers are inevitable? Which of these potentials is going to happen?

The truth is, I don't know, and anyone who tells you they do is a liar. What I can do is talk about some investing styles and how you can invest for each one. Thus, you're going to have to define your own comfort level and make the investments that are appropriate for you.

Investment Risk Level #1—Get Out and Stay Out

One way to invest for these emergencies is to be extremely conservative—simply get out of the markets. If you have this investing mindset, you put most of your money in short-term Treasuries, with some in physical gold as an inflation hedge.

Staying out of the stock market is not necessarily a bad strategy. You avoid the risks from short-term disasters—man-made or natural—that could shake investor confidence and send stocks tumbling.

On the other hand, disaster may not arrive on our doorsteps tomorrow, or next month, or next year. The magicians on Wall Street and illusionists in Washington are adept at pulling the wool over the eyes of a public that is desperate to be fooled into a sense of normalcy.

Heck, I don't have a crystal ball, and neither do you. The day of reckoning may not come for years; it may not come in your lifetime. That's not likely, but you have to at least admit the possibility.

And there are circumstances where you may wish to keep at least some of your money in the markets, working and growing. That brings us to . . .

Investment Risk Level #2—Long-Term Buy and Hold

Some of us need to grow our capital, and cash won't do that. But what kind of investing do you want to do—buy some solid funds (or even stocks) for the long term, or trade in and out? There is no one-size-fits-all right answer. It all depends on your investing style and appetite for risk.

Wall Street is busy telling us that buy-and-hold is dead. That's because Wall Street makes its bread and butter getting investors to trade as much as possible. I believe in a mix of investing styles, just as I believe in a mix of investments in my (or any) portfolio. And buy-and-hold has a place in your portfolio *if* you believe in long-term trends.

Those trends include the five emergencies I mentioned earlier. But they also include mega-trends that are shaping our world and will likely continue to do so no matter if the U.S. economy prospers or slumps. I'll share some ideas for long-term buy-and-holds with you in just a bit.

First, let's talk about areas of potentially enormous opportunity in the years ahead for buy-and-hold investors.

Invest With Mega-Trends in Mind.   There are big trends taking place regardless of economic cycles. In his 1982 landmark book *Megatrends*, author John Naisbitt forecast five major shifts:

1. Industrial society to information society
2. National economy to world economy
3. Hierarchies to networking
4. North (developed countries) to South (developing countries)
5. Simple choices to multiple options

These trends have all been realized, some more than others. And they shaped not only the world we live in, but also the world in which we invest. Google, for example, is riding both the information society and the multiple options mega-trend. Multinational corporations like IBM and McDonald's are doing well thanks to the world economy.

Trends don't last forever, and new mega-trends take shape. For example, a great wall of baby boomers, born between 1946 and 1964, are approaching retirement age. The oldest baby boomers turn 63 in 2009, and when the trend peaks in 2030, the number of people over age 65 will zoom to 71.5 million—one in every five Americans.

Another mega-trend is the shifting demographic of the United States—we are becoming a browner country. (See Table 5.2.)

More immigrants are coming from Latin America, and those immigrants are having more children per capita than previous immigrants. The percentage of Asians is rising rapidly as well. And even if we go into a prolonged economic slump, these demographic shifts won't alter much.

A third mega-trend is the rise not just of Pacific Rim nations but also of their consumers, led by China. Even if the United States

Table 5.2   American Workforce Projections

	White (non-Hispanic)	Hispanic	Black	Asians
2010	65%	16%	13%	7.3%
2050	53%	24%	14%	11%

Source: Bureau of Census.

can't get its act together to sell into that market, China is probably going to be ascendant at least for the early part of this century. And that means, at least for the next decade or so, Chinese consumers will be competing with first-world citizens for scarce resources. Indian consumers will also be bidding for finished goods and therefore driving up natural resources. A prolonged economic slump will have a different effect on those countries than on developed countries. For example, in China, most of the new cars sold go to first-time buyers. In the United States, most cars are replacement vehicles—so when hard times hit, Americans are more prone to hold on to their old cars and not buy new ones.

There are funds you can buy that specialize in Chinese stocks, Indian stocks, and/or pan-Asian stocks. If you believe in this megatrend, and you are a buy-and-hold investor, you might want to add one of those funds to your portfolio.

These are some less obvious mega-trends.

There is the Commodity Super Cycle that I talked about earlier. When discussing the best U.S. stocks and international stocks, I tend to favor natural resource stocks—simply because, along with the cyclical forces that should drive copper, oil, and other commodity prices higher, the world is running low on some important natural resources.

Figure 5.2, from a senior research scientist at TNO Defense, Security and Safety in the Netherlands, shows global supplies of common minerals projected using recent extraction rates. There is less than a 20-year supply of strontium, silver, antimony, gold, zinc, arsenic, tin, indium, zirconium, and lead. This is in addition to the looming crisis in crude oil.

Sure, we can find new supplies of these resources. But that takes time, energy, and money—and our civilization could face shortages of all three going forward.

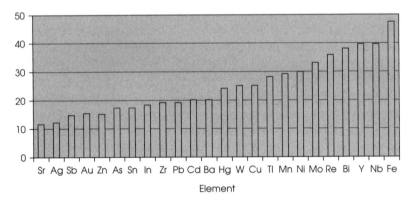

Figure 5.2   Years Remaining of Vital Minerals at 2% Annual Primary Growth
Source: Andre Diederen, writing for The Oil Drum Europe, May 4, 2009.

However, you shouldn't limit yourself to just natural resources. Sometimes technology is a better investment, sometimes banks (!) are a better investment. After one bubble bursts, another eventually arises—if history is any guide— not in the investment that was the center of the previous bubble. The implosion of the Tulip Mania in Holland and the South Seas bubble were not followed by reinflation of tulip prices or shares of the South Seas Company stock.

Likewise, after the dot-com bubble burst, the Nasdaq didn't reflate. There are stocks from the dot-com daze that are far from their old highs, and will likely never see them again. And some— Pets.com comes to mind—disappear forever.

Mega-trends hold a great deal of profit potential for long-term investors. But you have to be able to stomach risk and ride the market's roller coaster without throwing up.

If your investment style is more short-term oriented, consider the following.

Investment Risk Level #3—Riding the Market's Waves

Eighty percent of market movements are due to trends and most of the other 20% is due to cycles. If you're quick, have a stomach for volatility, know when to cut your losses and take gains, you can ride investment cycles, or waves.

I think we'll see investment waves going forward. A crisis or series of crises will come to a head and send markets crashing. The government will respond by turning on the fire hoses of money and sending broad markets higher. Global demand for commodities will likely ramp up the stocks of hard asset companies, but then the bubble will burst again and send prices spiraling downward.

Remember, recessions begin at the peak of economic activity when all economic data looks its best. On the flip side, things always look worst at the bottom. And thanks to the Central Banks and their fire hoses of money, when economic strength starts to build, the surge can come with the power and swiftness of a tidal wave.

In an economic crisis, we can see waves up and down like a storm-tossed sea. For example, from 1929 to 1933, we saw a massive cram-down in the Dow Jones Industrial Average, with declines of 45.4%, 49.4%, and 54.9%. But in the same market, we also saw big rallies of 39.3%, 52.2%, and even 100.7%! (See Table 5.3.)

Table 5.3   1929 to 1933 Dow Jones Industrial Rally and Decline

Eight Large Declines			
High	Low	H/L Percentage Difference	H/L % Decline
386.1	195.35	190.75	49.40%
297.25	207.74	89.51	30.11%
247.21	154.45	92.76	37.52%
196.96	119.81	77.15	39.17%
156.74	85.51	71.23	45.44%
119.15	69.85	49.30	41.38%
89.87	40.56	49.31	54.87%
81.39	49.68	31.71	38.96%

Eight Large Rallies			
High	Low	H/L Percentage Difference	H/L % Rise
195.35	297.25	101.90	52.16%
207.74	247.21	39.47	19.00%
154.45	196.96	42.51	27.52%
119.81	156.74	36.93	30.82%
85.51	119.15	33.64	39.34%
69.85	89.87	20.02	28.66%
40.56	81.39	40.83	100.67%
49.68	110.53	60.85	122.48%

One of those rallies—from October 1929 to April 1930—lasted *five* months and racked up a 52.2% gain. And that was before the Depression really got rolling.

To see a detailed chart of these rallies, go to http://tinyurl .com/5266a8. If you want to sit out the market's spastic dance, I don't blame you, not one bit. But if you want to try and ride these waves, you can make some serious money.

Six Things Every Investor Must Know About the Stock Market

There are a few things you should know about the stock market before you decide how you want to invest.

> **Don't obsess about catching the market's tops and bottoms.** As Frank Holmes of U.S. Global Investors is fond of saying, the best place to pick real tops and nice bottoms is on Miami's South Beach. In the market, eh—it's a bit more difficult.
>
> So traders fall back on other indicators—price action, volume action, momentum indicators, moving averages, and more. For example, depending on your time frame, a simple short-term moving average can tell you when to get in and when to get out. Many technical analysts use daily charts like the 20-day moving average—if it's trending up and your stock or fund is above it, that's a good time to buy. If the 20-day moving average is going down, and your stock or fund is below it, that's a time to sell.
>
> But that's just one way of judging the market. There are hundreds of others, as well as proprietary buying and selling programs, and they all have one thing in common—*none* of them work all the time. I think if you can find a buy-and-sell indicator that consistently works more than 60% of the time, you're ahead of the game.
>
> **Be flexible.** My hard-and-fast rule is not to have any hard-and-fast rules. The market is changing all the time. What worked yesterday won't work tomorrow. That's a very scary thing if you're not flexible. If you're flexible, you can start doing whatever works at the moment. It will make your life less stressful.
>
> So, what's the biggest variable in the market? Other people.

The stock market is a study in crowd psychology. And the fact is, crowds are extremely emotional and not very logical. The emotions of people within the crowd affect the emotions of others in the group. What will make them fearful or greedy one day won't bother them the next because the crowd dynamic will overwhelm their individual responses.

Now, consider this crowd behavior in the context of a market in crisis. Everything is revved up and accelerated like the market is a kid buzzing on too much sugar. Emotions will shift from pessimism bordering on total despair to optimism, euphoria, and even foolhardiness in a matter of weeks, even days. The emotional mood of the market can do an about-face even when the underlying fundamentals don't change that much.

The hard part for investors is balancing the extreme emotions and the likelihood that they persist against making prudent buys and keeping risks contained. While following the crowd is usually a great way to make money, doing so always becomes costly chaos at some point. We need to respect the crowd but maintain objectivity and be ready to stand aside when they start to shift.

If you want to make money, you have to be ready for more irrational exuberance but you also must be prepared to move quickly when it fizzles.

If all else is equal, choose value. Being a *value investor*, that is, buying things when they're relatively cheap, sounds like a no-brainer. But there are plenty of times when value is out of favor with the market, or the market doesn't agree with you that a certain investment is undervalued. One of the most bitter pills I've ever swallowed in the market is to buy something because I thought it was cheap only to see it get a lot cheaper.

So what denotes value? That depends on the investment. What makes a gold miner cheap, for example, is different from what makes a technology company a bargain.

Dividends can be a sign of real value. You buy stocks and funds, why? Because you expect them to go up. When you invest in dividend-paying stocks and funds, you have the added benefit of getting paid a regular fixed amount while you wait for your pick to work out. And if the investment goes down before you sell it, the dividend cushions the blow.

Dividends are not always good; sometimes they're too good to be true. It's a market truism that the best yields are paid by the worst performing industry sector. Even within a sector, a dividend yield that is way above the average paid by a stock's peers shows that everyone knows the company is in trouble and is going to cut its dividend—so they're already selling the stock.

You can look for sectors and industries where it's normal to pay out above-average dividends—for example, utilities. But a utility that pays one of the highest dividend yields in the entire industry is probably a utility in trouble.

The thing a value investor should do is look for stocks with steadily increasing dividends, or a fund that holds a basket of top-notch dividend-paying stocks.

A stock doesn't have to pay a dividend to be of real value. I know plenty of miners, for example that are dirt cheap and in the growth stage of their business cycle. They aren't paying dividends because they're using all their cash to grow their companies. But dividends can have a place in a value investor's portfolio.

Finally, I strongly believe that you, as an individual, are in charge of your own investing destiny. Don't buy something just because a guy on TV likes it, and don't buy a fund just because it is mentioned in a book (like this one). I'm going to give some broad investing guidelines and I'll be using funds as examples, but keep in mind that this wild and woolly market could have reversed a couple of times between when I write these words and when you read them.

The market moves in cycles. As Mark Twain famously said, "history doesn't repeat, but it sometimes rhymes." If you can spot a sector at a bottom of a cycle, that will make your life easier. Stockcharts.com has a good sector rotation tool that lets you see the money flowing out of one sector and into another. You can find it at http://tinyurl.com/25rqp.

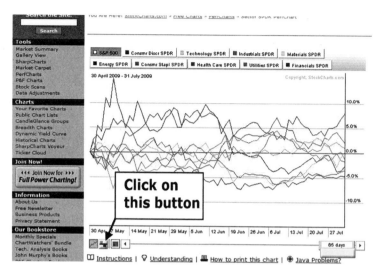

Figure 5.3   Sector SPDR PerfChart

Go to www.stockcharts.com. Once there, click on "free charts." Use the navigation bar on the left-hand side of the page to go to PerfCharts. (See Figure 5.3.)

Scroll down the page and find AMEX Sector SPDRs. Click on that link. This will pull up a chart showing how each of the sectors is performing. On the bottom bar, you'll see a row of boxes. Click on the second one.

This should bring up a chart that looks Figure 5.4, with columns representing each of the sector SPDRs. By moving the slider on the lower right back and forth, you can see money flow in and out of the different sectors (you can also set the slider for different time frames—30 days works well, but find what works best for you).

If you can identify the best-performing sectors, you can use exchange-traded funds (ETFs) to rotate from one to the next. I'll talk more about ETFs in just a bit.

There are other cycles as well. For example, there are seasonal cycles. Have you ever heard the phrase "sell in May and go away"? That's because November, December, January, February, March, and April tend to be the best months for market performance, while May through October tend to underperform.

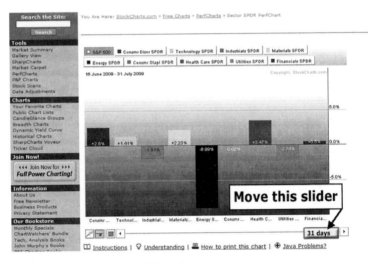

Figure 5.4   Sector SPDR PerfChart

According to the 2009 Stock Trader's Almanac, in 58 years of ups and downs, the six months of November through April saw the S&P 500 gain 1,098.03 points. The other six months saw the S&P 500 gain only 269.49 points during those 58 years.

If you want to break it out month by month, the chart in Figure 5.5, put together by Plexus Asset Management, shows the performance over the past 50 years.

The *good* six-month period shows an average return of 7.9%, while the *bad* six-month period only shows a return of 2.5%.

And there are much bigger cycles at work; there are cycles within cycles for individual issues, the broader markets, and beyond. Just like there are zigs and zags in the market, there are ups and downs in the global economy.

One that we're in right now is the Commodity Super Cycle. Research by Morgan Stanley has shown that commodity super cycles can last 20 to 25 years. The current super cycle started in the late 1990s.

Other commodity bull markets in modern history, roughly spanning 1906 to 1923, 1933 to 1955, and 1968 to

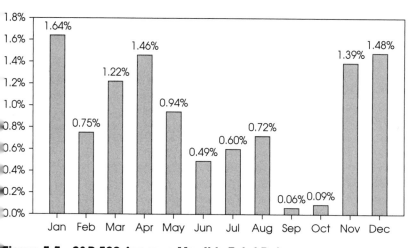

Figure 5.5   S&P 500 Average Monthly Total Return
Source: Plexus Asset Management (based on data from Professor Robert Shiller and I-Net Bridge).

1982, lasted more than twice as long as the current run. They also included some sharp corrections before they ran their course.

Should You Buy Funds or Individual Stocks?

In the section above, I outlined broad guidelines for investing. Now you'll have to make a choice between funds and stocks, or choose both.

In a mutual fund, you hope that some smart guy or gal is doing the work or you—going over the books of companies, checking out their position in the industry, getting a feel for the macroeconomic picture, and so on.

In an exchange-traded fund, you buy a basket of stocks that tries to mimic the action of a specific industry, sector, or investing class.

In individual stocks, you look for the best companies, the ones that will outperform the competition. Individual stocks are a lot more risky than mutual funds or ETFs; if a stock blows up, it can suck all the money you invested in it down a black hole. It's very hard for a fund to do that.

For casual investors—people who aren't paying attention to the markets all the time—I think funds are the way to go, especially exchange-traded funds.

If you buy individual stocks, you'll have to do extra homework, and take some extra steps to protect yourself.

Six Stock Investor Do's

What do I mean by homework? Here are some things you might want to consider doing with each stock you buy. If you do these consistently, you have a better chance of going to the head of the class.

- **Call the company.** Most publicly traded companies have a designated Investor Relations (IR) representative (or they *should* have one). This person's job is to answer questions from doofuses like you and me. Make their day and give them a call. You'll find the company's IR contact number on its web site. Call the company, ask questions, make sure you understand management's strategy and outlook, and see what to expect in the coming months. That should minimize the ugly surprises.

  If you feel self-conscious about calling, here are a few guidelines:

  1. Ask for the IR rep by name. You know this because you got this from the web site. This makes sure you don't get fobbed off on a secretary.
  2. Have a thorough knowledge of the company *before* you call. Know what they do, who the corporate officers are, if they made money in the most recent quarter, and what kind of guidance they gave for this quarter.
  3. Know what questions you are going to ask. Nothing puts an IR rep's teeth on edge like a rambling phone call. If you are already researching a company, you probably have specific questions about: new projects, sales visibility, whether the company is going to have to roll over any debt, and how it is going to spend the cash it already has, to name a few.

  I find calling a company works best with small-cap companies (which can be treasure troves of value). Most of the interesting stuff about the big companies is already out in the public sphere.

- **Scale in to a position.** Some traders buy and sell all at once. They find a stock that they like, the stock of which they can afford $5,000 worth, and they put all $5,000 into that stock.

  A better approach might be to split your purchase into two or even three parts, and make your purchase over days or weeks. That way, if the stock or market tanks, you still have some ammo to pick up more shares when they get cheaper.

  Scaling in allows you to keep your options open. It gives you time to think about the decision you made, and maybe rethink what you are doing with the rest of the money.

- **Take small bites and be ready to spit it out.** Keep your investment size on any one trade small, use protective stops, and exit if your stop is hit. Why? Because, Mister Genius, there is always the risk that you are dead, flat-out wrong.

  If you bet 100% of your money every time you traded, and you were right 99 out of 100 times, you would *still* end up broke because you put all your money into each trade, and the losing trade flatlines your account.

  On the other hand, if your strategy is to invest 10% of your holdings into 10 different stocks, and sell any position immediately if any of these shares drops more than 10%, you will preserve most of your capital even if the market goes completely against you.

  Am I saying this 10% formula is the right strategy for you? No! It depends on how much money you have to invest, your stomach for risk, and other factors.

- **Be skeptical of the lying liars on Internet message boards.** Internet message boards are a great place for investors to get together and share ideas. Unfortunately, they've turned into a forum for pump-and-dump artists to fleece the unwary and short sellers to use unfounded rumors and innuendo to scare people out of good stocks.

  There *are* good places to get information on stocks. MSN Money, Yahoo! Finance, Google Finance, Kitco, 321.gold, and I'll proudly add Weiss Research and UncommonWisdomDaily .com, for whom I work, to that list. There are plenty of other good investment web sites and blogs. But when you're on the

Internet message boards, treat every post you see as if it's written by a pathological liar. In other words, don't even believe a *hello* until you check it out.

- **When you're right, sit tight.** The legendary stock operator Jesse Livermore wrote: "Men who can both be right and sit tight are uncommon. I found it one of the hardest things to learn." In other words, don't sell too soon. Overtrading will nibble away at your account like a flock of rabid ducks.

- **Diversify, diversify, diversify**. Use your stock portfolio only as part of a bigger investment picture. I talked about splitting your stock portfolio into tenths. You could do that, but only after you've already divided up your wealth so just a portion of the whole is in stocks.

There are many ways to divide your personal finance pie. For example, you could divide your wealth into fifths:

1. Physical gold and silver
2. Ready cash or short-term treasuries
3. Currencies or currency funds
4. Best U.S. stocks
5. Best international stocks

This way, you have the opportunity to profit if you're right, and also to protect yourself if you're wrong.

The alternative can be very bad indeed. I know a gal who's a personal banker, which basically means she handles money for very wealthy clients.

A married couple who were clients of hers, with $35 million or so in the account, came in to the office. They were getting 5% on their money on deposit with her, and they wanted at least 6.5%.

She called all the way up the chain of command, but couldn't do better than 5.5%. The greedy couple called her some names, withdrew their money, and put it with someone else. This other guy, they told her, promised them at least a 20% return on their investments!

Maybe you've heard of this other guy? His name is Bernie Madoff. Of course, his investment plan turned out to be a total fraud, a giant Ponzi scheme, and the greedy couple got a big fat zero return on their money.

The lesson there is that the only people who should invest all their eggs in one basket are chicken farmers, and I'm not even sure how true that is for them.

Let's talk about diversification and asset allocation a bit more, and how you can use exchange-traded funds to achieve that goal.

Divide and Conquer with Asset Allocation

Asset allocation is the strategy of dividing your investment portfolio among major asset classes—for example, large-cap stocks, small-cap stocks, international stocks, and fixed income. At the same time, you choose your investing style—value or growth. Unless you are going to manage your investments on a daily basis, or have someone else do it for you, it's likely that proper asset allocation will really make the difference in your portfolio. In other words, the results you are going to achieve will most likely be determined by how you've invested your assets, and not necessarily your ability to pick individual investment winners.

You will have to make some choices. Choices like . . .

Which market cap are you comfortable with? Large-cap, mid-cap, or small-cap?

Are you comfortable with growth stocks, value stocks, or a mix of both? There are mutual funds and exchange-traded funds that are various combinations of market cap and investing style; you'll find some examples in Table 5.4.

Unless you've spotted a huge trend, today's winner is probably not going to do so well tomorrow. Diversity within a broad portfolio is good. Feel free to add focus or increase exposure to one sector or industry about which you feel strongly. As you can see by looking at Table 5.4, ETFs let you target different areas of the market, and you can mix and match them to suit your style.

Diversity is also good across international borders. If the ETFs in your portfolio don't have an international component, perhaps you should add an international fund.

Bonds are the anchor of any portfolio. Younger investors don't need much of an anchor—they want to move fast. The longer your boat's been sailing, the bigger an anchor you likely want.

One rule of thumb that many advisors use to determine the proportion a person should allocate to stocks is to subtract the person's

Table 5.4   ETFs Offer Market Cap and Style Choices

ETF	Ticker	Expense Ratio
Large-Cap Value ETFs		
iShares Russell 1000 Value	IWD	0.2 %
streetTRACKS Dow Jones U.S. Large Cap Value	ELV	0.21%
iShares S&P/Barra 500 Value	IVE	0.18%
Large-Cap Growth ETFs		
iShares Russell 1000 Growth	IWF	0.2 %
streetTRACKS Dow Jones U.S. Large Cap Growth	ELG	0.21%
iShares S&P/Barra 500 Growth	IVW	0.18%
Small-Cap Value ETFs		
iShares Russell 2000 Value	IWN	0.25%
streetTRACKS Dow Jones U.S. Small Cap Value	DSV	0.26%
iShares S&P/Barra SmallCap 600 Value	IJS	0.25%
Small-Cap Growth ETFs		
iShares Russell 2000 Growth	IWO	0.25%
streetTRACKS Dow Jones U.S. Small Cap Growth	DSG	0.26%
iShares S&P/Barra SmallCap 600 Growth	IJT	0.25%

age from 100. In other words, the theory goes that if you're 35, you should put 65% of your money into stocks and the remaining 35% into bonds, real estate, and cash. But that doesn't take into account factors like whether you're a parent or whether your spouse works. Don't get boxed in by others' expectations—do what works best for you.

These are all strategies that have worked in the past. In the future, if we are descending into a time of political, social, and economic upheaval, these tried-and-true strategies may no longer apply.

This is why so many investors and traders have adopted shorter-term horizons, namely moving in to the market when they think it is in rally mode, and moving out when they think the cycles have turned and the market is headed down.

But even if you try to ride the market's waves, it's probably still best to diversify.

So far we've talked about the five emergencies that could shape the market, the U.S. economy, and the global economy for years to come; deciding which kind of investor you are; six things every stock investor needs to know; and six investor *do's*.

Hedging Your Bets—Inverse ETFs

There's one more kind of ETF you need to know about—inverse ETFs. These are designed to go up when whatever they track goes down and vice versa. There are inverse or ultra-inverse (leveraged) ETFs for the broad indices, real estate, financials, consumer goods, semiconductors, technology, and even emerging markets. They can be used in two ways:

1. Speculatively, because you believe the broad market or a specific sector or commodity is going lower
2. To hedge your existing investments—for protection against declines in specific industry sectors where you are already invested

Some examples:

- If you have a broadly diversified domestic portfolio, you could use DOG or DXD, which move inversely to the Dow Jones Industrial Average, or SH, SDS, or RSW, which move inversely to the S&P 500 Index.
- If you have a lot of technology stocks, you could use the inverse ETF with the symbol REW.
- If you have a lot of small-cap stocks, you could use the SDD inverse ETF.

Overall, how much you invest depends on your own investing style and stomach for risk. Importantly, inverse ETFs are trading vehicles to catch short-term trends—not long-term investments.

Now, let's look at some ETFs that could help your portfolio survive and even thrive in various disasters *and* trends.

ETFs for All Sorts of Markets

Some investors use sector ETFs for conservative asset allocation strategies. Others use them to speculate. Whatever you prefer, ETFs can be a good addition to an active portfolio.

One aspect of them is they let you target areas of the economy you think will do well over the next few years, and you can even use them to invest for the five emergencies.

Energy.   If you think a new energy crisis is coming, there are different ways to play it. Many ETFs and ETNs say they track the price of oil, but sadly, that's just not true. Funds like iPath S&P GSCI Crude Oil Total Return ETN (OIL), PowerShares DB Oil ETF (DBO), and United States Oil Fund (USO) are being front-run by the big money on Wall Street so regularly that they lag oil's performance rather badly. On the other hand, if oil is trending higher, these funds trend higher, too. So they're an easy way to catch the general trend of oil, if not the total performance.

Another fund to consider is the PowerShares DB Energy Fund (DBE). It holds a basket of futures contracts on light sweet crude oil, heating oil, Brent crude oil, gasoline, and natural gas. It's meant to track the energy sector as a whole, not just crude.

There are also ETFs that track baskets of stocks in the energy sector—the Oil Services HOLDRs (OIH), Energy Select SPDR (XLE) and SPDR Oil and Gas Exploration and Drilling ETF (XOP), just to name three. These also lagged oil in a recent two-year period, but they may have periods of out-performance.

One final idea is to invest in Canadian royalty trusts that trade on the New York Stock Exchange. They pay high dividend yields of up to 10% to 15% annually. Not only are the dividends paid monthly, which allows for a better dividend income compounding, but some of them also allow investors to purchase shares through dividend reinvestment plans (DRIPs) at discounted prices. Unlike U.S. trusts, Canadian royalty trusts can purchase new assets and make acquisitions.

U.S. investors are at a disadvantage; the Canadian government applies a 15% nonresident withholding tax on distributions to U.S. investors. The good news is that U.S. investors can apply for a refund for at least a portion of the amount withheld. Many Canadian trusts provide information for income tax filing instructions for U.S. unit-holders on their web sites, so check them out before you buy.

Now for the bad news—there is a big change coming in 2011. Canada is changing the law, raising taxes on income trusts to a rate similar to corporations. Canadian royalty trusts are now under pressure to convert to corporations before the end of 2012, and that's what many of them, like Penn West Energy Trust (PWE on the NYSE), are doing.

Other high-yield Canadian Trusts I like include Harvest Energy Trust (HTE), Enerplus Resources Fund (ERF), Baytex Energy Trust (BTE), and Pengrowth Energy Trust (PGH). If you're interested in them, check with your accountant first to make sure the tax situation makes sense for you.

And sure enough, there is a fund that holds Canadian royalty trusts—the Claymore/SWM Canadian Energy Income ETF (ENY). It holds trusts as well as some big individual names in Canadian energy, and it pays monthly dividends.

Bottom line: I find energy ETFs are good trades if you think (1) oil is trending higher, and (2) you're not hung up on the fact that these funds will underperform crude oil itself. They are best for short-term trades; they're good at catching short-term fluctuations in the market, and there are inverse ETFs you can use if you think energy is going to make a short-term move to the downside.

If I had to pick energy ETFs for the long haul, I like the Claymore/SWM Canadian Energy Income ETF (ENY) for its dividend, and the PowerShares DB Energy Fund (DBE).

One more thing to consider: Everything is so interconnected now; a severe equity sell-off will probably drag down crude and energy stocks.

Water.   There are a bunch of water ETFs: PICO Holdings (PICO is a water hoarding play in the Nevada desert); First Trust ISE Water Index Fund (FIW) and PowerShares Water Resources Portfolio (PHO), which are very similar U.S.-focused funds; and the Claymore S&P Global Water Index ETF (CGW), which is more global. There are others, as well.

Food.   A half-dozen or so ETFs all hold various mixes of futures in grains and other agricultural products. The PowerShares DB Agriculture ETF (DBA), iPath Dow Jones AIG-Agriculture ETN (JJA), and iPath Dow Jones AIG-Grains ETN (JJG) are all good ways to play a bull market in food. If you prefer makers of agricultural machinery, there is the Market Vectors Agribusiness ETF (MOO).

And if you think agriculture prices are going lower, you can try the PowerShares DB Agriculture Double Short ETN (AGA) for a short-term trade.

Climate/Green Tech.   There are carbon-trading ETFs, but at this writing they're as illiquid as granite. Maybe they'll perk up. In the meantime, consider solar and other alternative energy plays: Claymore/Mac Global Solar Energy (TAN), the Market Vectors Solar Energy ETF (KWT), Market Vectors Global Alternative Energy ETF (GEX), and First-Trust ISE Global Wind Energy Index Fund (FAN).

These are the same funds that should do well if the United States invests in a green-tech-led industrial renaissance like I discussed earlier. Another fund to consider is the PowerShares Cleantech Portfolio (PZD). This tracks a basket of companies in alternative energy and efficiency, advanced materials, air and water purification, eco-friendly agriculture, power transmission, and more.

Commodity Super Cycle.   The iShares S&P GSCI Commodity-Indexed Trust ETF (GSG) tracks the S&P GSCI Total Return Index. This has a wide basket of components—everything from crude oil to industrial metals to precious metals, agriculture, and livestock.

PowerShares offers the PowerShares DB Commodity Index Fund (DBC),[10] which tracks the Deutsche Bank Liquid Commodity Index. It holds a basket of futures on crude oil, heating oil, gold, aluminum, corn, wheat, Brent crude, copper, natural gas, RBOB gasoline, silver, soybeans, sugar, and zinc.

Both of these funds charge 0.75% in annual fees.

An ETF that holds stocks and is a play on the commodity super cycle is the Claymore/Delta Global Shipping Index (SEA). Like the name says, this fund invests in companies in the global shipping industry. A commodity bull market is associated with higher volumes of international shipping, which should be good for the SEA. The SEA has an expense ratio of 0.65%.

Short commodity ETFs include the UltraShort DJ-AIG Commodity (CMD), but there are others, as well.

Treasuries/Debt.   There are three basic reasons to consider investing in a bond exchange traded fund:

1. If you're older, you may appreciate the stability that comes
   from income-generating investments; they can provide a relatively steady stream of income.
2. If you want to decrease overall portfolio volatility because
   bonds and stocks often don't move in concert with each other.
3. If you think bonds are going down, you can use an inverse or
   ultra-inverse fund—a fund designed to move up when bonds
   go down.

Bond funds include short-term treasury bonds (SHY), medium-
term treasury bonds (IEF), long-term treasury bonds (TLT), inflation-protected treasuries (TIP), and corporate bonds (LQD). If
you think Treasury bonds are going lower in price (which means
higher in yield—yield always moves inverse to price), you could use
the UltraShort 20+ Year Treasury ProShares (TBT).

Inflation and Hyperinflation.   The aforementioned TIP is a good
inflation-protected fund. But if and when we get to hyperinflation,
you'll probably want to be in gold, oil, and agricultural commodity
funds. You already have some suggestions for oil and agriculture.
For gold, you can consider funds that hold physical metal, like the
SPDR Gold Shares (GLD) and iShares Comex Gold (IAU), or a
fund that holds gold miners, like the Market Vectors Gold Miners
ETF (GDX).

If you think gold is going lower, you can play that with the DB
Gold Double Short ETN (DZZ) or the less-liquid (and un-lever-
aged) DB Gold Short ETN (DGZ).

Dividends.   You have to be careful—at times, value and sector
ETFs pay out more than ETFs designated as dividend ETFs. In just
a bit, I'll give you a list of web sites that will help you screen ETFs
for, among other things, dividend payouts.

Importantly, remember that risk is more important than yield.
A 5% yield does not make up for a 20% loss. Yields can change,
especially in *toxic* sectors.

Pros and Cons of Exchange-Traded Funds (ETFs)

Exchange-traded funds, also known as ETFs, are like an improved version of mutual funds. ETFs aren't only for stocks. Any class of asset that has a published index around it and is liquid can be made into an ETF. ETFs cover markets including bonds and real estate, commodities including gold, silver, and oil, and even currencies.

Going under the hood, ETFs are investment holding companies or futures contracts. A custodial bank holds the basket of stocks and other assets in the fund's account for the fund manager to monitor. These baskets are normally quite large, and sufficient to purchase 10,000 to 50,000 shares of the ETF. When those holdings rise in value, so does the ETF price. When those holdings drop in value, the ETF price falls.

These funds trade throughout the day over an exchange. Most ETFs track an index, such as the Standard & Poor's 500 index or the Philadelphia Semiconductor index. Because they are passively managed, ETFs have low annual expenses. They are not closed-end funds, and the fund companies do not redeem shares for cash.

ETFs are generally valued at close to their net asset value (NAV), although they sometimes trade at a slight discount or premium.

Five other things to consider:

1. ETFs offer you the diversification, convenience, and everything else you love about mutual funds—*without* the high cost and trading restrictions. Unlike mutual funds, ETFs almost never demand high minimum investments; never nick you for ridiculous loads, 12-b1 fees, or management fees; and never impose limits on what time of the day you can buy or sell!
2. Expense ratios average 40 basis points for ETFs. Some cost even less. Expenses for actively managed mutual funds average more than *double* that—150 basis points, or 1.5%.
3. ETFs offer you loss protection. You can use *stops* to help protect your principal and your profits. You can also aim to get in cheap with limit *buy* orders.
4. Plus, there are now ETFs that make you money when stock prices fall. You never have to go short yourself. You just buy an ETF like any other. The more the market falls, the more money you stand to make.
5. ETFs and ETNs that hold baskets of futures contracts on commodities will generally underperform those commodities. That's because the big players on Wall Street know when

those ETFs roll over their contracts and they front-run them. However, these funds can still let you ride the general trend in a commodity, up or down.

There are exceptions to every rule. And some mutual funds have managers exceptional enough that they're worth using. For example, The U.S. Global Investors (www.usfunds.com) family of mutual funds, run by Frank Holmes, are excellent funds that mix innovative strategies and smart investing ideas. But match any mutual fund you're considering up against a comparable ETF if you can find one, and see which is the real bargain.

Some of the more popular ETFs include the SPDR S&P Dividend ETF (SDY), PowerShares Dividend Achievers (PFM), and Vanguard Dividend Appreciation ETF (VIG).

The Asia/China Boom.   The iShares FTSE/Xinhua China 25 Index (FXI) is the granddaddy of China funds. Other options include the PowerShares Golden Dragon Halter USX China (PGJ), which primarily holds ADRs (American Depositary Receipts) of Chinese companies listed in the United States. The Hong Kong ETF (EWH) is overweighted with financial and real-estate firms based in Hong Kong, but is still good for tracking Chinese economic growth.

Web Tools for ETFs

There are some excellent free Web tools you can use to screen for the best ETFs to fit your investing style and current market conditions.

First—Morningstar's ETF Screener.   Morningstar made its name as a mutual fund site, and it's carried that expertise over to ETFs.

Go to Morningstar.com. You'll see a row of buttons on top. Click on the one that says *Tools*. Under the heading *Basic Screener*, you'll find a link to Morningstar's ETF screener.

Here, you'll find the screening criteria: Fund group, Morningstar Category, Expense Ratio, Year-to-Date Return, 1-year-return, 5-year return. And you can set other criteria as well. If, for example, you like natural resources, you might change the

Morningstar category to *Natural Resources,* and put the expense ratio at *less than or equal to 0.5%.* All the rest of the screening criteria you would leave as *any.* Then, click the button at the bottom to view your results.

You can also click on the categories along the top to sort the funds. Let's say you click on *Market Year-to-Date Return,* because the trend is your friend. Another important category is the one on the far right, *Total Assets.* You don't want to get into a fund that is too small. Any fund with total assets of low double-digits or worse, single-digits, should be crossed off your list immediately.

Why is that? Because it's just as important to be able to get out of a fund as it is to get into it. And a fund with low total assets will usually have a big spread between the bid and the ask. That means you get dinged on the way in and the way out.

Morningstar is a good screening tool, but it only shows you the most popular funds. Morningstar's ETF research is very basic. Maybe that's all you want. If you're looking for more information, then you can move on to other web sites.

Let's look at another one now—Yahoo! Finance.

Yahoo! Finance ETF Screener.   Go to finance.yahoo.com. Under the *Investing* tab, you'll find ETFs. There you can sort ETFs by all sorts of categories.

If you're in a bear market kind of mood, this is a great place to find out which funds perform best over three-month, year-to-date, and other time frames. Clicking on any of the fund names takes you to Yahoo!'s Summary page on that fund, which is really best in class.

But we're not done yet.

MSN ETF Screener.   When you use the MSN site, you should use the Internet Explorer browser, because Microsoft's web site was apparently designed by a bunch of control freaks who hate Firefox and other non-Microsoft browsers.

Anyway, point your Web browser to Moneycentral.msn.com. Down the page you'll see a lot of links, including one that says *ETF Research.*

One thing I like about this site is it tells you which ETFs are the leaders and laggards on any given day. This gives you a good idea of what is working in the market. To find this, look on the left-hand column for a link called *Top Performers.* Once you click on the link, you'll find there are many different categories. You can also look at what the funds are holding, check out the Morningstar rating if the fund has one, and organize by category, price, and performance over a number of time frames.

Many of the better performers have higher Morningstar ratings. It's funny how that works out, isn't it? Basically, looking for a good balance between returns and Morningstar ratings is a good first step.

These are three different ETF screeners, each with its own approach to finding the best funds. I don't have a particular favorite; and I've been known to use all three when I'm doing my fund research. You'll have to explore and kick the tires, and see which one works best for you.

The Least You Can Do

- Educate yourself! Define your own comfort level of risk and reward—which of the three levels that I discussed in this chapter suits you?
- If you're going to invest in stocks, be aware of the six things every investor must know about the stock market.
- If you prefer exchange-traded funds (ETFs), see the Pros and Cons of ETFs sidebar.
- Asset allocation is a way to remove risk from your portfolio—and ETFs make it easier.

PART

III

BE PREPARED—
GRUB AND GEAR

CHAPTER 6

Water

When the well is dry, they know the worth of water.
—Benjamin Franklin

Let's talk about some questions you should ask yourself about your water supply *before* a crisis hits, ways to purify water at home and on the road, and more.

There are a number of essentials to survival. Water is the first essential—without water, you'll be dead in three days. Then you need food; without food, even if you're a fat American, you'll last only a couple of weeks. Clothes are essential unless you live in Tahiti, and if you live in Tahiti, you lucky bastard, you'll still need sunscreen and a hat. Finally, there is gear—tents, knives, tools and more. The only things that are absolutely essential are food and water. And yet, those are the two things that modern civilized people take for granted; as a result, they never have enough of either food or water stored for when the manure hits the fan. That's why people will dodge police and national guardsmen to go loot a grocery store after an emergency. If you follow my recommendations, that won't be you, which really improves the odds of you *not* ending up as a premature corpse and being used as a bad example for others.

In a major disaster, it's easy for the power grid to get knocked out. Once the power is gone so is pumped water (including drinking and wastewater), street lights, store lights, house lights, refrigeration, heating systems, security systems, telecommunication systems, gasoline pumps, and more. Stores will close (no electricity to run the cash register, lights, or freezers), so you will not be able to buy the food, water, medication, and supplies you are used to having conveniently available 24 hours a day.

Unless you topped off your tank before the disaster hit, you will not be able to drive to an area outside the disaster zone. Gasoline pumps will not be operational—all you will have is what is in your tank. Your refrigerated food will spoil within a day, your sewage could back up and you will have no fans to remove the smell and the heat. If you live in the hot parts of the country, you'll have no A/C or ice; in the colder parts of the country, you'll have no heat. You will run out of food as soon as your pantry is empty, and for most Americans, that's within three days. The only water you will have to drink, or clean with, is what you had in bottles before the outage occurred.

Well, you can always call the cops, right? Sorry, in a real emergency, they're too busy. In a really bad emergency, the phones, even cell phones, probably won't work.

So here's the question you need to ask yourself: If civilization isn't there, what will you need?

It sounds crazy to think you might not have water, but we're talking clean water that is fit to drink, and it can run out rather quickly in a crisis. Just ask the survivors of Hurricane Katrina.

Before a crisis starts, here are some questions to ask:

- Are you sure you'll always be able to pay your water bill?
- If you have a well, does it run on electricity? How safe is that power source?
- If you live in a dry area, how sure are you that your water supply is secure?

These are questions worth asking ahead of time, because you can't live without water. Water is the most important element for your body's survival. A person can lose all reserve carbohydrate and fat, and about half the body's protein without being in real danger (though it would be *really* uncomfortable). Losing water, which amounts to 10% to 22% of your body weight, would be fatal.

Basically, you have three choices: You can get water from under the ground, on top of the ground, or the sky. It is worth understanding fully where your water comes from and where you might get it in an emergency. If your water isn't supplied by your local town, then you'll have to face other concerns, such as well pollution, pesticide run-off, mercury contamination, and more. If your water comes from a municipality, that supply could be threatened by a large-scale disaster, or even a protracted power outage.

Following are some other questions you should ask.

How Much Water Do I Need?

You'd be amazed how much water you use in your everyday life. My home state of Florida uses 174 gallons per person per day.[1] But I live in a state with more than its share of crazy people and golf courses, and crazy people on golf courses.

Here are some other figures:

- The average person uses over 100 gallons of water per day; that includes water for drinking, washing, cooking, and cleaning— the works.
- The World Health Organization says 26.5 gallons of potable water per person is needed daily for minimal health and sanitation standards.
- The U.S. army has done studies that have found that troop- use averages 14.5 gallons per soldier, per day.
- A common recommendation for emergency survival situations is at least 2 gallons per person per day.

If you're facing a short-term emergency, you need at least three days' worth of water for each family member, including pets. A *bare minimum* is one quart, but you'd be more comfortable with two gallons each per day.

On the other hand, you might want to stock more than that, especially if you're keen on bathing.

I'd be more comfortable storing a week's worth of water. A week's worth of water for four people and a dog would be 70 gallons of water.

Metal containers can leave water with an unpleasant taste. So, most people store water in plastic jugs or other containers. Make sure that you use food-grade plastic. If you recycle old plastic bottles, remember that whatever was in it originally has probably soaked into the plastic, so make sure to use only ones that held stuff you'd drink again, like water, milk, soda pop, etc.

Containers should be filled to the top to help prevent algae growth. Store water out of direct sunlight in a cool part of your home. But avoid freezing, because that can rupture containers.

How Long Can Water Be Stored Before It Is Replaced?

The shelf life of water depends on the original quality of the water, the temperature at which it is stored, how much light it is exposed to. Darker containers will make water last longer. Store-bought bottled, distilled, or purified water should be good for at least two years, and maybe three, though some may evaporate. Ordinary chlorinated tap water can last at least six months in storage.

In the past, a common recommendation was to add a few drops of household chlorine bleach or iodine to a bottle of water to sterilize it. It turns out iodine can be toxic and chlorine bleach is potentially toxic *and* a cancer hazard (oops!) and so that isn't anything you want to do long term.

How come chlorine is used in city water then? Well, (1) it's not household chlorine bleach, and (2) it's in city water in very small amounts—a parts-per-million basis.

Water Purifiers

Now we're talking! Rather than store dozens of gallons of water in your house, you can buy a water purifier. Portable water purification devices are self-contained units that are used by military personnel, explorers, missionaries, and others who must obtain drinking water

Can Water Go Bad?

Sure it can, if you keep it too close to solvents or chemicals, or keep it too long. Stored water may eventually develop a disagreeable appearance, taste, or odor. As the saying goes, "If the water tastes funky, don't give it to your monkey."

Other tips: You should probably split up your water stash, in case some gets damaged or you can't access it. In a real emergency, you can always drink water drained from a hot water heater or from the flush tank of a toilet (not the bowl). Water from a swimming pool can cause diarrhea due to high chlorine content, but it's fine for bathing.

from untreated sources (rivers, lakes, etc). Water purifiers make ordinary ground water drinkable (the scientific term is *potable*). And they're a good alternative for elderly or infirm people who have difficulty lugging around big gallon jugs of water.

Carbon water filters. This form of filter comprises possibly 95% of those in use domestically. They are simple to install, relatively economical, and depending on micron level, will filter out the most deadly of contaminants, including bacteria like Cryptosporidium and Guardia. Anything one micron rating or below will inhibit Cryptosporidium and Guardia as the cysts are larger than this in size. Viruses cannot be inhibited by a filter with a micron rating of more than 0.01 microns.

An average charcoal filter will last a family six to nine months. Some charcoal filters are enhanced by the use of activated nano-silver, which provides extra antibacterial protection, killing around 650 known types of organisms.

A cheap, useful carbon filter is a simple RV water filter. These are designed to hook inline with a garden hose and fill up an RV's water storage tank. As of this writing, you can buy these for about $25 each, and they're available at

Another Water Storage Tip

Not all water is created equal. The water that stores best and for the longest period of time is higher in alkaline.

You can test the alkalinity of your water using litmus paper, which is sold in some pharmacies. A pH below 6.8 indicates acidity, while a pH above 6.8 indicates alkalinity. Water from different parts of the country can vary widely in pH levels.

To do the test, dip red litmus paper in the water you wish to store. If the strip changes in color from pink to violet or blue, then your water alkalinity is fine.

If your water has low alkalinity/high acidity, then you can fix that by adding small amounts of baking soda to each container of water. It shouldn't change the taste of the water.

If you're on the lazy side—come on, embrace your inner couch potato—you can skip the water testing and just add two teaspoons of baking soda to each gallon of water. Mix well and store.

any RV store or Wal-Mart. Remember that if the water is run through too fast, the filter will not be effective. It takes about one minute to fill up a one-gallon jug using a carbon RV water filter.

However, if you're serious about this, don't use an ordinary garden hose. Some garden hoses can contain lead or other harmful chemicals. Again, an RV store can supply you with a proper hose.

Types of Filters

Pitcher-type filter. BRITA, PUR, Culligan, and Braun all make pitcher-type water filters. They remove a lot of impurities, but they aren't water purifiers. Still, if you don't have anything else, they're better than nothing. And they're good for everyday use, because they can remove the chlorine taste from household tap water. The filters are replaceable, and prices vary.

Ceramic Filters. Some ceramic water filters come as a cartridge that fits a normal bench top filter. At the core of the ceramic filter element is diatomaceous earth, a fossil substance made up of tiny silicon shells left by trillions of microscopic, one-celled algae called diatoms that have inhabited the earth for the last 150 million years. Flow rates of ceramic water filters are slower than many other filters. However, the flow rate of the ceramic filter can be renewed by brushing its outer surface under running water. As the top layer of ceramic and contaminants are brushed off and flushed away, a new layer becomes available.[2]

British Berkefeld. A portable ceramic filter system, and the granddaddy of gravity water filter systems, the Berkefeld has a history dating back to the 1800s. It was originally developed by Mr. Henry Doulton to purify London drinking water, which was drawn from the Thames, a river that was heavily contaminated with raw sewage; cholera and typhoid epidemics were rampant. Queen Victoria was one of Doulton's first customers. Really, when you get down to it, Mr. Doulton's water purifier probably did more for British health than a legion of doctors.

The British Berkefeld is known as the water filter of choice by missionaries and relief agencies around the world. You can pour creek water in this filter and a short time later have clean, good tasting water. How? The Berkefeld has ceramic filters with a pore structure designed to remove very fine particles and bacteria. It can be used when camping or where there is no municipally treated water. The gravity feed system also works when water pressure is too low for other filters.

The Berkefeld is constructed of high-grade, polished stainless steel making it hygienic, durable, and easy to clean. The two piece housing is portable and can be used virtually anywhere, anytime. It takes minutes to assemble and can provide up to 24 gallons of safe drinking water each day. Its ceramic filter can be cleaned and reused.

This is my family's choice for a water purifier. Very little can break and no pumping is required. If you are moving around a lot, you might want another system, but if you're staying put, the Berkefeld will do the job. It's also good for picnics and other outdoor gatherings.

Another choice that's a lot cheaper is the Katadyn Base Camp Water Filter. You simply fill up the 2.6-gallon bag and hang it from a tree. Gravity will draw the water through the filters and it come out clean from the tube.

Other options: If you want to go high-tech, you can get water purifiers based on reverse osmosis, ultraviolet radiation, magnetics, infrared, catalytic purifiers, ionization, and more. All of these have one thing in common: They require electricity, which may be in short supply during an emergency.

A SteriPEN, which looks roughly like a pen, destroys viruses, bacteria, and common microbes in water. It requires batteries, and it's supposed to work well. According to the manufacturer, a SteriPEN has the advantages of no pumping, no chemicals, no test strips, no timekeeping, no lubricating, and no replacement filters. All you have to do is push the water purifier's button (once for 32 ounces, twice for 16 ounces), place the pen-like lamp in clear water, and stir until an indicator light turns green. This would work well whether you're staying in one place or on-the-go.

"Oh Crap! The World Is Ending and I Didn't Store Water!"

If you experience a disaster, don't have any water stored, and are worried your water supply will be cut off abruptly, here's what to do: Find and wash as many plastic, glass, fiberglass, or enamel-lined containers as you can. Soft-drink bottles and food-grade drums work well. If you're worried about the quality of the water, and you're doing this on a short-term basis only, forget my earlier warning about the long-term adverse effects of household bleach in water and add eight drops of household bleach (containing 5.25% sodium hypochlorite) per gallon of water. This amount of bleach will kill microorganisms, but it won't make you sick. Seal the containers and store them in a cool, dark place.

Portable Water Purifier

There are a bunch of portable water purifiers on the market—just go to Amazon.com and search for *portable water purifier*. They tend to be more pricey than the others I've mentioned already. I'd avoid ones with hoses because that's always the first thing to break, but it's a matter of personal choice. That said, I think one of the best you can buy is the Katadyn Pocket Water Microfilter. It has hoses, but it also has a lifetime warrantee; this makes it four times more expensive than its competitors, so I guess you get what you pay for.

Another, less expensive choice is the Katadyn ExStream XR Water Bottle Purifier. This has a three-stage filter built into the bottle, and it's good for 125 refills. By the time you need to change the filter, you should either be someplace safe or you probably have bigger problems.

If you think your *end of life as we know it* story will include a lot of travel, a portable water filter is the way to go.

Hobo Water Purifier

If you find yourself stuck without a water filtration system and a powerful and growing thirst, take some comfort in the fact that our ancestors dealt with this situation successfully. One solution is to construct a *hobo water purifier*. Here's what to do . . .

Find the cleanest water you can. Strain the water through paper towels, paper coffee filters, or several layers of clean cloth into

Four Alternative Ways to Store Water in an Emergency

If you don't want to keep bottles of water around the house, and you're pretty sure your water won't be cut off right away, you can buy a container ahead of time and fill it up when you need it. Options include the following:

1. **WaterBob:** The WaterBob is a 100-gallon bag made of 4-mil, food-grade plastic that fits in your bathtub. You can fill it in about 20 minutes using your bathtub faucet. An included siphon pump is used to dispense the water into jugs or pitchers. The WaterBob costs $30 (cost per gallon $0.30). To find out more about it, go to http://tinyurl.com/d572r4.

2. **Aquatank:** This bladder comes in different sizes from 30 gallons to 300 gallons. It's advertised as being made from an advanced food-grade material so it won't affect the odor or taste of the stored water. A 300-gallon bladder costs about $300 (cost per gallon $1). To find out more, go to http://tinyurl.com/c4k6ks.

3. **Home Emergency Water System (HEWS):** This is a two-ply plastic bladder system that holds more than 45 gallons of water. Each HEWS system comes with a siphon pump and sanitary alcohol swab (cost per gallon $1.12). To find out more, go to http://tinyurl.com/dhaqh7.

4. **Five-gallon collapsible water container:** This kind of container is made of heavy-duty polyethylene and is easily portable. It costs about $6 (cost per gallon $1.2). To find out more, go to http://tinyurl.com/dfocbf.

Source: Watercrunch.blogspot.com.

a container to remove any sediment or flaking material. Then boil the water vigorously for 10 minutes. Boiling water will kill bacteria as well as other disease-causing microorganisms that are commonly found in rivers and lakes, but would scare the crap out of you if you saw them through a microscope. Add one additional minute for each 10,000 feet of altitude, depending on where you live.

Bottom line: Disaster may never come, so I wouldn't overspend on many areas of equipment, but some type of water stockpile and/or purification system is a must. If and when TSHTF, you'll die without it. If disaster never comes, then you have water stored, and there are a million and one uses for it.

The Least You Can Do

- Buy cheap supermarket bottled water—two gallons of water per day for three days for every person in your household, plus pets. Distilled or purified water is best, water labeled "drinking water" is okay, too.
- Write the date the water *expires* in magic marker on the plastic jugs of water.
- Make sure none of the bottles leak.
- Find a fairly cool place to store it in your house where it won't heat up to 130 degrees Fahrenheit.

7

Food Storage for Couch Potatoes

A cabin with plenty of food is better than a hungry castle.
—Irish saying

In this chapter, we're going to explore food storage. We'll cover bulk storage, dry goods, canned goods, dehydrated foods and ready-to-eat meals, and pantry essentials. We'll also cover cooking without electricity.

Even if you don't have a lot of money to spare, dedicating a few extra dollars from your budget every month to build a small food stockpile is a good idea. It's not just for survival planning. A food stockpile will also help you save time and money.

A well-stocked, well-organized pantry avoids last-minute dashes to the store, which means you save time and gasoline. It also makes eating out less tempting, so it can help you save money and lose weight.

Saving money is also known as frugality, a word that seems to have picked up bad connotations in the consumer-obsessed United States. So let's use the word *spartaneity*, a back-to-basics, less-is-more approach to living in bleak economic times, and that's reflected in my food storage choices. I didn't invent the word, but it pretty much sums up what should be a winning approach for any suburban, couch-potato survivalist.

Frugality or spartaneity is about creating a comfortable standard of living, which provides for you and yours while allowing you to save as much money as possible. What's more, you can potentially make back the cost of the book in the first week by improving your shopping habits.

Spartaneity begins in the pantry, for the reasons I've outlined above, namely that having a well-stocked, well-organized cupboard will save you time and money.

There are three different ways to store large amounts of food, and I'm in favor of two of them. I like bulk storage, or buying food in large lots and storing it at home. I also like the idea of beefing up your pantry through smart shopping, which we'll explore more in Chapter 8.

You can also buy the Meal, Ready-to-Eat (MRE)—a form of food that comes in a lightweight pouch, lasts for a very long time, and can sometimes even cook itself (if it has a self-heating feature). MREs tend to be expensive, though. If you have more money than time, you might want to consider MREs. If you have some time, you can build up your pantry and bulk storage without spending too much money.

Make sure your food storage can survive a loss of power. Food in your refrigerator or freezer can't be considered long-term food storage unless you have a backup generator and the fuel to run it. Even then, it will only last as long as your fuel.

How to Begin

On average, a person needs about 2,400 food calories per day. Most people prefer to consume between four and five pounds of food per day. Obtaining a proper balance of proteins, vitamins, and nutrients requires a variety of food sources. Some typical survival food comes dry and is prepared in water to make it edible, such as rice and beans, while other foods are usually eaten fresh and full of water weight, such as vegetables and fruits.

Here's an important thing to consider: All the survival rations in the world won't do you any good if you won't or can't eat them. Will you eat Spam? Or canned lima beans? You have to eat the food you store, and store food you will eat. It is useless to buy a lot of survival foods just because they are inexpensive if you or your family doesn't like them. The best advice is to store the food you eat, and to get in the habit of eating the food you store.

A severe emergency, when you no longer have heat, electricity, running water, and may be running for your life, is not the time to strain your body by changing your diet. If you try to suddenly go from grazing on fast foods and frozen pizza to living on MREs, it's pretty much guaranteed that your digestive system is going to revolt, and the results will not be pretty. And if you're living on a diet of Pop-Tarts, Cheetos, and Hot Pockets—well, you're a miracle of science. That said, you should go ahead and include some of those foods that you like in your long-term storage.

So what should you store? Start keeping track of what you eat. Do this for two weeks, and you can use that to plan your food storage.

If you want to take a more scientific approach, you can use Table 7.1 to start estimating your needs.

Begin with the basics, the lowest-cost essentials that are simple to acquire and will help keep you going in the tough times. Whole grains, rice, and beans are the bulk of many long-term food storage larders. Whole grains and brown rice are superior because they are packed with nutrients, unlike their counterparts.

Next, add dried and/or canned vegetables. Get some oils in there like olive, vegetable or peanut oil, because you'll need something to use when frying your food. Do you eat meat? Add canned, dried or freeze-dried meat, fish, and chicken to your stockpile. You'll also want to include dried fruit, peanut butter, and other snacks, especially energy-boosting foods. This includes chocolate. Even if you don't eat chocolate, put some in storage because you can always use it for barter.

Table 7.1 Average Food Consumption per Person

Food	Pounds per Year	Ounces per Day (dry)	Ounces per Day (wet)	Calories per Pound	Calories per Year	Calories per Day
grains	270	11.8	35.5	1,550	418,500	1147
dry beans	90	3.9	11.8	1,600	144,000	395
oils	25	1.1	1.1	4,000	100,000	274
sprouting seeds	30	1.3	3.9	1,600	48,000	132
fruit and vegetables	400	1.8	17.5	200	80,000	219
eggs	30	1.3	1.3	650	19,500	53
meats	40	1.8	1.8	950	37,000	101
Totals	**915**	**24.3**	**74.3**		**888,400**	**2,434**

Weights given are most common available form; grains are normally dry, vegetables wet.
Source: TheOilDrumCampfire.com.

Also include coffee or tea. It's easy enough to boil water even if you lose power.

You can find an Internet calculator that will help you figure out how much food you should store. One place to visit is Internet Grocer: http://www.internet-grocer.net/planner.htm. Internet Grocer also sells canned, dehydrated, and freeze-dried foods.

So you've started stacking up lots of boxes in the pantry. This will be good for six months or a year, tops. Now, it's time to take the next step and get some real survival containers, such as food-grade plastic pails with air-tight lids. These will preserve the foods, protect them from bug infestation, and can survive many disasters that might befall you.

Bulk Storage

Storage life of food will depend on the type of foods stored, their condition and age at the time of storage, how you choose to store them, and the temperature at which you store them. Even dry foods can deteriorate and spoil, with the major causes being incursion of moisture, oxygen, high temperatures, light, and animal infestation.

Storage containers need to be *food grade*, meaning they won't deteriorate and contaminate food, and they will be able to seal completely. A common and inexpensive container is the plastic bucket (HDPE, type 2) with a rubber gasket lid manufactured specifically for holding food. While this type of plastic is a relatively poor barrier to oxygen, these buckets have good resistance to impact, acids, fats, oil, and moisture.

Used buckets may be contaminated with non-food items, so be careful. Bucket lids may need a prying wrench to open, or a more expensive option is to buy screw-top lids. You may want a scooper to remove grain from five-gallon buckets and into kitchen containers. Alternatives to the plastic bucket include one- or half-gallon glass jars and metal cans, but these are not as widely available.

Optimum food storage temperature (unless you're talking frozen food) is 40 degrees. Most of us don't have access to 40-degree root cellars. The storage lengths I'll give you below are for northern room-temperature storage, or an average 70 degrees Fahrenheit. Every 10 degrees above that halves storage life. So, storing your food in an un-air-conditioned garage in Florida or Arizona is just asking for trouble.

If you store foods without using oxygen absorbers or some other kind of vacuum sealer, you can expect storage lengths along the following lines:

- White flour—six to 12 months
- Wheat flour—three months or longer if kept in the fridge (Note: I don't like the taste of wheat flour kept in the fridge.)
- Popcorn—two years
- Baking soda—up to 18 months, but go by the expiration date when possible
- Ground spices—one year
- Whole herbs and spices—two years

If you store mainly what you normally eat, and keep rotating your stock, then your food is unlikely to spoil. The best strategy to keep your food stores fresh is one of lifestyle and habits—for example, a diet primarily based on whole grains and beans, seasonally available foods, and drawing from bulk household supplies of sweeteners, oils, and preserved out-of-season produce will naturally foster a smart storage plan. Primarily local sources of meat, egg, and dairy products might be healthy additions, too. If you store several months of food or more, clearly label the containers by date and content and always eat from the older stores and refresh periodically to maintain your buffer.

As you can see in Table 7.2, this is going to be okay if all you're going to do is keep a year's worth of food and you rotate your stock. If you have more ambitious ideas, that takes more planning.

Table 7.2   Food Potential Storage Life

Food	Length
Honey, sugar, salt	>20 years
Dry beans, whole grains	5–20 years
Processed oil, non-fat powdered milk	5 years
Pasta, dried fruits	2–3 years
Unshelled raw nuts, dry yeast, jams, Canned fruit, pickles	18 months
Liquid oils, nut butters	1 year
Fresh produce (potatoes, garlic, onions, winter squash)*	6 months

* Only if cooler than 70 degrees F.
Source: TheOilDrumCampfire.com.

If you want to keep more than a year's worth of food on hand, I highly recommend you store at least some of your food in five-gallon plastic food-grade buckets.

If you're storing food in a bucket, make sure the bucket is lined with a food-grade plastic liner, available from companies that carry these kinds of supplies.

These buckets should have an air-tight lid with an oxygen absorber placed inside. Oxygen absorbers require a little explanation before use. They are purchased in air-tight containers. Once exposed to the air, they absorb oxygen for three days to two weeks, depending on the brand. Then they quit. If this occurs in a sealed bucket, it will create a vacuum.

Place the oxygen absorber on top of the food inside an open zip-lock bag. Seal the lid, then tape the label of whatever you store to either the top of the lid or the front of the bucket, depending on your storage system, and write the expiration date on it. Bulk foods stored in this way can be stored, generally speaking, for seven years, but some foods can last much longer.

Vitamin and nutrient content will deteriorate over time, faster than the food goes bad. Most canned foods will lose over half of their nutrient content after the first three to five years in storage. The food will still be perfectly fine to eat but will contain less nutritional value when consumed.

Of course, you're smart enough to rotate your stock. Whatever you store, even in your long-term storage, you are going to open it up in the next five years and eat it, right? Because otherwise, it's a damned waste of time.

Make sure your food storage can survive a loss of power. Food in your refrigerator or freezer is not long-term food storage unless you have a backup generator and the fuel to run it. Even then, it will only last as long as your fuel.

One More Bucket Idea

If you are putting together *bug-out* bags for your car (see Chapter 14), you also may want to put together a bug-out food storage bucket. Put a red stripe on the bucket (or some other marker) to indicate this is the bucket you are going to grab when you are evacuating your house. You might want to put some comfort foods in there—you're going to be stressed out as it is. And yes, chocolate is a survival food. The foods in your bug-out bucket should be ones that can be eaten without cooking or that require no more than 10 minutes of cooking in boiling water or over a flame.

You might want to consider storing more food than you need. If TSHTF, then cans of food might be used as a currency, at least for a short while.

Buckets aren't the only storage solution. Another plastic solution is the soda, juice, and water bottles, which you probably use a lot in your house. These are commonly made from PET plastic. Properly cleaned and with screw-top lids, PET plastic containers will keep nearly any kind of food, provided the containers are stored in a dark location. PET plastics are nearly always transparent to light, and light will cut down on the length of time you can store food.

Mylar bags are also very good, and nearly impervious to oxygen. Many survivalists store food inside heat-sealed Mylar bags, which are then placed inside five-gallon plastic buckets; obviously, that's only for long-term storage.

Dry-Bulk Foods—Pros

- Very inexpensive—the cheapest of the options here.

Dry-Bulk Foods—Cons

- Storage time is limited; you have to actively rotate your stock.
- If not stored properly, these can spoil and/or attract vermin.
- Require the most preparation time of the options here.

Money-Saving Tip

A gamma seal lid has heavy-duty construction that allows it to be reusable. Over 150 million five-gallon pails are manufactured each year. Millions are discarded. If you can find empty, discarded pails, clean them properly to make them food-safe and dry them; then you only have to buy the lids, which you can find from numerous online vendors.

Gamma seal lids come in different colors. Consider color-coordinating your food storage for easier use.

Canned Goods

Most canned goods sold in U.S. supermarkets are guaranteed for 10 years. However, Del Monte and other corporations have done research that shows canned foods sealed forty years or longer are just fine to eat.

In reality, canned goods can be fit to eat unless the can bulges or rusts all the way through. Canned goods also have the advantage of being good after being dusted with radioactive fallout (eek!), chemical agents (ack!), or biological contaminants (argh!). Just wash the can thoroughly before opening, maybe in that distilled water you stored because you read Chapter 6.

However, while cans *may* last a long time, they won't if improperly stored. Steel cans must not be put in long-term storage on concrete, or in cardboard boxes, or in a damp area, because this can cause the cans to rust. If the rust goes all the way through the skin

The Canned Cheeseburger Conundrum

One of the problems that people face when doing food storage is that it's very hard to store their favorite meals. Some you can do with ingenuity. When my sister was in the Peace Corps in Mali (not the Hawaiian island—that's Maui; Mali is a pestilent hellhole in Africa), I mailed her a pizza. In a box, I placed a prepackaged pizza pie sealed in plastic, a can of pizza sauce, a bag of shredded cheese, a can of parmesan cheese, and a package of sliced pepperoni. I labeled the whole thing *Bibles*, and a month later, she got it. My sister was *very* appreciative.

But how do you put a hamburger in long-term storage? Well, you can get an MRE that's hamburger-ish. Or you can use ingenuity. Would you believe in such a thing as a canned cheeseburger?

- Lightly fry small hamburger patties.
- Stack them into wide-mouth jars (the cooked patty should be just small enough to fit through the mouth of the jar).
- Layer the patties with finely chopped onion or garlic if you like.
- When ready to use, refry them, adding cheese if desired.

They aren't the same as the regular hamburgers your family is used to, but they're still good. And it's the cheapest choice for putting hamburgers into long-term food storage.

of the can, the food within them will become worthless or downright poisonous.

Also, if you're preparing for WTSHTF, remember to stash more than one nonelectric can opener.

Home Canning

Home canning is a great way to preserve foods from your garden to eat all year round, and a great way to add to your home stockpiles. It's relatively easy to do; the only equipment you'll probably have to buy is jars and lids. You can download a whole tutorial on it at http://tinyurl.com/dz85qo.

Canned Foods—Pros

- Last a long time—up to 10 years.
- Can be an inexpensive option, depending on how you do it.

Canned Foods—Cons

- Need more storage room than most other options.

Dehydrated Foods

Dehydrated foods, along with pickling and home canning, are what our ancestors used before some smart guys figured out how to freeze, vacuum-pack, and freeze-dry food. Dehydration works fine; dehydrated foods sealed in an airtight container can easily last a year, and it's something you can do on the cheap.

First, invest in an electric food dehydrator. Then, cut the food in thin slices and dry it where insects can't get to it. Once well dried, you can store dehydrated food in airtight jars or sealed gallon or five-gallon containers.

But what if you're *really* cheap? Spartaneity is in, dude! Well, the great thing is you can dehydrate foods real cheap by simply *air-drying* them, *if your climate permits*. Some examples:

- **Sun-drying:** This is ideal for fruits such as apricots, peaches, grapes, and figs. Sun-drying requires a number of hot (85 degrees or higher) days with relatively low humidity. Spread thin pieces of fruit evenly across a shallow pan and cover with a cheesecloth to keep the food safe from bugs and birds. Sunny porches, balconies, and even flat roofs are all natural places to dry food. Alternately, you can put boxes in the backseat of a car and lay the tray on top, with full exposure to the sun through the back windshield.

- **Oven-drying:** This involves drying food at temperatures between 130 and 150 degrees. (Some older ovens may not have temperature settings this low.) As in sun-drying, distribute pieces of food in a shallow pan or dish. You may want to check the food periodically for adequate dehydration.
- **Solar dehydrator:** You can build a solar dehydrator for food preservation instead of using an electric one. Here's a nifty one: http://tinyurl.com/3d2yhg.

If the temperature is too low or the humidity too high when sun- or oven-drying, the food may dry too slowly or even spoil. When the temperature is too high, it could cook the food and make it hard on the outside, while leaving the inside moist and vulnerable to molding or other forms of spoilage from microorganisms.

To prepare dehydrated food, just add water. The food should reconstitute itself by soaking in water for approximately 15 to 20 minutes. Then, cook and serve. Many reconstituted dehydrated foods are a little darker in color, more fragrant, and sweeter in taste. Do not expect food dried at home to look or taste like commercially dried food. It's better than that, but naturally, it won't taste the same as fresh food.

Dehydrated foods will last from one season to the next. If you dry enough garden tomatoes this year, you can eat them until next year when fresh ones are again dropping from the vines.

Dehydrated Foods—Pros

- Inexpensive—especially when you can grow many foods from seeds.
- Cheap—one of the cheapest alternatives you have here.

Dehydrated Foods—Cons

- Storage time is less than other options.

Storing Fresh Fruits and Vegetables

You don't have to dehydrate and/or preserve all your vegetables. Mature potatoes, onions, and hard-shell squashes can last three to four months or longer in a cool (45 to 50 degrees F), dry place. However, there are a few things to keep in mind:

- Don't rinse your potatoes before storing them. If you do rinse them, they're more likely to sprout. Potatoes will also sprout as a result of exposure to light or warm temperatures.
- When storing potatoes, put them in a bag (a paper bag will do fine) and throw in half an apple. The apple will absorb moisture and allow the potatoes to last longer.
- While it's good to put half an apple with your potatoes, avoid storing apples with other vegetables. Apples and some other fruits release a gas (ethylene), which causes ripening. Likewise, avoid storing potatoes close to onions because they produce gases that spoil both.
- Sweet potatoes don't last in storage as long as regular potatoes, but they can still last two to three months if stored properly.
- According to studies, fruits and vegetables grown in soil with high potash levels store better and longer than others.

Not all vegetables store the same under the same conditions. For example, carrots, turnips, eggplants, and beets store best under cold and moist conditions. Potatoes, cabbage, and apples like it cool but not too moist. Garlic, onions, and soybeans like it warmer and a bit dryer than most other vegetables, whereas pumpkins, sweet potatoes, and winter squash like staying dry, period. You'll have to experiment and realize that you won't be able to store everything you harvest in the same place.

A good site for finding storage times for foods of all types—fresh, canned, packaged, or frozen—is Still Tasty (http://www.stilltasty.com). It bills itself as *the ultimate shelf life guide*, and it covers a wide range of foods.

In an emergency worst-case scenario, you can push the storage of many fresh foods out much further. Don't be fooled by guides that give carrots, for example, a mere seven to 14 days in the refrigerator, even when wrapped in plastic bags. If you're not persnickety, you can handle eating carrots if they've been stored in a cool spot for a couple months. They will likely be rubbery, but you can boil or fry them up to gather in their vitamins. And if you're sitting around after an emergency, you may have plenty of time to preserve those carrots by canning them, or using them in vinegar or relishes, *before* they get rubbery. Here are some very general guidelines on how long fresh food can last under optimal storage conditions—just remember it all depends on your own food storage conditions.

- Beets—four to five months
- Broccoli—two weeks
- Brussels Sprouts—three to five weeks
- Cabbage—three to four months
- Chinese Cabbage—one to two months
- Carrots—two months
- Cauliflower—two to four weeks
- Celery—two months
- Cucumbers—two to three weeks
- Eggplant—two weeks
- Jerusalem Artichokes—one to two months
- Onions—three to four months
- Parsnips—one to two months
- Pepper—three to four months
- Sweet Potatoes—three to four months
- Potatoes—four to six months
- Pumpkin—three to four months
- Radishes—two to three months
- Rutabagas—two to four months
- Soybeans—four to six months
- Squash—four to six months
- Tomatoes—one to two months
- Turnips—four to six months

The worst environment to store fresh fruits and vegetables is in high temperatures and high humidity. This combination is an excellent growing environment for bacteria, molds, and yeasts. The cooler and dryer you can keep foods, the longer they will last.

A root cellar, if you're lucky enough to have one or to be able to build one, is perfect for storing fresh food. You can download a PDF on storing food in a root cellar at the Maryland Cooperative Extension web site: http://tinyurl.com/cb8jhm.[1]

Another excellent resource is the book *Root Cellaring: Natural Cold Storage of Fruits and Vegetables* by Mike and Nancy Bubel.

Root cellars keep foods cool and somewhat damp; while the foods stored in a root cellar don't last as long as they would in a dry cellar, they don't shrivel. Shriveled food can still be quite nutritious. Moldy food should be avoided. As soon as you see a rotting or molding section of any vegetable, get rid of it. Slice off the bad part and eat the rest, or throw it into the compost heap.

MREs—Meals, Ready-to-Eat

As mentioned earlier, a Meal, Ready-to-Eat (MRE) is a lightweight pouch of precooked food. MREs are lightweight because they come in foil pouches instead of cans. They are precooked so they can be eaten cold, or you can dunk them in boiling water or set them next to a small fire for a few minutes and have a hot meal. Some MREs have their own heating systems built in to the packaging.

The military MREs are 2,000 calories per meal. Civilian camping meals don't provide as much actual food value but have the advantage of tasting better. The disadvantage of MREs is the expense. These pouches can be stored for seven years.

Meals, Ready-to-Eat—Pros

- Fastest preparation time possible; can be heated quickly.
- You can order them online in minutes and have them delivered to your house. Actual storage time will take under an hour.

Meals, Ready-to-Eat—Cons

- Expensive—the most expensive of all the options here.
- Last five to seven years—less than some alternatives.
- Taste may take some getting used to.

Freeze-Dried Food

A variation on MREs is freeze-dried, pre-cooked food canned in nitrogen. These will last pretty much forever. The advantage of freeze-dried nitrogen packed canned foods is they're good as long as the can is good, they're lightweight because they're freeze dried, they require no cooking because they're precooked, and many people think they taste great, much better than other types of MREs! You can buy these from different suppliers; Mountain House is one of the best-known vendors, found at MountainHouse.com. Mountain House products store well in their pre-packed cases, each containing six cans. You can also buy freeze-dried, pre-cooked food in the camping section of large sporting goods stores.

Freeze-Dried means that the food is held at just above freezing, while in a vacuum chamber. In a vacuum, the moisture is removed quickly, to a point where it is much drier than most other dehydrated foods. Because the food is not allowed to freeze, ice crystals do not form in the cells of the food. It is these ice crystals that can cause frozen foods to loose their texture and become mushy, because the ice crystals rupture the cell walls in the food. Freeze-dried food, when water is added, returns more closely to original freshness than do other dehydrated foods.

Nitrogen-packed foods take it one step farther—almost all of the oxygen in them is replaced with nitrogen. It is the oxygen that causes most foods to spoil, as most microbes and insects require oxygen to live. When this method of preserving food is combined with freeze-drying, the result is food that will keep for *very* long periods of time and maintain its nutritional value and flavor. There is nothing bad to say about these methods of food preservation except that nitrogen-packed, freeze-dried foods tend to be expensive.

Freeze-Dried Foods—Pros

- Easy to store—nitrogen-packed freeze-dried foods can last up to 30 years.
- Simple to prepare—just add water.
- Close to original food taste.
- You can order them online in minutes and have them delivered to your house. Actual storage time will take under an hour.

Freeze-Dried Foods—Cons

- More expensive than some alternatives, although less expensive than others.

Emergency Pantry Essentials You *Must* Have

Some people find it hard to get started in food storage. So here's a list of things just to push you down the path. Store as much of each as you have space for. Buy single-serving sizes whenever possible, because you can't depend on refrigeration after the containers have been opened.

Basic Emergency Food Pantry

- Canned or dried meats. Beef jerky or beef sticks are good sources of long-storing protein, as is Spam and canned chicken.
- Canned fish. Canned tuna is an excellent source of protein and omega-3 fatty acids.
- Canned beans. If you're a vegetarian and don't (or can't) eat beef, chicken, or fish, remember that canned beans are an excellent source of vegetarian nutrition. However, humans do not have the ability to digest beans well, and in some people this causes a lot of gas. This could add stress to a survival situation, especially in closed spaces. So if you're stocking up on beans, you might want to stock some Beano. That's an over-the-counter preparation containing an enzyme that helps your body digest the sugar in beans and some vegetables. Beano is not useful for gas caused by foods other than beans and certain vegetables.
- Canned fruits. Peaches, pears, applesauce, and more are good sources of vitamin C and other nutrients.
- Canned vegetables. Vegetables are also good sources of vitamins.
- Dried fruits.
- Whole grain crackers. These can be used as replacements for bread.
- Peanut butter is a staple and goes well with crackers.
- Nuts. I'm talking whole or cracked almonds, walnuts, cashews, and pecans; they have protein, fiber, and healthful fats.
- Packages of peanut-butter and cheese crackers for snacks.
- Water. In case your regular water supply becomes contaminated, store several bottles of water in your emergency pantry.
- Granola bars.
- Dry cereals.
- Juice boxes. Single-serving-sized juice that doesn't need to be refrigerated is helpful. Choose 100% fruit juices; it's best to avoid ones made primarily of corn syrup.

(Continued)

(Continued)

- Multivitamins. A bottle of multivitamins can help supply any missing nutrients.
- Basic spices. Salt, pepper, oregano, basil, etc.—whatever you like to cook with. Also remember baking soda, baking powder, and other baking essentials if you're going to turn flour into baked goods.
- Paper plates, plastic cups, bowls, and flatware. If you have room, you might also want to store flashlights, fresh batteries, candles, matches, first-aid kits, and any other emergency supplies you may need.
- A nonelectric can opener. Maybe two.
- Bug-Out Bucket. As mentioned earlier, you should have a bucket filled with food you'll take with you should you decide to evacuate your home.

Below is a list of optional food items that you may want to store:

- Boxed milk. If you have kids, boxes of milk treated with Ultra High Temperature (UHT) pasteurization are great to stock up on.
- Baby food/formula, as well as diapers and wipes. If you have a baby, these aren't optional at all.
- A camping stove or small grill that you can use in a safe area to heat foods. There might not be room for this in your emergency pantry, but have one ready in case you have to rough it. If you have a camping stove, remember to keep grill utensils and a pot or pan stored with it.

Remember—you have to periodically check the foods in your emergency food pantry, so you don't keep foods that have passed their expiration dates. And again, it's good to store only foods you'll eat.

Six Mistakes People Make in Food Storage

Here are six mistakes that people often make when storing food.

1. **Not enough variety.** Some people rush to store wheat, beans, Spam, salt, and honey—and not much else. But you will get tired of the same foods over and over again. This is called appetite fatigue. Variety is the key to successful food storage. If you are storing for the short term, remember to stockpile snacks you'll eat. In your long-term food storage, remember to

put flavorings, including things like soup recipe mix, bullion, onion flakes, crushed garlic, tomato paste, and other ingredients you will add to food you're going to cook, as well as basics like cooking oil and baking powder.

2. **No vitamins.** A package of good-quality multivitamins doesn't take up much room and is vital, especially when you're under stress. Remember to get separate kids' vitamins if you have children. These can be rotated regularly.

3. **No *temptation* foods.** I may be on a diet, but if TSHTF, then I want chocolate, dammit! And cheese. Whatever tantalizes your taste buds—potato chips, Doritos, Cheetos, Hostess Ding Dongs—store some of those in your pantry. If you don't want to be tempted by having them around, seal them in a bucket. They're great for calming yourself down when stress levels are rising. And if you're denying yourself your snacks now for waistline reasons, maybe you'll have something to look forward to if and when the Apocalypse comes.

4. **Lack of balance.** Buying all your beans at once, and nothing else until next month, is just setting yourself up for disaster if TSHTF in the meantime. Get a one-month supply of everything you need; then you can start adding with large-volume purchases of single items.

5. **Improper storage.** Sticking a bag of rice in the back of your closet is not proper food storage, except for the insects and rodents that will make a meal of it. Moisture will get anything stored improperly in your garage or cellar. If you use plastic buckets, use a food-grade plastic liner—never trash-can liners, as these are treated with pesticides.

6. **Not using your stockpile.** Putting all that food away and forgetting about it is just wasting your money. First of all, you won't be able to stomach that stored food if you suddenly switch from whatever you're eating now to your stockpiles. Secondly, it's all too easy for forgotten food stores to go stale, and then go bad, and ultimately, be worthless.

Other Cool Tools You Can Use

Along with your dehydrator and water purifier, here are some other tools and gadgets you may want to consider when undertaking long-term food storage.

Kitchenware. Let's start with hand-operated can openers, cast iron or heavy pots, a kettle, pans, skillets, Dutch ovens, a grate to use over open fire, as well as long-handled cooking utensils (again, for using over an open fire). Also consider saving coffee cans, jars, and other rodent-proof storage containers.

Home vacuum-packaging system. Just like it sounds, these are gadgets that vacuum-pack food. Why would you want to do that? Because it reduces oxygen, which in turn helps foods last longer and retain nutritional value. The better ones seal and shut off automatically. One brand, Food Saver, sold on Amazon.com, gets rave reviews. Food Saver claims to keep food fresh up to five times longer than traditional storage methods like Tupperware or plastic wrap.

Another version, Handi-Vac, is made by Reynolds. Some users say that the Handi-Vac is easier to use than the Food Saver; it's certainly cheaper, *and* it takes up less counter space. You'll find both products have their fans. However, Handi-Vac has significantly more negative reviews than Food Saver. You'll have to make your own decision on this one.

Hand-operated wheat grinder/flour mill. I've seen survivalist web sites rave about these, so I'm adding them to the list. But keep in mind:
- It's hard to grow enough wheat to feed you and your loved ones in the suburbs.
- This book is based on my outlook, which is that while we could go through some horrific times that could last for months, eventually civilization will return to a semblance of normalcy.

That said, if you're going whole-hog survivalist, and you've moved out to a farm, you might want a wheat grinder. Grinders sell for under $100, but it would make sense to buy the more expensive models. A recent review of grinders came up with two top choices: the Country Living Grain Mill and the Family Grain Mill. Both can be electrified later. Don't fall for a cheap one; you'll get frustrated and it will get thrown in the back of a closet, where it will stay.

Depending on the model, it takes between five and 15 minutes to grind enough flour to make one loaf of bread. A bushel of wheat kernels weighs about 60 pounds, and it will net about

50 pounds of whole wheat flour, enough to provide about 70 loaves of bread. So, if you're going to grow your own wheat, you'll need about five bushels per year for every loaf per day. As I hinted at earlier, grinding wheat is not in my survival plan.

The Joy of Alternative Cooking—Cooking Without Electricity

So you've stored your food. Now, let's say there's an emergency and the power goes out . . . for a long time. How are you going to cook that food?

You can stock up on MREs with a built-in heating system. Or you can discover the joy of alternative cooking.

The first option is to cook on your gas grill, charcoal grill, or camp stove. You can do it; just remember to use it in a well-ventilated area and keep cooking mitts handy for handling pots over an open flame. But you'd also better stock up on fuel, whether it's LP gas or charcoal. You probably need at least enough to get you through a week, cooking every meal. A month's supply would be better.

But what if the power grid is down for longer? Then you might want to look at some *real* alternative ways to cook.

The Solar Oven

You can cook things over a gas stove for a while, or charcoal—plan to use both. But if an emergency drags on for weeks, those fuels may get scarce. At that point, you may want to go solar.

There are many varieties of solar ovens. By one count, there are over 65 major designs and hundreds of variations on those basic designs. All solar cookers share some basic principles:

- **Concentrating sunlight.** A mirror, or some type of reflective metal, is used to concentrate light and heat from the sun into a small cooking area, making the energy more concentrated and therefore more potent.
- **Converting light to heat.** Any black on the inside of a solar cooker, as well as certain materials for pots, will improve the effectiveness of turning light into heat. A black pan will absorb almost all of the sun's light and turn it into heat, substantially improving the effectiveness of the cooker.

- **Trapping heat.** Isolating the air inside the cooker from the air outside the cooker makes an important difference. Using a clear solid, like a plastic bag or a glass cover, will allow light to enter, but once the light is absorbed and converted to heat, a plastic bag or glass cover will trap the heat inside. This makes it possible to reach similar temperatures on cold and windy days as on hot days.

You've probably already seen a solar oven in action. Your car becomes a solar oven on hot days as the sun's rays enter the car, are converted to heat, and trapped inside. I've even seen recipes on the Web for baking cookies on your car's dashboard.

Now, you can buy a top-of-the-line solar oven at SolarDirect. com. However, the cost of a solar oven from that outfit, including shipping, was about $275 including shipping when I checked. And when I saw that price tag, I about coughed up a lung: $275 for a solar oven? That had better be one darned good oven, because you can *make* a pretty good one for next to nothing.

Do what you want, but *I'm* not spending nearly $300 for a solar oven. So, let's go over some cheaper options:

- **Do-it-Yourself Solar Cooker.** InTheWake.com is a good survivalist web site, with some nifty plans for a solar cooker. (See Figure 7.1.)

  Figure 7.1 shows a *panel cooker*. The reflective part of the cooker can be made by folding aluminum foil over corrugated cardboard. If you don't like using aluminum foil because it tends to bend and wrinkle, consider using *aluminum-type* duct tape, which you can purchase at your local hardware store.

  The web site recommends placing a black pot in a clear plastic bag when you use the stove, as this allows for better heat retention. A simple wire frame can prevent the bag from touching (and melting) on the pot. It will also keep the pot off of the ground, reducing heat losses from conduction. This solar design (as well as the others) can also be used to boil or disinfect water for safety.

  You can find out more about this solar cooker, as well as InTheWake's other cooking ideas, at http://www.inthewake .org/b1cooking.html.

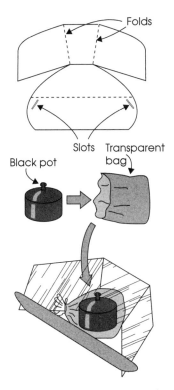

Figure 7.1   Folding Solar Cooker

You can buy a very similar solar cooker, factory-made, from Solar Cookers International for $25 plus shipping. To order one, point your Web browser to the Solar Cookers International Marketplace at http://tinyurl.com/cy9ezv.

And you can find plans to build many different types of solar cookers and solar ovens at Solar Cookers International's archive: http://solarcooking.org/plans.

If you try solar cooking and enjoy it, you really need to check out the solarcooking.org web site. It has *everything*.

Two things to keep in mind: First, a solar oven isn't going to work on a rainy day. Second, cooking with a solar oven takes a lot longer than a normal electric or gas oven. Table 7.3 shows some comparative cooking times.

Cooking time will vary, depending on how hot you can get the solar oven, and foods like chickpeas and split peas need to be pre-soaked. But you get the idea—a solar oven is

Table 7.3 Comparable Cooking Times

Food	Stove top time	Solar oven time
White rice	20 minutes	1 hour
Brown rice	50 minutes	2 hours
Wild rice	50 minutes	2 hours
Lentils	30 minutes	2 hours
Chick peas	1.5 hours	5 hours
Split peas	30 minutes	2 hours

Source: The OilDrumCampfire.com.

going to take time. Fast cooking time is a luxury of the modern age. Our forefathers were used to meals that took all day to cook, and we might have to get used to that as well.

- **Prize-Winning Kyoto Box Oven.** This won the $75,000 Kyoto prize awarded to the best idea to fight global warming. It is the brainchild of Kenya-based entrepreneur Jon Bøhmer and costs all of $6. Basically, the Kyoto Box is made from two boxes, one inside the other with an acrylic cover, which lets in the sun's power and traps it.

  Black paint on the inner box and silver foil on the outer box help concentrate the heat, while a layer of straw or newspaper between the two provides insulation.

  In other words, it's a simple solar oven. You can build ones just like it using plans found at Solar Cookers International. But heck, if the dude gets a $75,000 prize for it, who am I to argue? And if it makes you feel better to buy a solar oven that wins prizes, go for it.

- **Parabolic Cooker.** This is a variation on a solar oven. The parabolic shape concentrates the sun's rays like a magnifying glass. You can go through the trouble of making a parabolic-shaped oven. Or you can find an abandoned DishNetwork Parabolic receiver; there may be some lying around after a big disaster.

  Once you make or buy one, line it with *aluminumized* duct tape, and voila. It should get hot enough at the focal point to ignite paper in just a few minutes. You may have to jerry-rig a platform or tripod to suspend your cooking pot at the focal point.

- **Haybox.** Sometimes disasters happen at the wrong time of year to use the sun's rays for cooking. In that case, you may

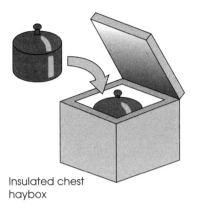

Insulated chest
haybox

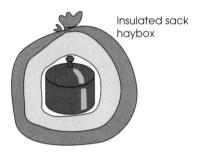

Insulated sack
haybox

Figure 7.2   Simple Haybox

want to use a haybox, an insulated container that can lead to significant fuel savings—up to 70%. The hay box is a good way to make stews and soups without using up too much of your existing fuel. (See Figure 7.2.)

A basic haybox is a simple gadget with a multistep process.

First, you heat the food, preferably using a cast-iron pot or some other container that will retain heat.

Then, put the container in the haybox. This can be an insulated cooler, though you'll probably want to stuff more insulation in there.

This insulation uses the heat in the food and the pot to cook the food even further.

Example: You bring a potato stew to a boil in a cast-iron pot on an open fire. Boil it for five minutes. Then put a lid on the pot and put the whole thing in a haybox. Wait one to two hours and the potato stew will cook itself.

You can make a haybox out of any material that won't melt when exposed to heat. Our forefathers used hay in a wooden frame, hence the name.

- **A fire pit.** This still requires fuel, but your fuel can be scrap wood or your neighbor's collection of ugly wooden lawn gnomes (when you think about it, garden gnomes are begging for a fiery end to their humiliating existence). Be sure to choose a location for your fire pit that isn't close to trees, a building, or anything that could catch fire from stray sparks (and there will be sparks). Naturally, avoid underground wires, cables, or pipes, and the flatter the spot, the better.

  Pick a spot for the center of the pit. Draw a circle around it that is about three to four feet wide.

  Remove the soil, dirt, and/or clay inside the circle and dig out the hole to a depth of about one foot. Be sure to keep the sides as straight as possible. If you have time, in the center of your fire pit, dig a hole that is six to eight inches square and 12 inches deep.

  Scrape out the bottom of your hole and pour in about four inches of small gravel or stones. Fill the hole in the center with the gravel as well. The gravel will help drain the fire pit and the hole in the center will improve the drainage.

  Add about three inches of sand or dry dirt on top of the gravel. The sand will help prevent any fire from spreading to roots under your pit.

  Surround the fire pit with at least two rows of concrete blocks stacked on top of each other. Then add a metal grate— one taken from your gas grill that you forgot to buy LP gas for will do just fine. If the grate isn't wide enough to bridge the cement blocks, you can stack it on blocks in the fire pit or bridge the gap with iron rods or other nonflammable supports on which you can rest the grate. Be sure to avoid touching hot metal when the fire is going.

  A fire pit isn't just for a post-crash lifestyle; it makes a nice addition to nights outside anytime. If you have the room, consider building one now. It will be easier to do if you're not stressed out, you can buy a grate to fit, and doing it now means you still have the option of a quick trip to the emergency room (always a possibility when I'm building anything) if things go wrong.

More Cooking Outside

If your survival plan includes cooking outside over an open fire, you might want to have the following ready ahead of time:

- Pot grips
- Kindling, including pocket lint
- Bark or paper
- Small twigs to feed the fire
- Small fire pan
- Leather gloves
- Non-synthetic clothing—clothing that won't burn if you a spark lands on you

To boil water over a campfire, put a flat rock in the fire. Heat it up. Use a stick with a barb on the end of it to lower a pot on to the fire (assuming the pot has a pail handle).

The Least You Can Do

- Store only the foods you'll eat. Start by storing enough for one month, then three months, and then longer if you have the room and desire.
- Begin with the basics—the low-cost essentials that are simple to get and store. Whole grains, rice, and beans are the bulk of many long-term food storage larders. Add dried, vacuum-sealed, or canned meats, chicken, or fish to your stockpile if you normally eat them. Likewise, add olive oil or vegetable oil and your usual spices. Comfort foods are fine, including chocolate, peanut butter, and other pre-packaged snacks.
- Do you drink coffee or tea? You'd better pack some that can be made with boiled water—an emergency is no time to get a caffeine jones.
- Acquire food storage containers, such as food-grade plastic pails with gamma seal lids. Put your food in them, seal tightly, and store the containers in an air-conditioned place. You might want to mark one container as a *bug-out* can to grab if you're jumping in the car and getting the heck out of Dodge.

C H A P T E R

Smart Shopping—How to Plan Ahead for Next Week's Meals (and Save Significant Money)

In this chapter, we'll talk about smart shopping, which is one of the basic tools of survivalists on a budget. We'll cover coupons, including how to use them and where to find the best coupon web sites. I'll give you seven tips to lower your grocery bill, tell you how to play the *drugstore game*, and, of course, tell you the least you can do.

Making the Change from Impulse Shopper to Smart Shopper

My wife, Cindy, started preparing for the worst in the way a suburban housewife knows best: shopping.

And by that, I do *not* mean she went wild with the credit cards and started hoarding anything and everything. She wanted to increase the amount of stuff we could get while decreasing the amount of money that she was spending, because the price of gas was really cutting into our budget.

Smart shopping became Cindy's part-time job. Yes, she clips coupons, but she also keeps track of sales, reads relevant blogs every day, and buys deals and loss leaders in large quantities when she can.

If nothing else, she figures she'll have our family well stocked with toothpaste, toilet paper, peanut butter, and SpaghettiOs—at least for short-term emergencies.

As for these shopping tips, you might already be following some of them, so this could be an easy transition. Improve your efforts in this area, and you'll set yourself up for success in one of the most vital areas of concern in a crisis.

People form shopping habits that are hard to break. Understand that change is easiest in increments. Do the least you can do at first, and then work your way up.

Step 1: Get a Flyer

Get a flyer from your grocery store, or perhaps flyers from two or three local grocery stores. There are a lot of ways to get these: in a local newspaper, in the mail, or online. But beware—just because a food item is featured in a flyer doesn't mean it's on sale. Research has shown that just putting a food in a flyer can send its sales up by 500%. So, grocery stores tend to feature a mix of sale and non-sale items in their flyers.

Step 2: Find Sales on Food and Items You Can Use

Once you have the flyers, go through them and mark any sales on food products that you and your family will actually use. Again, buying stuff you won't eat or use, even if it's cheap, isn't a good strategy. It won't save you money and will waste space in your food storage.

The only time when it *is* a good strategy is if you think the world is going into such a decline that ordinary money isn't going to be useful anymore. In that case, stock up on health and beauty products to use as currencies and bribes. You also might want to buy more toilet paper than you can use in a year.

A great web site for leading you to sales in your local grocery stores is http://www.mygrocerydeals.com.

Step 3: Find Coupons

Coupons can turn your local grocery store's sales into giveaways. My wife is able to find items that are Buy-One-Get-One free (BOGO), and *then* find a coupon that makes the first item 50% off or more. In a really good deal, she brings home two free items—legally!

The trick is that when a store has a BOGO sale, you are allowed to use two coupons—one for each item.

The average manufacturer's coupon for grocery items has a face value of $1.08, according to NCH Marketing, a coupon-processing firm. Yet of the 281 billion coupons distributed in 2008, only 2.6 billion were redeemed. Obviously, a lot of people are missing out on these savings.

There are web sites that specialize in finding amazing coupon deals. Again, you can google, or you can use some of the following web sites, which Cindy finds useful.

Great Web Sites That Lead You to Coupon Deals

- **Coupon Cravings:** www.couponcravings.com
- **Common Sense With Money:** www.commonsensewithmoney.com
- **Mommy Snacks.Net:** http://mommysnacks.net
- **Money Saving Mom:** www.moneysavingmom.com

And there are also coupons you'll just find online. Here are three of Cindy's favorite web sites for **online coupons**:

- **Coupon Chief:** www.couponchief.com
- **Rather-Be-Shopping.com:** www.rather-be-shopping.com
- **Coupons.com:** www.coupons.com

Finally, if you want to find the food coupons from the Sunday newspaper without buying the Sunday newspaper, check out:

- **CoolSavings.com:** www.coolsavings.com
- **Valpak:** www.valpak.com
- **Smartsource.com:** www.smartsource.com

You generally have to supply personal information to register, so familiarize yourself with privacy policies, and use a separate e-mail address from your personal one.

When you find a really good deal where you can combine sales and coupons to get free products, you can purchase more coupons that you need on eBay. (Well, legally you can't actually buy the coupons; you are paying for someone else to cut them out for you.) One time Cindy picked up 15 BOGO coupons for crackers for $3 a box, then combined them with a BOGO sale at our local grocery store, and walked away with 30 boxes of crackers for nothing.

Remember: Don't let coupons encourage you to buy products you wouldn't otherwise buy.

You can use the coupons to find deals on staples and other items you want to use to build up your stockpiles. With the money you save through sales, meal-planning and super-coupon shopping, you should have enough to start bulking up your cupboards.

Step 4: Be Flexible About Brands

You might be buying the same ol' brand of peanut butter or toothpaste out of habit. But is it really your family's favorite—and more importantly, is it the cheapest you can get? Be willing to try different brands when a coupon and sale combination makes something super cheap or free. You might find that a specific brand won't matter. Or you will discover some new product you didn't know existed.

Of course, you and your family will find some products for which you just have a strong preference. For us, there's only one brand of frozen pizza, but we've found we'll use nearly any kind of toothpaste.

Step 5: Build Meals Around What Is on Sale

After you see what's on sale in a given week, you'll know what you're working with. Then you can find recipes that utilize these ingredients plus the food you've got stored. Use recipe search engines (google *recipe search engine*) like FoodieView and enter combinations of the on-sale ingredients that sound interesting. These ideas will provide the backbone for several meals throughout the week.

Step 6: Create a Weeklong Meal Plan

Make a weeklong meal-planning worksheet and fill in the dinners first based on the meals you can make from sale items. Remember to keep your weeknight meals pretty easy; unless you have a lot of free time, it's best to save the more challenging recipes for the weekend.

Given all that, it's pretty easy to fill in the rest of the squares on your meal plan. Cindy usually only needs to come up with five suppers per week and two to three lunches per week (our family uses leftovers for other lunches).

Step 7: Make a Shopping List from the Meal Plan

Once the meal plan is in place, go through and list all of the ingredients for all of the recipes you'll make and then cross off the things you already have in your pantry or refrigerator. You won't save money by accidentally buying things you already have on hand.

Also, check your staples—flour, milk, yeast, juice boxes, and so on—and add replenishments to the list.

Step 8: Go Grocery Shopping—and Stick to Your List

Once you have the list in place, it's simple. Take it to the grocery store and stick to your list! Nip impulse buying in the bud; it's hard to do, but controlling your impulse shopping will save you a ton of money.

Sticking to your list will also make grocery shopping itself substantially quicker. In the end, when you go home, unpack your groceries, and put that meal plan up on the fridge, you should find that overall, it hasn't taken you any more time than a grocery trip without planning would have taken. Plus, you now have a clear plan for a week's worth of meals and you've saved money at the grocery store.

Strategies for Stocking Up

- Buy a few things each week.
- Focus on what's on sale.
- Buy in bulk (you can do this with a friend to save even more).
- You can stockpile some items when you are able to take advantage of combining sales and coupons. Otherwise, do your stockpile shopping at warehouse clubs, Wal-Mart, or bulk-order from online.
- Buy double or triple or even more when items are on sale. Sales work in cycles. When a staple such as peanut butter, of which your family eats a lot, goes on a big sale, buy up a few

months supply. Before you run out of it, it'll be on sale again. You'll never have to pay full price for the regular nonperishable items that you need.

Eight Tips to Lowering Your Grocery Bills

1. Make a list and stick to it. And avoid shopping hungry—you'll be less tempted to overbuy. Especially beware the last-minute temptations at the checkout counter.
2. Substitute store brands for name brands when possible. They're significantly cheaper (25% cheaper on average) and often as good as their brand-name counterparts.
3. Compare prices in different areas of the store. For example, research by Consumer Reports has shown that cheese at the deli counter is often pricier than cheese in the dairy case.[1]
4. Trade convenience for cost. Prepped and precut foods often cost more. Similarly, you'll pay extra for single servings, such as cereal in disposable bowls.
5. Endcaps don't mean bargains. Don't automatically buy the foods you seen featured on endcaps in the grocery aisle. Often, products prominently displayed at the ends of aisles aren't actually on sale. Endcaps can also be a destination for merchandise about to expire, so check expiration dates carefully.
6. Bigger isn't necessarily better for prices. Big packages are often more economical, but not always, according to research. A Federal Trade Commission study showed that canned tuna, peanut butter, ketchup, canned coffee, and frozen orange juice frequently turned out to be costlier in larger containers. Comparing unit prices (per ounce, etc.) is especially important when one size is on sale.
7. Clip coupons. One 25-cent coupon isn't worth the hassle. Several 25-cent coupons and a few one-dollar-off coupons, especially when combined with buy-one-get-one-free deals, add up, especially if you do it every week.
8. Get a store card, if available. With a preferred-shopper card, you receive automatic discounts on products in the store circular without clipping coupons. Just remember that these programs request personal information, which means that the chain can track your purchases.

The Drugstore Game—How to Make Drugstores Pay *You*

It's called the drugstore game because it's a way to save money when buying products at national drugstore chains, and sometimes even make money! According to the Food Marketing Institute, half of retailers now offer customers savings through card programs, with discounts such as two-for-one sales, members-only specials, and reward points toward future purchases. Some stores will double the value of manufacturers' coupons if you have that store's bonus card.

Working the drugstore deals can stretch your grocery budget. You'll start getting so many super deals and even free stuff at the drugstore that you'll have more money left over to spend on food.

CVS and Walgreens have similar deals where they give you coupons based on the time and/or money you've spent in the store, which you can then put toward future purchases. At CVS, they refer to these as ExtraCare rewards, or Extra Bucks. Extra Bucks print at the bottom of your cash register receipt every three months, so all you have to do is keep your eyes peeled and hang onto your receipt! You can then use them just like cash on your next visit to any CVS. At Walgreens, these are known as Register Rewards.

The catch at CVS is that you have to sign up for a card so they can track your purchases and limit how many deals you get. The catch at Walgreens is that you can't use Register Rewards to buy the same product again, so you can't keep rolling over the same deal.

RiteAid and other smaller drugstore chains have similar special programs as well.

My Wife's Advice

Here's how it works: When you are just starting out, you will pay out of pocket for the first one or two deals. After that, though, you can use any Extra Bucks you have earned to help pay for your next deal. Your goal is to earn enough to cover the price of future deals so that you never pay any money out of pocket again. This is what's called, *building your Extra Bucks.*

For example, one week CVS may have Softsoap Spa bodywash on sale for $4.99. This is a good regular price for bodywash, but by buying this product at this time you will earn $4.99 back in Extra Bucks.

So, you got the bodywash that you needed anyway. Then you can turn it around and buy milk and toothpaste with the Extra Bucks. Ultimately, you got three items you needed for $4.99. Sweet deal.

But it's even better if you *work* your Extra Bucks. Say Advil has its own ExtraCare rewards deal going on. You use that $4.99 in rewards to buy the pain reliever, and you get another $4.99 on your register receipt. You didn't spend any of your own money on this deal, and you still have $4.99 toward another future purchase. (You might have to pay a few cents for taxes.)

You can make this deal even better if you have been collecting your coupons and reading the money-saving blogs. Say that Advil is $4.99 and Crest toothpaste is $2.50, and they both have ExtraCare rewards offers on them. You find that you have coupons for $1.50 off Advil and $1.00 off Crest. When you take these two items to the cash register, after the coupon amounts are figured into your purchase, you owe a bit more than $4.99 (because of tax). You pay with your $4.99 in Extra Bucks and a few coins, and you have these two products, plus another $7.49 in Extra Bucks for your *next* purchase. This particular scenario is known as a *money maker*. You won't get rich playing the Drugstore Game, but the only things better than free products are products where you profit a couple bucks just buying them.

There are a few web sites you can visit where people will post all of the free deals and actually put together deals for you that will earn you the most money back.

1. **Money Saving Mom** (www.moneysavingmom.com)
2. **Wags to Riches** (www.wagstoriches.com)

These are Cindy's two favorite sites for drugstore deals. They are great resources for a beginner, explaining in even more detail how to work the deals.

Here's more advice from Cindy:

1. **Start small:** When you are just beginning, don't do any big deals, and only work the ones that are going to be free or are items you absolutely would have been buying anyway. You can work your way up to bigger, more complicated deals after you understand how everything really works.

2. **Be careful of coupon expiration dates:** Extra Bucks and Walgreens' Register Rewards (RRs) expire, usually a couple weeks after you get them. So keep an eye on the expiration dates and keep the receipts handy. Sometimes you'll have to take a deal that just breaks even in order to get newer Extra Bucks or RRs. Or sometimes, you'll just have to burn them—but don't waste them. By burning them, I mean going to the drugstore and stocking up on some necessities like Band-Aids, envelopes, or milk. Or heck, treat your kid to some cookies or yourself to a magazine. With your soon-to-expire Extra Bucks or RRs, you'll have free (or discounted) supplies or luxuries.

3. **Stockpile the items you get so you never have to pay full price again:** Your goal is to stockpile the nonperishable necessities. Imagine never having to pay full price—or any price if you work it well—on things that everyone needs, like toothpaste, shampoo, razors, and toilet paper. You save money because you never have to run out and buy them in an emergency. These frequently go on special, so it's easy to stockpile. If and when bad times come, you'll be sitting pretty—with clean teeth to boot—when store shelves are empty. Plus, beauty and health products will be major currency if things get really tough, as happened in post-Soviet Russia.

4. **Buy items you don't need.** Occasionally Cindy will buy products that have deals even though it's not something we need or use. She picks up these nonperishable items if they will make money, so she can build up more ExtraCare rewards or at least roll them over. You could also save these items to barter with later. Or, you can be generous and give to a friend or to a charity.

Fake It Until You Make It

It's not easy to change gears from U.S. suburban family to hard-core survivalist with 10 buckets each of wheat, beans, and rice. We didn't just suddenly program our suburban All-American consumer personalities to *deny*. We started out clipping some coupons and keeping our eyes on sales. Over those first few weeks, when we began learning the system at the grocery store or the awesome DrugStore Game, we started seeing how cheap or FREE we can get stuff. We were hooked.

After a while, like us, you'll refuse to pay too much for anything. You know you've got supplies at home, and you know a coveted item will go on sale later. Impulse shopping will decline! Yet another way that you will save money.

Cindy told me:

> Back when I kinda sorta watched what I was buying, I was saving —according to the grocery store—about 20% to 25% each time I went. I thought that was pretty good. But once I started using coupons more frequently and lining it up with sales, I started saving about 33% consistently, and on good days, I can save 50%.
>
> For the past year, I've bought MORE food and not spent more money. And now, because we have a good stockpile, I don't go shopping as often, unless it's something we need or I find a great deal to replenish our stockpile. And I am spending even less money.

Buying Food Online

You can actually buy bulk food online, and if you're trying to build up your food storage, you can't beat it.

Take inventory of the dry food items you use the most often. These are the items you should consider buying bulk online. Some examples include pasta, rice, flour, nuts, spices, and crackers.

Consider buying the largest amount of food you can—perhaps as much as you can eat in a year. The more you buy bulk, the less the cost per ounce. You could even work with some like-minded family or friends to increase your bulk purchase.

Remember to include shipping costs in your calculations. That's another reason to buy in the largest quantity possible.

The following are web sites that specialize in selling food in bulk.

Bulk Food Web Sites

- BulkFoods.com—everything from beans to seeds to snack mixes to candy.
- FoodServiceDirect.com—they're a restaurant supplier, so they sell by the case.
- PleasantHillGrain.com—a large display of food and equipment for home food stockpilers.

- GrainLady.com—a web site that sells bulk grains as well as kitchen mills and other equipment.

Three Sites for Prepackaged Foods in Bulk

I am all in favor of bulk storage because it saves you money; and if you buy what you normally eat and rotate your stock, it works fine. These next three sites are for when things are going to heck in a handcart and you want to get ready in a hurry.

1. **The Internet Grocer** (http://internet-grocer.net): This site sells canned, dehydrated, and freeze-dried foods. You can buy canned meats, cheese, butter, and more, as well as their popular *One Year Food Supply for Four Persons.*
2. YourFoodStorage.com (http://www.yourfoodstorage.com): This site will sell you prepackaged supplies for up to 10 people a year at a time, as well as storage shelves, wheat grinders, water ionizers, and more.
3. Efoodsdirect.com (http://www.efoodsdirect.com): This site not only sells food in bulk (including items like *1-year adult basic dehydrated bulk food supply*), but it also sells the Berkey Water Purifier and other useful products.

The Least You Can Do

Below is a list of the bare minimum things you can do in order to become a more efficient food shopper.

- Get store flyers and find foods on sale.
- Find coupons in newspaper and shopping circulars. See if they can be combined with any buy-one-get-one free offers or other sale items at the store.
- Build meals around what is on sale.
- Create a weeklong menu plan. Some of the meals can be from sale items, while others should be built around foods in your pantry.
- Make a shopping list from the meal plan.
- When you go shopping, stick to your list.
- Pay attention to your receipts at drugstores—you might be missing out on valuable coupons and rewards!

CHAPTER

Gardening

Gardening requires lots of water—most of it in the form of perspiration.

—Lou Erickson

Many survivalists have vegetable gardens, because we've clued in to the fact that food may become scarce in the future and much of what you can buy at the grocery store is crap. Tasteless, tasteless, crap!

I won't scare you with the details of how lettuce on sale at a grocery store may be contaminated with rocket fuel,[1] how toxic chemicals on plastic pallets could be leeching into fruits and vegetables,[2] or how foreign food packers are shipping us products contaminated with E. coli bacteria.[3] The fact is, growing your own food is just plain healthier. But it's also a good survival strategy.

Starting a vegetable garden requires a modest financial investment, and that investment can be reduced if you're willing to put in more time. Most of the money you spend will be in the beginning. And the long-term benefits are incredible. You'll save money on groceries, while providing easy access to healthy, even organic, produce. Plus, gardening is a fun, rewarding hobby for all ages.[4]

There are whole books on gardening—what we're going to concentrate on this book is small-scale suburban gardening. The point of gardening in a suburban or urban environment, as I see it, is *not* to replace *all* of your food. That isn't really a feasible goal on most

175

suburban lots. Instead, your garden will supplement your stored food with the kinds of foods you are used to eating.

In this chapter, we're going to cover topics like the basics of starting a vegetable garden, how to grow a lot of food in a small space, how not to overspend when gardening, why you should grow heirloom seeds, what to do if you have no yard, how global warming will affect your garden, and I'll also give you a list of useful gardening *dos* and my picks for the 10 best garden crops for beginners.

Thanks to the United States' worst-since-the-Great Depression recession, plenty of people are already catching the gardening bug. The National Gardening Association (NGA), a nonprofit research group, estimates that 43 million of the nation's 111 million households grew at least some of their own fruits and vegetables in 2009—a rise of more than 19% over the previous year. More than half of those who are taking up gardening (54%) say they are trying to save on food bills, according to the NGA's annual report.

A Lot of Food in a Small Space

The United States' rekindled romance with gardening is proving to be a boon for some companies, such as Burpee & Co., the nation's biggest seed retailer. The company projected its sales would jump by as much as 20% in 2009. And sure enough, with the recession and tight budgets in mind, Burpee sold its Money Garden, a $10 pack of seeds that will produce more than $650 worth of vegetables, according to the company. Each envelope contained six packets of seeds:

1. Carrot Big Top
2. Tomato Steak Sandwich
3. Pea Super Snappy
4. Lettuce Burpee Big
5. Bean Heavyweight II
6. Pepper Home Run

If you want to buy seeds from them, you can find Burpee's catalog online (http://www.burpee.com).

Some other facts . . .

You don't need much land to garden. The survey by the National Gardening Association shows that 57% of U.S. home gardens were smaller than 100 square feet.

The NGA projected that the average garden could produce 300 pounds of fresh produce worth $600, a return of $530 based on an average investment of $70. And if you don't have *any* room for a garden on your property, you can always join a community garden if there is one in your town. This is often a good option for urban gardeners. You can search for one in your neighborhood at the American Community Gardening Association: http://www.communitygarden.org.

To provide enough produce for a family of four, the Oregon State Extension Service says you'll need a 30 × 30 foot garden.[5] If you also plan to supply your table *and* can, freeze, or dehydrate your vegetables, you may need a garden twice this size. However, the bigger your garden, the more time you're going to have to spend on it on a weekly basis.

The traditional method of vegetable garden design is to plant long rows. Most home gardeners now opt for planting in beds rather than rows. This method allows you to concentrate your compost on the area where the plants are growing rather than wasting it on the paths between the rows. Walking between the rows also ruins the soil structure, so beds are really a better way to go.

The beds should be small enough so that you can easily reach in to weed and harvest all the plants without stepping on the bed itself.

If you have a problem with too much water in your garden, raising your beds by about eight to 12 inches will improve drainage and the soil will stay warmer in colder weather, such as early spring. If your problem is sandy, too-dry soil, you can line the bottom of a raised garden bed with cloth or newspaper to aid water retention.

Victory gardens are back in style. Michelle Obama planted the first White House Victory Garden since Eleanor Roosevelt planted one in 1943. It's estimated that 40% to 50% of the fruits and vegetables consumed in the United States in 1942 to 1945 were homegrown. Back then, they were known as Victory Gardens because citizens were helping the war effort by growing their own food. Now, a victory garden of your own could help you in a battle with finances.

It's about more than saving money. Growing your own food could be your best investment right now—it's hard to lose money, and the food you get will be a big improvement over the stuff you find on supermarket shelves: no pesticides, no chemicals—just good old dirt and non-genetically modified seeds. The fresh vegetables, hard work and dirty hands are better for your kids, too.

Five hours a week will cover most gardening chores in an average suburban garden. This is after the initial planting and before harvesting; the time for those tasks will depend on what you plant and your skill level. Can you spare five hours a week? After spending a few evenings and a weekend building raised beds and filling planters with soil, my wife and I now only spend a couple hours a week watering the garden, weeding, and cutting back dead leaves.

Nielsen Media Research says that the average American watches 142 hours of TV in a month, which is close to five hours *per day*. Switch just a few of those hours from couch potato to actually growing potatoes, with a little fresh air and exercise thrown in, and we'd probably see the nation's obesity rate go down significantly.

If you really don't have time for a regular vegetable garden, consider planting fruit or nut trees; they require little in the way of heavy work, and nearly all of the work you have to do comes at harvest time. On the other hand, fruit trees take a long time to start producing fruit, and we may get to WTSHTF before your trees are ready.

Tips for Getting Started

Getting started is easy, and the garden department at Home Depot, Lowe's, or your local nursery is a good place to ask questions. Here are a bunch more tips:

1. **Good soil for a good garden.** I highly recommend you either use potting soil (if you're doing container gardening) or get your soil tested. A basic soil test is inexpensive, costing as little as four to six dollars, and the results will indicate exactly what you need to add to your soil so you can grow healthy

crops and reap big harvests. A quick study by a professional soil tester will tell you about the pH and nutrient content of your particular patch of earth. From there, you can add the right nutrients and get your crop off to a good start. You can find a soil test laboratory at the OrganicGardening.com web site: http://tinyurl.com/dhxgy6. If there isn't a soil test laboratory near you, you might want to consider just replacing the top layer of dirt in your garden with good quality soil.

2. **Get free government help.** The U.S. Department of Agriculture has Cooperative Extension System offices all over the place. There you can find out about what crops grow best in your area and also tap a treasure trove of agriculture information and advice. To find the local CES office near you, visit http://www.csrees.usda.gov/Extension/index.html.

3. **Start small and start smart.** Gardening and horticulture doesn't have to be back-breaking work, it depends upon how you approach it and how much you tackle.

   Using mulched, raised garden beds, for example, cuts down on the need to do a lot of weeding and also gets you off your knees. The Colorado State Master Gardener program has a great explanation of how to do this, which you can download from the Master Gardener web site: http://tinyurl .com/cc3a7l.[6]

4. **Don't overspend.** It's easy to go crazy at the garden store and buy everything, so remember to buy only what you need. Here are some money-saving gardening tips:
   - You can pick up second-hand gardening equipment (like pots and tools) quite cheaply at garage sales.
   - Plan before you buy, so plants and seeds do not go to waste.
   - Don't buy more than you need. Not only equipment, but also seeds—you'd be amazed how long you can stretch out a packet of seeds in a small garden. You can store seeds from year to year, depending on the type.
   - Egg cartons make great seed starters. You can push up on the bottom of the carton to release each individual plant when it's time to transplant.
   - Use the library. You don't have to buy every gardening book in the world. Many of them are available at your local library.

- Make your own compost bin. It's as cheap as buying a trash can with a lid. You can find do-it-yourself guides all over the Web for this; here's one as an example: http://tinyurl .com/dmk56j. Along with being a great way to recycle your kitchen waste, a compost bin will be a cheap source of excellent compost. If you want your kitchen waste to break down faster, add worms. If a good amount of compost is incorporated into the soil, less water is needed. Compost holds six times its weight in water. This is an inexpensive way to make your soil much better for healthy plants
- Potatoes, lettuce, radishes, and garlic are quite hardy and you don't need to buy much special equipment (like greenhouses or climbing frames). I'm growing all of them.
- Share rental costs. If you need to rent a tiller or other garden-ing tool, see if a neighbor, family member, or friend needs it, too. Splitting the rental cost or space can save a lot of money.
- Got slugs? Kill them with beer. Fill beer in a small empty container, about the size of those disposable Ziploc con-tainers or a small butter tub. Dig down into the soil so the top of the container is flush with the ground. Leave it over-night and the slugs will drown in the liquid. Refill it and keep it up until you do not see any more slugs!
- Cut the bottom off a plastic gallon milk jug and place over a young plant—it will work like a miniature greenhouse. Leave off the cap to provide air circulation. Once the plant is large enough to survive on its own, remove the jug.

5. **Find out what to plant and when.** Your local gardening store is a wealth of information on this; likewise, if you can find a local gardening club, you'll be ahead of the game. I also recommend checking out MotherEarthNews.com. It is chock full of great gardening tips, and importantly, it has an online guide to tell you when to plant and what crops to plant in your part of the country. You can find that by pointing your Web browser to http://tinyurl.com/cdcx7l.

Why You Should Grow *Heirloom Seed* Plants

Heirloom seeds and plants are varieties that were commonly grown before the advent of industrial farming. If you are a gardener, it is very important that you use these kinds of seeds.

Before agriculture was industrialized, our forefathers grew a wide variety of plants. The yields were lower, but this variety was a strength—diseases that would kill one type of corn didn't kill another type of corn.

Big agriculture changed all that. Today, most crops are grown in large, monocultural plots. Only a few varieties of each type of crop are grown. These varieties are often selected for their productivity, their ability to withstand mechanical picking and cross-country shipping, and their tolerance to drought, frost, or pesticides.

They're also protected by patents. I won't go into why Monsanto may be the most evil U.S. corporation ever. Plenty of other people cover what Monsanto does regarding patents (see http://tinyurl .com/dbmpc2). What both Monsanto and its critics can agree on is that the company does provide the seeds for 90% of the world's genetically modified crops. It will go to any lengths to protect those patents, including sue farmers for growing seeds the wind planted on their land from their neighbors' crops.

The fact is that Monsanto's dominance is making the United States dependent on seeds that the company controls—seeds that cannot be harvested from a grown plant to sow a new crop. Seeds from most modern hybrids, as genetically modified crops are called, result in seeds that range from sterile to ones that have unpredictable gene expression.

So, if civilization collapsed, and you had to grow a new crop from vegetables in your garden, and those vegetables grew from Monsanto seeds, you might have some difficulty.

In case you're wondering, Burpee—a Philadelphia-based family seed company for over 100 years—is not owned by Monsanto. Burpee is privately owned, but the company *does* carry some Seminis seeds, and Monsanto now owns Seminis.

Plenty of heirloom seeds can still produce impressive yields. You'll be doing yourself and the planet a favor if you grow them.

There are free online guides to gardening. Along with MotherEarthNews.com, here are a few others I've found useful:

- **The Garden Helper:** http://www.thegardenhelper.com/ gardeningguides.html
- **Victory Seed Company:** http://www.victoryseeds.com (a source of heirloom seeds)
- **MasterGardening.com:** http://mastergardening.com

"But I Have No Yard!"

Ah, the mournful wail of the zero-lot-line suburbanite. If you really *don't* have space for a standard garden, you can always try micro-gardening—intensive gardening in a small space. You don't have to grow *all* of your own food. But anyone has the room for a small garden, even if they live in a condo (okay, that's a *really* small garden).

Here are some micro-gardening tips . . .

A garden can be a collection of large pots. Even better, if you can build an enclosed area as small as three feet by three feet, you can build a raised bed garden. Make it as large as possible in your small space. Home Depot sells eight-foot-long landscape four-by-four lumber for cheap. They'll cut those boards to size for you, and you can nail them together. I used six-inch nails. My sister, who also does raised bed gardening, uses plain' ol boards and much shorter nails.

Once you build the enclosure, line the bottom of it with thick cloth, such as landscape fabric or rock wool. Or, use multiple layers of newspapers and cardboard if you don't have the cloth. This will help your raised garden bed retain moisture so you won't have to water it so much.

Fill it with a mixture of top soil and fertilizer, or you can use a pre-mixed planting soil. You can estimate the amount you will need by multiplying the width by the length by the height to determine the cubic feet of soil needed. For example, if your garden is four feet by eight feet by two feet, you would need approximately 64 cubic feet of soil. Unless you're investing in some fancy-pants wood for the enclosure, the soil will probably be the most expensive thing in your micro garden.

For the price of eight pieces of lumber, some nails, and potting soil, you can have a great raised-bed box garden. Once the soil is in place, mark off sections of the garden for each of the selected vegetables. Don't crowd the garden —plants need space to grow.

How Global Warming Will Affect Your Garden

Every gardening book refers to plant hardiness zones, also known as climate zones or growing zones. Calculated by the USDA, the hardiness map divides North America into 11 latitudinal zones, each representing a 10°F range of *average annual minimum temperature*—the coldest lows that can be expected in that area. Zones 2 through 10 are each subdivided into two sections—*a* and *b*—that represent 5°F ranges. Zone 11 (southern Mexico and much of Hawaii) is tropical, with winter lows above 40°F.

Basically, plant hardiness zones are a guide to help you know which plants will grow where you live, so you don't plant things that will soon die just because they can't handle your region's temperatures.

Get in the zone.

So that sounds simple enough. Except, thanks to global warming, the hardiness zones are moving. The National Arbor Day Foundation has released an updated hardiness zone map. (See Figure 9.1.)

You can find the original at the Arbor Day Foundation web site: http://arborday.org/media/zones.cfm. And you can see how global warming changed the Arbor Day Foundation's map in this online animation: http://www.arborday.org/media/mapchanges.cfm.

The USDA originally rejected the Arbor Day Foundation map, but that was during the Bush Administration, which seemed to think it could clap real hard and wish global warming out of existence. Now, finally, the USDA should follow with an official map of its own. A sneak preview of the new USDA map raised hackles among some gardening experts who have seen it. For example, Washington D.C., which previously was a climate fence-sitter, has been swallowed by a southern climate zone, the same zone as North Carolina.

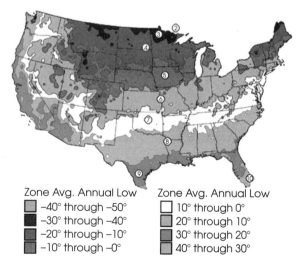

Zone Avg. Annual Low	Zone Avg. Annual Low
■ −40° through −50°	☐ 10° through 0°
■ −30° through −40°	■ 20° through 10°
■ −20° through −10°	■ 30° through 20°
■ −10° through −0°	■ 40° through 30°

Figure 9.1   Global Warming Moves Planting Zones North

Source: National Arbor Day Foundation.

Along with the fact that plant hardiness zones are sliding all over the map, there are other problems that global warming raises for gardeners.

- Earlier spring warming does not rule out sudden drops in temperature. If the trees are blooming earlier, a sudden cold spell can bring the risk of frost damage to flowers and developing fruit.
- There's increased danger of drought and extreme precipitation events—what some scientists now call *global weirding*.
- Weeds like poison ivy and ragweed are thriving. With higher temps and increased CO_2, ragweed produces 10 times the amount of pollen.
- Invasive plants like English ivy and Japanese honeysuckle are thriving under the changed conditions.
- Canada thistle has become more resistant to herbicides, requiring three times the dosage in the presence of higher carbon dioxide.

The point is, local climates are changing, as are the plants that thrive in them. What worked for your grandfather may not work for you. It makes it all the more important to do your research. Local nurseries should have the scoop on what's working in your area now.

A Useful List of Gardening Do's

I'm not a great gardener. But there are a few things I've picked up. So here's my list of Gardening Do's—you may find them useful.

> **Chose the best available site for your garden.** Situate your vegetable garden in a sunny place (six to 10 hours of sunshine per day) and start growing food early in the spring. Keep planting all summer long so something fresh and tasty is always ready to harvest. If you can, place the garden near your kitchen. It will be easy to go pick a few things you need, and you can spy on the garden from your window.

> **Be aggressive with weeds.** Weeds rob your plants of water and nutrients, so it's very important to keep them at bay. The

best way to remove weeds is to chop off the top of the weed at ground level. You might have to repeat this a few times, but the weed will die eventually.

Use mulch. Organic mulches such as grass clippings, wood chips, old leaves, compost or straws help improve the soil by adding organic matter as they decompose. Mulch also may encourage the growth of worms and other beneficial soil organisms that can help improve soil structure and the availability of nutrients for plants. Mulch should also cut down on weeding and watering.

Water enough (but not too much). Proper watering is the most difficult part of growing a garden. Roots need to stay moist, but not too moist since roots do not grow in the soil but in the air between it. In other words, with too much water your can actually drown your plants. Complicating things, the visual signs of overwatering are the exact same as under-watering—wilted leaves and yellowish color.

The key is the soil. If you have sandy soil, you're going to water about twice as often as loamy soil and three times as much as soil that contains a lot of clay.

A guideline is that mature plants need one to two inches of rain per week in summer (more for hot climates). You should provide whatever portion of this moisture is lacking. One inch of rain equals 65 gallons per 100 square feet of garden space. A rule of thumb is to water your vegetables at least twice a week. With adequate organic soil content, the garden should be able to go two to seven days between irrigations. But this is just a guide. Along with soil composition, the time of the season, stage of plant development, and many other factors affect the amount of water required.

A drip system, which is an irrigation method that delivers small amounts of water to the roots of plants, will make your life easier, though it involves time, effort, and expense at the start. A drip system on a mulched garden reduces water need by around 50%.

Finally, water on a consistent schedule: It is easy to forget the last time you watered your garden, and watering a few days late or early can have a significant effect on your harvest.

Fertilize! In addition to water, air, and sunshine, plants need nutrients. Nitrogen (N), phosphorus (P), and potassium or potash (K) are the common fertilizer nutrients. These three—N, P, and K—are the most heavily used nutrients, and you'll need to apply them every year.

How to Plant a Three Sisters Garden

The Native Americans knew how to farm and how to farm well—they taught the pilgrims a thing or two. One of the basic native farming traditions in the Northeast, where I grew up, is the *Three Sisters Garden*.

The three sisters are corn, beans, and squash. The old legend goes that they were originally three sisters who could only grow and thrive together. What the natives were telling us is these are great complimentary plants, as they build on each other's strengths.

Corn provides a natural pole for bean vines to climb. Beans are *nitrogen fixers*, adding nitrogen to the ground, which helps the next year's corn crop. And squash has lots of shallow vines and leaves, which keep weeds down and prevent soil moisture from evaporating.

If you want to try gardening native style, here's what to do:

- Use a hoe to create a mound of soil approximately five feet across and one foot high.
- Add compost to the soil if needed and level off the top of the mound.
- Plant four to six corn seeds in holes at the center of the mound, six to eight inches apart and one-inch deep.
- Wait for corn to sprout and reach approximately six-inches high before planting beans. Plant four bean seeds four inches from base of corn stalks, evenly spaced around stalks.
- At the outer edge of the mound, plant three squash seeds evenly spaced around perimeter of the mound. Don't plant the squash directly on the edge. Instead, place them approximately six to eight inches in from the edge of the mound.

Foot traffic near root systems is decreased in this method of gardening, which prevents soil from becoming compacted like it does in row gardening.

Source: Jacqueline Cross, How to Grow a Three Sisters Garden, suite101 .com, Nov. 10, 2008, http://vegetablegardens.suite101.com/article.cfm/ three_sisters_gardening.

Before planting, it's common to use one pound of fertilizer containing N-P-K for each 100 square feet. The fertilizer might be labeled (20-20-20)—20% by weight each of nitrogen, phosphorus, and potassium and potash. There are many fertilizer mixes; another common one is ammonium sulfate (16-20-0), and many gardeners use two pounds of 16-20-0 for every 100 square feet. You can see where I'm going with this: Check with your local garden shop to see what kind of fertilizer you should be using and how much. Sulfur (S), Calcium (Ca), and magnesium (Mg) may also be needed, but you'll find that out when you do your soil testing. You can also use organic fertilizers—plant compost or manure.

Plan your garden so you have vegetables throughout the entire season. Check with your local garden shop to see what grows well at different times of the season in your area. And MotherEarthNews.com has an online guide at http://tinyurl.com/cdcx7l. Some crops, like corn, have short harvest periods, so depending on where you live, you can make several successive plantings for staggered harvests.

Plant disease-resistant varieties that are adapted to your area.[7] Again, your local garden shop will know what plants are best suited to survive the diseases and pests in your area.

Use companion plants. There are some plants that, when planted close together, will benefit each other. The Iroquois used the *three sisters*—beans, corn, and squash (see sidebar). Many organic farmers still swear by the three sisters today.

Some More Tips

Likewise, there are certain combinations of plants that will inhibit the growth of one or both types of plants. Here are a few combinations to avoid:

- Potatoes—inhibit growth of tomatoes and squash
- Beans—inhibit growth of onions

- Broccoli—inhibits growth of tomatoes
- Carrots—inhibit growth of dill

Some other tips . . .

Soak seeds to get a jump on the season. Before germinating, seeds need to drink up moisture, just as if drenched by spring rains. Once they become plump and swollen, the little embryo inside will begin to grow.

Large seeds can be chipped or nicked with a knife to aid in germination. If they're too hard to nick easily, try rubbing them between pieces of sandpaper.

Small seeds can drown easily. Try starting the seeds in a mix containing sand or perlite, a volcanic material that creates tiny air tunnels which allows moisture and oxygen to flow freely to roots.

Especially in cold climates, you might want to start with large seedlings grown on your windowsill or purchased at a nursery (if you have more money than time). This works especially well for tomatoes and peppers.

Not every vegetable needs to be started as a seedling. Squash, zucchini, pumpkins, and cucumbers are best started by direct sowing in the ground.

If you grow too much food, then lucky you. Home canning is an excellent solution. The USDA has a great FREE guide to canning that you can find online at the National Center for Home Food Preservation web site: http://www.uga.edu/nchfp/publications/publications_usda.html. There are whole books on canning if you're really interested. You can also check into dehydrating and preserving your homegrown foods. Or, be generous, and share with your neighbors or a local food bank.

In addition to giving you a fresh vegetable supply to stretch out your food stockpiles, gardening will calm your frayed nerves and put food on your table. That's a change from the chemical-soaked Frankenfood being sold at your grocery store. And remember, you can't eat gold or silver, but you can eat your own vegetables.

And if disaster never comes, then you've saved money, eaten more healthily, learned some new skills, and had fun in your own backyard.

10 Best Garden Crops for Beginners

I don't have the best green thumb in the world, but there are plants that even I can't kill. Here are some to consider for your gardening.

1. **Radishes.** Radishes do well even in not-so-great garden soil and are ready to harvest in only a few weeks. Plant the seeds in spring and fall.

2. **Green beans.** These are easy to grow and prolific. If you get a big crop, they freeze well, and they're also delicious when pickled as dilly beans. Start with seeds after all danger of frost has passed.

3. **Onions.** Start with onion sets, and if they do well, you can harvest bulb onions. If not, you can always eat the greens.

4. **Strawberries.** Perfectly ripe strawberries are unbelievably sweet, and the plants are surprisingly hardy. Buy bare-root plants in early spring. Put this perennial in a sunny spot and keep it well weeded.

5. **Peppers.** Both hot peppers and bell peppers are easy to grow. Start with plants and let peppers from the same plant ripen for different lengths of time to get a range of colors and flavors.

6. **Bush zucchini.** This squash won't take up as much room in your garden as many other types, and it's very prolific. Start from seeds or transplants. You won't need more than a few plants for a bumper crop.

7. **Tomatoes.** There's just no substitute for a perfectly ripe homegrown tomato, and it's hard to go wrong when you start with strong plants. If you get a big crop, consider canning or freezing.

8. **Basil.** Many herbs are easy to grow, but basil is a good choice because it's a nice complement to tomatoes. Basil is easy to grow from seeds or from transplants.

9. **Potatoes.** These are an easy-to-grow staple that stores well when kept cool. A simple and low-maintenance approach is to plant potatoes in straw rather than soil. Seeds are whole or cut sections of potatoes, sold in early spring.

10. **Salad greens** (lettuce, spinach, arugula, and corn salad). Pick your favorite, or try a mix? Many companies sell mixed packets for summer and winter gardening. Plant the seeds in spring and fall, and you can pick salads almost year-round.

Source: MotherEarthNews.com.

The Least You Can Do

- Consider starting a small garden—even if you begin with just one pot and one vegetable. You'll eat healthier, fresher food.
- Don't overspend. Buy what you need, but you can scrounge a lot of supplies and share rental costs on equipment with friends.
- Do basic research at Home Depot, Lowe's, or your neighborhood gardening store. They can tell you what to plant and when.
- If you're new at gardening, consider sticking to the list of *10 Best Garden Crops for Beginners*. Taking on too much and trying to grow difficult crops could discourage you.

PART
IV

HEALTH, HOME, AND EDUCATION

CHAPTER 10

Health, Medicine, and Disease

After a brief period of turmoil in which the usual helpless and useless patients who consume the lion's share of medical care dollars die out in a Darwinian mass extinction, we can at last get down to the serious business of making our statistics look good.

—Anonymous

We've got a lot of ground to cover in this chapter. I'll tell you about what medical professionals are doing to prepare for a WTSHTF scenario, Seven Medical Tips for smart suburban survivalists, what you should keep in a traveling medicine bag, and why you should think twice before buying from an Internet pharmacy. I'll also tell you about medicinal plants you can grow yourself, and 23 Home remedies from the spice rack. Finally, we'll take a look at pandemics, epidemics, and how to protect yourself and your family in the event of either one.

When TSHTF, your family's immediate safety, food, and water will probably be your top three priorities. But medicine should be high on the list, as well.

Why? Well, you're used to living in a world where medicine is plentiful and (mostly) cheap. And the odds are better than average that you or someone in your family is taking medicine for a chronic condition. More than half of all *insured* Americans are taking prescription medicines regularly for chronic health problems.[1]

Research shows that that last year, 51% of insured U.S. children and adults were taking one or more prescription drugs for a chronic condition, up from 50% the previous four years and 47% in 2001. Most of the drugs are taken daily.

Now here's the scary part: Our government discourages stockpiling of prescription drugs. If civilization breaks down, those drugs will become unavailable in a hurry.

There are many drugs that you can buy without a prescription in foreign countries (Mexico, for instance) that you cannot buy in the United States. Our government simply doesn't trust us because our medical professionals, who write the laws, are arrogant enough to think only they know best. For the same reason, your doctor won't prescribe more than three months' worth of most prescription medications, and sometimes less. There is some logic behind the caution—more people die from overdoses of prescription drugs every year than die from overdoses of illegal drugs. But this situation makes it tough to build a stockpile for long-term emergencies.

And my lawyer's head would explode if I didn't mention that medicine is something that should *only* be practiced by trained professionals. That being said . . .

Medical Professionals Are Worried About *Something More Serious*

I talked to Nannette Lavoie-Vaughan, certified Nurse Practitioner and CEO of Nurse Nan Consulting. She and other health practitioners have been talking a lot about this problem recently.

Since Nan does a lot of work with nursing homes, that's where she focuses her planning. Nursing homes carry, *at most*, one month's supply of each patient's drugs.

"It a hot topic for people in the nursing home field," Nan told me. "If transportation is disrupted, drug supplies will run out pretty quickly."

"All nursing homes are required by federal law to come up with a disaster manual and a disaster plan. It used to be for hurricanes and tornadoes. Now, we are realizing that it could be something more serious. It could be bioterrorism or something else. We live in an age where anything can happen."

Nursing homes are not allowed to stockpile large amounts of medication, Nan explains. They are supplied by what are called *dispensing pharmacies*, which keep close track of the drugs.

Just-in-time inventory practices and our highly centralized society make things worse, Nan explains. North Carolina, where she works, is served by just three major dispensing pharmacies. If one of those suffers a major disruption, patients might not get the medicine they need. People could start dying pretty quickly.

And nursing homes themselves could face armed attack. "Nursing homes do have drugs on hand that are mind-altering," she says. "In a time of civil unrest, like post-Katrina, nursing homes could become a target" for armed individuals or gangs.

Nursing homes may be especially vulnerable, but anyone who needs medicine—that is to say, the majority of Americans—is also at risk.

The first thing to do is to make sure you and your family need as little medicine as possible.

Seven Medical Tips for Smart Suburban Survivalists

Some of the best medical care you can get is preventative medical care. With that in mind, let's look at seven medical tips for suburban survivalists.

1. **Get in shape NOW!** Lose weight and build up your endurance. You might have to walk five or 10 or many more miles with a backpack loaded with stuff as you escape whatever calamity strikes your home. Also, losing weight means you'll be at less risk of diabetes and several other diseases. If you're diabetic and civilization collapses, your odds are grim.

   Obesity puts you at risk of heart disease, asthma, arthritis, Alzheimer's disease, depression, high blood pressure, hormonal imbalance and infertility, sleep apnea, stroke, incontinence, and a list of cancers longer than your arm. Also, if you're being chased by an angry mob with pitchforks, guess who gets caught first? The fat guy, that's who.

   It reminds me of an old joke we used to tell in Maine. Two guys go camping. The next morning, they wake up to find a bear has wandered in to the camp and, having already eaten their food, is looking at the humans hungrily. Wisely, the campers decide to run away. One of them stops to put on his sneakers. The other camper can't believe it. "You damned fool!" he hissed at his friend. "Even with sneakers, you'll never outrun a bear."

"I don't have to outrun the bear," his friend said. "I just have to outrun you."

The point is, being overweight slows you down and makes you a liability to your friends and family, as well as putting you at risk of heart attacks and other medical crises that won't be easily treated WTSHTF.

2. **Change your diet.** This goes hand in hand with getting in shape, but you really want to change your diet *before* a crisis occurs. Learn to eat what you have stockpiled. This will help with rotating your stock. Put down the Cheetos and start eating healthier snacks. If you've followed my recommendation and planted a garden, you could have lots of healthy snacks growing in your own backyard.

Benjamin Franklin said, "An apple a day keeps the doctor away." Start snacking on apples, bananas, and grapes, and you'll feel better. Start eating radishes and carrots you grow in your own garden and you'll feel better and have a real sense of accomplishment.

It's hard to diet in a land of abundance. Weight Watchers has helped me. Exercise is also good—30 minutes a day is recommended.

3. **Don't get *too* skinny.** That is, if you're really planning on hard times. Why? Because each two pounds of extra weight you carry gives you enough energy to survive for three to five days, as long as you have enough water and vitamin pills. Get fit enough to run away if you have to, but a few extra pounds won't kill you and may save your life.

4. **Stop smoking.** The government is already making it hard enough on smokers, and if you quit, you'll have more money to spend on building up your survival stash. Along with lung cancer, smoking is linked to damage to your arterial walls, high blood pressure, asthma, and you name it. Smoking also makes it hard to run.

5. **Get a medical checkup.** It's important to know and understand what your body needs, and a visit to your health-care provider can provide that information. If your doctor is like mine, he's

a prick who will marvel aloud that you're not dead yet, but he'll also give you a baseline of information and alert you to any unfortunate developments you might miss on your own.

A survivalist I know went hard-core, bought a farm far from civilization, stocked it to the gills with survival gear, and then found out he had a chronic disease that would kill him unless he moved close to where he could get regular treatments. That changes your priorities. Maybe he should have gone for the checkup before he bought the farm, eh?

6. **Get CPR/First-Aid Training.** If the paramedics aren't answering the phone, it's all down to you. A Cardio-Pulmonary Resuscitation (CPR) class will teach you critical, life-saving skills. For example, you'll learn the ABC method for CPR:

> **A = Airway.** Check to be sure the person is breathing. They must have a clear passage for the air to get in through their nose or mouth and down into their lungs. When we are awake and conscious, we automatically maintain our airway. If a person is unconscious, they cannot do this for themselves. There are various ways to clear the airway. First, be sure the tongue is not too far back into the throat area. This can be fixed by tilting the head backwards. This manually changes the angle of the airway so that the tongue is no longer a problem. Next, be sure there is no object blocking the airway. This can be remedied by using appropriate back slaps or abdominal thrusts, after learning how, where, and when these are to be done.

> **B = Breathing.** If the victim is breathing, great! If not, the rescuer needs to begin artificial respiration, or *rescue breathing*.

> **C = Circulation.** To check circulation, the rescuer would need to check the victim's pulse. If there is none, this is the time to begin CPR, or cardiopulmonary resuscitation. CPR is a method of breathing for the patient as well as massaging the heart to help the blood move through the body until it can do so again on its own.

This short description is not enough. You're going to need hands-on training to become proficient at CPR. Taking CPR and First-Aid Training is well worth it for anyone. You can learn everything from the small (the correct way to bandage a cut) to the big (keeping a person alive). And the fact is, in a disaster, the only doctor or nurse your family may be able to depend on is *you.*

The Red Cross offers CPR and First-Aid courses that won't break your piggy bank. You can find out more by pointing your Web browser to http://tinyurl.com/cfzetl or calling 1-800-787-8002.

7. **Get medicines for your pets.** Along with protecting your pet, veterinarian supplies are more easily obtained that human prescriptions and can be used for your own needs in a pinch. I'm not endorsing this, but it bears mentioning. Use your own judgment.

Nurse Nan's Traveling Medicine Bag

Nan says everyone should keep over-the-counter medicines on hand for emergencies. These you can stockpile. Her list includes packages of:

- Aspirin. "It has so many different properties," Nan explains. "Pain control, fever control, and it works as a blood thinner for people with high blood pressure."
- Topical antibiotic ointment, like Neosporin.
- Antidiarrheal medicine, like Imodium AD or Kaopectate. "They're handy for bad water or food poisoning," Nan says.
- Nausea medicine, like Pepto Bismol or Mylanta.
- Anti-allergy medications, like Claritin and Zyrtec. "If there's any airborne threats or people have trouble breathing, these would be good to have."
- Multivitamins. "You don't know what your access to food will be in a crisis situation."
- Your current medical information. Nan recommends putting a list of all the current medications you take and a list of all your medical diagnoses in a little plastic bag, as well as a living will and a *do-not-resuscitate* form if that's your choice.
- You'll also want to stock a traveling medical kit with your basic bandages, gauze pads, medical adhesive tape, alcohol prep pads, a small pair of scissors, and any medicines you use on a regular basis.

Remember to rotate the medicines in your bag regularly so they don't go beyond their expiration dates.

Nan also suggests keeping the same list of your medicines and diagnoses in a plastic bag in your freezer and putting a sticker on your door that says *Medical information in freezer*; that way, paramedics know to look for it there if and when there is a fire or other emergency at your house.

I think you should actually consider having three medical kits: The first is a small, basic kit for your bug-out bag that includes Nan's list of medicines as well as other basic first-aid supplies. This is one you'll take traveling and can be stored in your car or close to the car. The second is your basic home medical supplies (see sidebar). The third should be an extensive medical kit stored with your survival gear for use at home when going to a hospital is too dangerous.

Survival Medical Kit

Below is a list of basic medical supplies no home should be without:

- Bandages
- Rolls of gauze
- Several sizes of sterile pads
- Medical adhesive tape
- Antibiotic ointment
- Alcohol prep pads and/or antiseptic pads
- Aspirin *and* non-aspirin pain relievers
- Children's aspirin
- Cough medicine
- Sore throat lozenges
- Burn medication
- Anti-itch treatment
- Athlete's Foot powder
- Poison Ivy medication (urishol)
- Sunscreen
- Diarrhea medication
- Eye drops
- Thermometer
- Small scissors
- Tweezers

- Safety pins
- Moleskin (for blisters)
- Rubber (latex) gloves. (Find out if you're allergic to latex—some people are—before you pack the gloves in your kit.
- Basic first-aid instructions

Your more advanced medical kit can be expected to include the items listed above as well as some or all of the following:

- Special bandages for trauma and field dressings
- Eye pads
- Sponges
- Cotton balls
- Burn treatments
- Rubbing alcohol
- Hydrogen peroxide
- Iodine
- Larger scissors
- Sterile sutures, in several sizes
- Mouth-to-mouth shield
- Instant hot pack
- Instant cold pack
- Prep pads
- Cold medication
- Decongestant
- Antihistamine
- Insect and snakebite poison extractor kit. Even if you've never seen one, you need one. Poisonous insects and snakes are all over the United States. Check out http://tinyurl.com/d8pbtn.
- Splint materials
- Potassium iodide (anti-radiation pills). There is no medicine that will effectively prevent radiation poisoning. However, potassium iodide can help protect you against radioactive iodine released in nuclear fallout or from nuclear accidents, which is highly carcinogenic and attacks the human thyroid.[2] Today, nearly half of the survivors of Nagasaki studied have identifiable thyroid disease.
- EpiPen (epinephrine). *You cannot get epinephrine without a prescription*, but if anyone in your family is at all at risk of

a severe allergic reaction, consider putting an EpiPen in your medical kit. Shellfish and bee stings are just two of the things that can cause severe allergic reactions in some people. The technical name for this severe allergic reaction is anaphylaxis. Victims suffer swelling of the throat or tongue, hives, and trouble breathing. When it strikes, life is at risk and time is short. The good news is you can administer epinephrine, using an EpiPen (single-shot injector) or Twinject (two doses of epinephrine). There are side effects, so consult your doctor.

• In-depth first-aid/surgical guide

You may also want to consider putting the following in your advanced medical kit. While you may be of the opinion that you would *never* be able to do surgery: (1) you'd be surprised what you can and will do when lives are depending on it, and (2) someone may be doing surgery on *you*:

• Forceps
• Scalpel—keep this well protected from exploring hands
• Hemostats
• Wound probe
• Surgical thread

You may also want to put some kind of anesthetic or whatever pain pills you can find in your emergency medical kit. The end of life as we know it will be made doubly difficult if you or someone you love is in intense pain.

And as with your other medical kits, remember to rotate the medicines in your bag regularly—moving the old ones to your home medicine shelf to be used up and putting new ones in the bag—so they don't go beyond their expiration dates.

Having a medical travel bag is just good common sense. This can make a difference when disaster strikes, and if you ever need it, it'll be worth every penny you've invested.

So let's say you've stocked up your medical kit as much as possible, you're losing weight, and you're getting in shape. You're still stuck with the fact that it's very difficult to stockpile medicine legally in this country.

Think Twice Before Buying from an Internet Pharmacy

You may be thinking of buying meds online at a web site called My Canadian Pharmacy. They advertise everywhere and you probably get spam from them in your e-mail inbox. Be forewarned that SpamWiki .com (http://spamwiki.com) reports My Canadian Pharmacy as "a longstanding Russian or possibly Ukrainian spam operation which has been relentlessly spamming email users around the world since at least the spring of 2004. The operators are currently wanted by numerous international law enforcement groups including Interpol and the FBI. They largely appear to be tied to credit card fraud and identity theft."

SpamWiki.com adds: "My Canadian Pharmacy is part of an umbrella group of web sites which purport to offer discounted pharmaceuticals to an unwitting public. They are notable in that literally every single word, every single claim are 100% false. They lie in the spam messages they send, they lie in telling you their site is secure, they lie when they say your order is on its way. Even the name itself—My Canadian Pharmacy—is a fallacy. No known connection to the country of Canada is present in anything this group has done."

Sounds like just the kind of people you want to give your credit card number to, eh?

There *are* reputable web sites for buying drugs online, but it's hard to do this without a prescription, not to mention illegal. In April of 2009, the Drug Enforcement Administration (DEA) began enforcing new regulations designed to target rogue Internet pharmacies. The new law amends the Controlled Substances Act by adding several new provisions aimed at preventing the illegal distribution of controlled substances through the Internet.

The new rules:

- Require at least one face-to-face medical evaluation before a patient can receive a prescription for a controlled substance via the Internet.
- Create new definitions of what can be considered as an online pharmacy and what it means to deliver, distribute, or dispense medication via the Internet.
- Expand regulatory requirements to online pharmaceutical sales.
- Establish prescription reporting requirements for online pharmacies.

The Drug Enforcement Administration (DEA) says it's trying to protect patients. Excuse me while I roll my eyes and think that maybe they're trying to protect the *profits* of fat-cat pharmaceutical companies and the members of the American Medical Association.

Nonetheless, the law is the law.

And that brings us back to the conundrum of how to stockpile drugs for a major disaster. One solution is to talk to your doc and explain that you want to have extras in case of emergency; maybe he or she will write you a refill sooner. Be sure to use your oldest meds first.

There is another solution: Grow your own.

Herb Garden—Medicinal Plants You Can Grow Yourself

Many people already use centuries-old natural remedies. They don't trust doctors, or the pharmaceutical companies, often for very good reasons. One solution is to learn to identify and grow your own medicinal herbs and prepare them to suit your needs. It's not hard, despite a sophisticated industry dedicated to telling you exactly the opposite. If you're willing to trust treatments that folk-healers used for generations, herbal medicine may be what you're looking for.

Medicinal herbs are what our forefathers used when they felt sick—along with bleeding themselves with leeches and drinking themselves insensible with rum. While leeches and rum aren't on the doctor's Rx pad anymore, even today, nearly 80% of drugs on the market are derived from plant material.

It is difficult for the home gardener to extract the medicinal parts of the plant. Echinacea, for instance, must be extracted by boiling only the roots, reducing it over a period of hours while skimming off the impurities. That's a lot of time and effort when you can buy it off the shelf at the drugstore.

However, down the road, if things go to heck in a handcart, medicinal herbs might well be worth the time and effort. They could even turn into a profitable side business for you if your neighbors are looking for cures for what ails them.

Here are some common medicinal herbs you can grow and what they are good for. Many are used as teas. Steeping teas in hot water is called *infusion*:

- **Angelica**—Dried leaves can be steeped in hot water to improve energy, stimulate circulation, and reduce flatulence. Angelica also has antibacterial and antifungal qualities.
- **Basil** (sweet)—Steep leaves in water for a few minutes to make a tea to help indigestion. Make a cold-oil infusion to massage sore muscles.
- **Calendula**—Flowers make a healing mouthwash for the gums. Mix a cream using calendula petals and plantain leaves for healing of cuts.
- **Catnip**—Make a tea to relieve colds and fevers. Also used to treat headaches and upset stomachs. Catnip also has mild sedative qualities, except for cats.
- **Chamomile**—Use in a tea as a mild sleep aid or to aid digestion. Make a cream to treat dry, rough skin.
- **Common Yarrow**—Infused tea fights colds and fevers. Make a cream with its flower petals to use on cuts and burns.
- **Coriander**—Chew leaves or infuse as a tea to relieve upset stomach. Also used as a mild sedative.
- **Feverfew**—Eat three to five leaves daily to reduce migraine headaches. Infuse as a tea to relieve muscle spasms or reduce fever.
- **Garlic**—I'm growing a lot of this herb in my vegetable garden. It has been shown to help a whole bunch of ills including high blood pressure. See sidebar for more on garlic.
- **Hawthorn**—Its berries, flowers, and leaves can be made into a tea that is an old-country treatment for high blood pressure. Hawthorn helps improve the contractility of the heart muscle, increase cardiac performance and output, and increases the heart's tolerance to oxygen deficiency.
- **Horehound**—Make a tonic of chopped horehound leaves and honey to treat sore throats. A cold infusion will help relieve heartburn.
- **Hyssop**—Make a cream to treat bruises and burns. Infuse as tea to treat colds, flu, bronchitis, and sore throats.

- **Lemon Balm**—Made into a tea or added to food, it calms the nerves and improves blood flow.
- **Purple Coneflower**—Also known as Echinacea, it's often infused into a hot tea to stimulate the immune system.
- **St. John's Wort**—Infuse as tea to treat depression or as a mild sedative. Makes a cream to treat bruises and skin inflammation.
- **Summer Savory**—Make a hot tea from this plant and gargle with it to treat a sore throat. Also drink as a tea to treat diarrhea and indigestion.
- **Thyme**—Make a tea sweetened with honey to help relieve sore throats and coughs. Infusion used to relieve hangovers.
- **Valerian**—Roots used to relieve nervous tension, anxiety, insomnia, and pain. Roots used in a cream to treat acne or skin rashes.

If you're going to make teas from herbs you grow in your garden, you'll need either a tea ball infuser or a mesh infuser. You can buy both on Amazon.com, and they're cheap.

You can buy seeds or starters for these herbs just about anywhere, and grow the ones you think you'll need. If you want to order a seed kit for a bunch of different medicinal herbs, you can find them for sale all over the Internet. Here's one example: http://www.herbkits.com/medicinal.htm, but be sure to check around for the best prices.

It's important to remember that not all herbs will help you, and many U.S. doctors will argue that none beat modern medicine. Some herbs are actually harmful for people with various ailments. For example, licorice and Asian ginseng are both suspected to *cause* high blood pressure in some individuals when not taken properly. And be cautious about mixing natural remedies with any prescription medicines, as there may be side effects.

Finally, you'll see that herbal treatments won't cover some serious diseases like diabetes. There is some new research showing that cinnamon (yes, cinnamon) may help treat diabetes, but I think it's beyond the ken of most backyard gardeners to extract cinnamon for use in treating diabetes.

There is one plant that deserves its own section—if you aren't growing this already, start now.

Aloe Vera—The First-Aid Station In Your Backyard

You can grow aloe vera in your backyard or even in your home, and it has many medicinal uses without processing. You might already have one of these plants in a pot on your porch!

Aloe-vera gel is used as a common ingredient in many commercially available first-aid products. Most people are probably most familiar with its use in lotions and sunburn creams. Extracts from aloe vera are said to help prevent bronchitis, sinusitis, and treat allergies. Aloe vera extracts also show antibacterial and antifungal properties. There is some preliminary evidence that aloe vera extracts may be useful in the treatment of diabetes.

Aloe vera is a succulent that is very drought-tolerant and resistant to most diseases and insects. About the only thing aloe won't tolerate is cold. But if you live up north, aloe can live in a pot in the warmth of your kitchen—it's that easy to grow and maintain.

23 Home Remedies from the Spice Rack

In a real pinch, medical relief may be as close as your spice rack. The web site Tipnut (http://tipnut.com) offers a collection of home remedies that you don't even have to grow, not if they're already sitting by your stove. This is not professional medical advice, and some spices and herbs may conflict with prescribed medicines. My lawyer will be very happy that I'm telling you to always check with a doctor before treating yourself with any home remedy.

1. **Allspice:** Relieves muscle aches and pains. First, grind Allspice into a powder and then add water to make a paste. Spread on a strip of clean muslin and apply to sore area.
2. **Anise:** Helps congestion from allergies, colds, or flu, and settles upset stomach with gas. Make a tea by steeping one teaspoon of anise seeds in one cup of boiling water. Strain before drinking. Also chew a couple anise seeds as needed for bad breath.
3. **Basil:** For relief of cough, make a tea of dried basil using one teaspoon per one cup boiling water. Steep, then strain, add a spoonful of honey, and drink.
4. **Bay Leaves:** Helps with dandruff. Make a rinse by crushing a handful of bay leaves to one liter water (first brought to boiling then removed from heat). Cover and steep for 20 minutes. Strain and cool. Apply to hair and leave for 45 to 60 minutes. Rinse clean.

5. **Black Ground Pepper:** Stops bleeding. Sprinkle a generous amount on a cut and voila!.
6. **Caraway Seeds:** Chew on a few seeds to help with flatulence. You can also make a tea by steeping one teaspoon seeds per cup of boiling water. Strain before drinking.
7. **Cardamom:** Digestive aid. Brew a tea with one teaspoon of cardamom and one cup boiling water. Steep. Drink tea with meals.
8. **Cayenne Pepper:** Sprinkle a pinch of cayenne pepper on meals to clear sinuses. Also a natural appetite suppressant that increases metabolism. Sprinkle cayenne pepper on a toothbrush or add to a glass of water to gargle and rinse mouth—helps prevent gum disease and speeds up healing gingivitis. For toothaches, make a paste with cayenne pepper and water, and apply to sore area.
9. **Celery Seed:** Relief from fluid retention. Make a diuretic tea by crushing roughly one-and-a-half teaspoons celery seed and steep in one cup boiling water (20 minutes). If you're menstrual cycle is running late, this infusion can be used to bring on menstruation. Also helps with high blood pressure and anxiety.
10. **Cinnamon:** Mix one-half teaspoon of cinnamon to coffee or tea to help raise good cholesterol levels. Arthritis pain: Try one-half teaspoon cinnamon mixed with one teaspoon honey. To help with heavy menstruating, add a bit of cinnamon to tea or coffee, or sprinkle on foods.
11. **Cloves:** Chew one clove for bad breath. For toothache pain, rest a clove against the sore area until pain goes away. You can also chew on three or four cloves to relieve nausea. To relieve a sore throat, slowly chew on a few cloves.
12. **Coriander:** Helps with high cholesterol. Boil one teaspoon of coriander seeds in one cup of water, and drink.
13. **Cumin:** Drink for cold relief. Boil one cup of water with a teaspoon of cumin seeds, and simmer for a few seconds. Strain and cool.
14. **Dill Seed:** Try swallowing one teaspoon of dill seed to stop hiccups. Mask bad breath by eating a bit of dill seed.
15. **Fennel Seeds:** Chew a couple fennel seeds for bad breath. For stomach cramp relief, you can brew a tea by steeping one teaspoon seeds per cup of boiling water. Strain before drinking. Crush seeds slightly when making tea. Fennel is also good for flatulence.

(Continued)

(Continued)

16. **Garlic Powder:** Mosquito Repellent. Make a garlic powder and water paste. Apply to pulse points, behind knees, on shoes and ankles, and a dab or two on your cheeks or somewhere on your face and neck—keep out of eyes.

17. **Ginger:** Helps with nausea. Brew a tea with one-half teaspoon ginger per cup of boiling water. Strain before drinking. If you have fresh ginger on hand, chewing a bit is more effective than ginger tea. For headache relief, make a paste of ground ginger and water, apply to temple area. Mix one-half teaspoon of ground ginger with one teaspoon of honey for cough relief. Drink tea or chew on a fresh piece of ginger to fight motion sickness.

18. **Mustard Powder:** To relieve congestion, mix one tablespoon of mustard powder with one liter of hot water then soak feet.

19. **Mint (peppermint or spearmint):** Helps with stomachaches and cramps. Brew a tea with one-and-a-half teaspoons dried mint per cup of boiling water. Strain before drinking.

20. **Sage:** Control hot flashes (caused by menopause) by drinking sage tea three times a day. Boil one-half teaspoon sage per one cup boiling water. Steep (10 minutes), strain, and drink.

21. **Salt:** Canker sore remedy. Apply salt directly to the sore or rinse your mouth a couple times a day with a strong salt-water solution. Warning: This stings. For mosquito bite relief, make a salt and water paste and then apply to bite area.

22. **Thyme:** Sooth a cough with thyme tea. Brew one tablespoon of dried thyme in one cup boiling water. Strain then drink (for sore throats, gargle with this tea). Helps relieve gas and stomach cramps. Brew a tea with one teaspoon dried thyme per one cup boiling water. Strain before drinking.

23. **Turmeric:** Fever relief. Mix one-half teaspoon turmeric powder with one cup of warmed milk, and add a teaspoon of honey.

See the original article, with links to other home remedies and cures, at http://tipnut.com/home-remedies-spice.

Garlic, The Survivalist's Wonder Herb!

Humble garlic is a member of the lily family. While not as easy to grow as aloe vera, growing garlic isn't too tough either.

Garlic is a treatment for many of the woes that afflict man—some people say it even fights cancer, though that's further than I'm willing to go. In any case, it belongs in every survivalist's garden. You can even grow it in a window box if you don't have a yard.

Garlic contains a large number of unique sulfur-containing compounds. When you crush garlic cloves, a strong odor is released; this is a sign that potent anti-microbial compounds are being produced—ajoene, allyl sulfides, and vinyldithiins. These sulfur compounds are thought to be the source of garlic's healthful benefits. Scientists have proven that garlic displays antibiotic, antifungal, and antiviral properties.

Here are some of the things garlic is good for:

- **High blood pressure:** Garlic lowers blood pressure by relaxing vein and artery walls. This action helps keep platelets from clumping together and improves blood flow, thereby reducing the risk of stroke. Garlic also decreases the levels of cholesterol and triglycerides, substances that increase the risk of cardiovascular diseases.
- **Arterial plaque:** Garlic's cardiovascular protective properties have been proven by many scientific studies. People over 50 years old who already had symptoms of atherosclerosis and who then consumed at least 900 mg per day of a standardized garlic supplement experienced significant reduction of arterial plaque formation.
- **High blood sugar:** Garlic increases insulin levels in the body. The result is lower blood sugar. Thus, garlic makes an excellent addition to the diet of people with diabetes. It will not take the place of insulin, anti-diabetes drugs, or a healthful diet, but garlic may help lower the need for additional insulin by reducing glycogen (stored sugar) release from the liver and by increasing the overall effectiveness of insulin.
- **Ear infections:** Place one to two drops of warm garlic oil in the ear canal several times a day at the onset of ear pain, and it will help speed the healing.
- **More medical wonders:** Garlic stokes the body's immune system, and is used to treat everything from the flu to herpes simplex (the virus responsible for cold sores) to vaginal yeast infections.

Soaking in a garlic infusion (tea) has been shown to even help treat athlete's foot. You crush a garlic bulb, and steep in four to five cups of hot water. (*Soak feet in garlic tea for 20 minutes, three times a day, and your athlete's foot will go away.*)

With all the good that comes with garlic, you can see why many people include garlic in their daily diets. Garlic aficionados add the herb to soups, salad dressings, and casseroles during the winter months to help prevent colds, or eat garlic at the first hint of a cold, cough, or flu. Garlic reduces congestion and may help break up mucus, which makes it effective against bronchitis.

Of course, you can overdo anything. Some people don't have a tolerance for garlic. But if you like garlic, make sure you grow it. You may need it if TSHTF.

Pandemics and Epidemics

Pandemics are illnesses spread across vast geographic areas. Epidemics are when a large part of any particular population gets sick. We'll probably see more pandemics and epidemics going forward. Why? Because each and every human being on Earth is a living, breathing germ factory. Germs are constantly mutating inside our bodies. Most of these mutations come to naught. But every now and then a mutation is successful, and that's when a new epidemic breaks out.

Be aware that the mass media will probably lie about the risks faced in a pandemic or epidemic. Why? In the early stages, they like to whip up fear to boost their ratings. In the later stages, the government will probably tell the media to not report developments so as to avoid panic, and the lapdogs in the media will probably go along.

It's probably best to do your own risk assessment. Before panicking, try to find out these five things:

1. What is this disease? Is it a new strain of an existing disease or something that's never been seen before? A new disease poses much higher risks.
2. What is the incubation period before symptoms show up? The longer the incubation period, the more likely the disease can spread undetected through a wide swath of the population.
3. How fast is it spreading? Are there 100 new cases in a week? 1,000? 10,000? Are some areas of the country or state more infected than others?

4. What is the contagion risk? Is the disease very contagious, spreading by air? Is it moderately contagious, spreading by flesh contact? Or is it less contagious, spreading by body fluids?
5. What is the mortality rate? A 50% mortality rate means half the people who contract the disease will die.

Assessing these factors, you can roughly figure: (1) if people in your area could be exposed to the disease, and (2) what your risk is if you are exposed to these hypothetical carriers.

If the risk for you and your family is high, be proactive. Schools in particular are breeding grounds for diseases. Consider keeping your kids home if the mortality rate is high and/or if risks are increasing that other kids may be coming to school with the disease. Local governments will be quickly closing schools, as was seen in the recent swine flu panic. Be prepared to have your child at home, and your work disrupted.

If you can work from home, you are much better off. There is always pressure on sick workers to *suck it up* and come in anyway. Likewise, the grocery store is going to be a germ fiesta—yet another reason to have stocked up on survival food ahead of time.

Government Tips for the Next Swine Flu Outbreak

The Center for Infection Disease Research and Policy (CIDRAP) and Pandemicflu.gov offer checklists for what families can do to get ready for a pandemic. The government is specifically worried about a swine flu pandemic, but their tips are general enough to cover other things. Many of their suggestions are similar to what survivalists are doing anyway, though naturally CIDRAP and Pandemicflu.gov are focused on disease prevention. Action items include:

- Learn about pandemic H1N1 (swine flu) influenza, its symptoms, how it spreads, and how to prevent infections.
- Stock up on water and nonperishable food. Although the recommendations vary from days' to months' worth, most experts agree it's important to have extra key supplies on hand.
- Ensure you have a supply of your prescription medicines.
- Keep other emergency and health supplies handy such as

(Continued)

(Continued)
flashlights, manual can openers, face masks, and painkillers.

- Make a list of people who are willing to help and can be contacted in case of emergencies.
- Make plans for potential disruptions at work, curtailed social gatherings, and school closures. (For example, is it possible to work from home if you are unable to go into work?)

Other useful skills for pandemic preparedness include learning how to care for the sick at home, using rehydration therapy and isolation measures.

Source: CIDRAP, "Promising Practices for Pandemic Planning," www.cidrap.umn
.edu/cidrap/content/influenza/swineflu/news/jun3009personprep-pp.html.

In a Real Epidemic, America's Health-Care System Will Be Overwhelmed

In recent flu seasons, hospital emergency departments have quickly reached their limits and there is little room for a surge in patients in either emergency rooms or inpatient beds. In other words, even a normal flu season sends our health-care system to the brink of crisis.

According to an article in *Public Health Reports:*[3]

> The federal pandemic influenza plan predicts that 30% of the population could be infected. The impact of this pandemic would quickly overwhelm the public health and health-care delivery systems in the U.S. and throughout the world.

The federal projection is that sometime in the next few years we could see a pandemic that would leave:

- 45 million people in need of outpatient care
- One to 10 million people in need of hospitalization
- 130,000 to one-and-a-half million people in need of intensive care

- 65,000 to 750,000 patients requiring mechanical ventilation
- Deaths numbering from 200,000 to two million

I don't think disease alone can bring down our civilization. However, disease can have a snowball effect on an existing crisis. As resources are stretched thin to deal with one crisis, the system that normally handles disease is stretched to the breaking point. If the number of unattended dead increases, the chance of the disease spreading goes up exponentially.

When a tipping point is reached, disease can run rampant like wildfire, because the resources will be insufficient to stop the onslaught worldwide.

The Diseases of the Future Could Be Horrendous

Along with the diseases bred in human guts and animals that are doped to the gills on antibiotics in factory farms (indeed, that's how Swine Flu got its start*), there is a new threat. The Associated Press says that amateur hobbyists called *biohackers* are now doing genetic engineering in their basements:[†]

Using homemade lab equipment and the wealth of scientific knowledge available online, these hobbyists are trying to create new life forms through genetic engineering—a field long dominated by Ph.D.'s toiling in university and corporate laboratories.

Obviously, this is just a skip and a jump from unleashing an environmental or medical disaster. It could happen unwittingly or wittingly. Some bright lad laboring in a basement laboratory in, say, the Middle East, could be brewing microscopic payback for enemies real or imagined.

This is just the latest twist in a long story. Our civilization is incredibly advanced and complex, and it would be ironic to see it humbled by the tiniest of creatures. But God seems to be disposed toward irony.

*From Brandon Keirn, "Swine Flu Ancestor Born on U.S. Factory Farm," *Wired*, May 1, 2009, www.wired.com/wiredscience/2009/05/swineflufarm.

†See ABC News/AP, "Hobbyists Are Trying Genetic Engineering at Home" Dec. 25, 2008, http://abcnews.go.com/Health/ColdandFluNews/wireStory? id=6527921.

How to Protect Yourself and Your Family

The government tips mentioned earlier are good as far as they go. There are three simple things you can do to protect your family, which include a mix of common sense and hard science.

1. **Keep your distance.** Remember all that stuff I told you about building a strong neighborhood? When an epidemic is loose, you don't want to turn your backs on your neighbors, but you do want to keep your distance.

   Experts in so-called *social distancing* strategies say such measures can cut the chance of an outbreak of potentially deadly infections in half, but only if steps are taken early. That's why cities close schools when only one infection is reported.

   For your own social distance, you want to stay at least three feet away from other people to avoid the infectious spray of droplets when someone coughs or sneezes. This will cut your risk of infection by 50%, according to government-sponsored studies.

   If you have more space, use it. Staying at least six feet away from others in public will cut your risk by two-thirds, according to the Centers for Disease Control.

   In the 1918 flu pandemic—the worst, deadliest flu outbreak in modern U.S. history—cities that closed schools, churches, and theaters during the early months of the deadly plague had peak weekly death rates about 50% lower than those of cities that imposed such measures later or not at all.

2. **Sanitize.** Wash your hands frequently in soap and hot water for around 20 seconds. The CDC estimates that 80% of all infections are spread by hands. Consider stocking up on hand sanitizer (with aloe) and latex gloves for when you have to go out in public.

3. **Stock up now.** Along with hand sanitizer and latex gloves, consider the following:

   - N95 Particulate Respirators. You can pick up a 30-pack of these on Amazon.com for cheap. They are an improvement over surgical masks in that they keep out bacteria. Be aware, however, that a virus is much, much smaller than bacteria and these masks cannot stop a virus. You'll also want rolls of bandage tape for sealing any mask edge gaps that form, which easily occurs with kids.

- A steam vaporizer. It keeps your respiratory system moist, allowing it to fight off bacteria.
- Vitamins D and C—both of which help you fight off diseases.
- If you haven't already built up your food stockpile, get cracking. If a plague is raging, all your preparation could be undone by a single trip to the grocery store.

What If Friends or Relatives Show Up at Your Door When a Plague Is Raging?

There's no way around this—if there's an epidemic making the rounds, and friends show up at your house, you're going to have to put them in quarantine for as long as it takes the disease symptoms to show up. Keep your distance while talking to them and find some place to put them. Your garage, if you have one, may do the trick. You already have survival food and gear—stick some of that in your garage and start the countdown. The disease's incubation period is one of the points in the five-part risk assessment mentioned earlier in this chapter.

The Least You Can Do

- Get a travel ditty bag. On the side, in magic marker, write: MEDICINE. In the bag, put packages of aspirin, Neosporin, Imodium AD, Pepto Bismol, Claritin, a small bottle of multivitamins, bandages, gauze pads, medical adhesive tape, alcohol prep pads, a small pair of scissors, a N95 Particulate Respirator, and any other medicines you use on a regular basis. Write down your doctor's name and contact info on a piece of paper, and add a list of any medications you are taking. Place it all in your bag, zip it up, and you're done.
- Put the bag where you can find it if you're running out the door. Remember to rotate the medicines in the bag before they expire.
- If you're slightly less lazy, get an aloe vera plant. They're simple to care for, hard to kill, and have many medicinal uses.

CHAPTER

Your House, Home Security, and Power

The best offense is a good defense.
—Anonymous

A house can be many things—a home, a stronghold against intruders, and a base of operations. In this chapter, I delve into ways to secure your house against intruders, how to hide valuables in your home, and what you can do to make your home and neighborhood safer if society starts to break down. I also discuss whether you need a gun, including some very basic information if you decide you do.

Then we'll examine two things that can turn your home into a castle (water and power), as well as tools you might want to buy for home repairs and improvements.

But before we get to all that, we have to talk about one thing that Americans *must* do: Stop thinking about homes as investments.

Free Yourself from Thinking of Your Home as an Investment

There are seven good reasons why the housing bubble isn't coming back. I'll explain them to you now. Your life will be much easier and less stressful if you can get the real estate monkey off your back.

The world has changed, and the days of flipping houses like rows of hamburgers are gone and probably not coming back in our lifetimes.

The first two years after the bursting of the housing bubble saw home prices fall about 30% from their peak. And nothing goes down forever, right? And maybe we'll see home prices bottom sometime in 2011 and 2012? I think that's actually optimistic! There are a couple of reasons why prices could start to rise at that time.

Reason #1: Simple Price Action, Enhanced by Time

Robert Shiller, an expert on housing prices and the author of *Irrational Exuberance*,[1] published a chart of how housing prices behaved for the last 120 years (adjusted for inflation). (See Figure 11.1.)

The house price line is on top. Prices are indexed against the 1880 price (left scale), and the chart is updated through the end of the fourth quarter of 2008. At that time, Schiller's analysis suggested that, as of early 2009, home prices had to fall *at least* another 20% just to get back to fair value.

Never mind the price spike—that was the housing bubble. Historically, home prices have risen annually in line with the Consumer Price Index. By 2009, the median value of a home, based

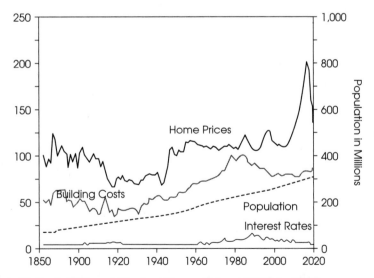

Figure 11.1   Inflation-Adjusted Home Prices 1880 to 2008

Source: Investorinsight.com.

on historical precedent, should have *risen* to $150,000. But at the end of 2008, the median value of a home was $180,000.

Sure, modern homes are bigger and more *modern* than they were in 1929. But they were bigger and more modern in 1969 than they were in 1929. The only way home prices can rise in real dollars is if incomes are going up as well, and they're not.

In short, while we could see temporary rallies, the easiest path for home prices is still down. And since there is usually overshoot to the downside after a bubble bursts, it could be much further down.

Reason #2: The Mortgage Default Tsunami

More than 2.3 million homeowners faced foreclosure proceedings in 2008, up more than 80% from 2007. A huge wave of ARMS-mortgage resets started in 2009 and will continue through mid-2012.

This tsunami of mortgage resets is one of the reasons why President Obama has created a $75 billion plan he says will prevent seven to nine million foreclosures. We aren't going to discuss the morals of bailing out people who bought too much house. I will point out that of homes that were delinquent in 2008 and then refinanced, more than half went back into foreclosure. Also, 40% of the homes sold at the peak of the bubble were second homes or investment properties. They won't be helped by Obama's mortgage initiative.

Obama's plan may ease some of the pain of the housing crisis, but won't make it go away. And it will probably weigh on the economy for years to come.

These two forces should weigh on home prices going forward, even if the economy recovers during that time. A lackluster economic recovery, naturally, will also throw cold water on the housing market.

But even *after* those two problems are worked out, there are five other reasons why the housing bubble—or any bubble—won't be reflating any time soon.

Reason#3: Deflation Hammers Home Prices!

In the United States, consumer prices started dropping in 2009, with the first monthly year-on-year drops since August 1955. At the same time, personal income also went down. Wages came under increasing pressure as employment declined; in the first quarter of 2009, employment dropped by the largest amount since current data series began in 1949. Falling wages and prices are deflationary. Deflation is terrible for home prices; as wages fall, rents follow, and home prices tag along behind.

Reason #4: Inflation Won't Help

Our current bout of deflation is probably going to end in runaway inflation. The federal debt is soaring to levels that would have seemed unimaginable just a decade ago. Through March 2009, the U.S. government and the Federal Reserve had spent, lent, or committed $12.8 trillion for the financial bailout.[2] The $787 billion stimulus package almost seems small by comparison,[3] but both the bailout and the stimulus will probably grow. As it monetizes its debt, the U.S. government will probably buy $1 trillion of its own debt in 2009 alone—talk about a snake eating its tail.

The federal debt was equivalent to 41% of GDP at the end of 2008. The Congressional Budget Office projects it will increase to 82% of GDP in 10 years. With no change in policy, it could hit 100% of GDP in just five more years.

This debt manifests itself as a flood of loose money sloshing through the system. When the economy compresses, that flood of money can be helpful. But when the economy bottoms and heads higher, all that extra money can ignite into an inflationary inferno— more money chases less goods, so prices ramp up and the value of the dollar goes down.

That means even if your home value goes up, it's struggling to keep pace in real terms. And if your home price doesn't go up, that will be even worse.

Here's an example why: The Dow Jones Industrial Average hit 1,000 in 1966. It didn't get there again for seven years, in 1973. The inflation from 1966 to 1973 was 37%. So investors may have made the same paper gains, but in real dollars, they were losing money.[4]

Reason #5: The Next Bubble Won't Be a Housing Bubble

The implosions of the Tulip Mania in Holland and the South Seas bubble were not followed by reinflation of tulip prices or shares of the South Seas Company stock.

Likewise, after the dot-com bubble burst, the Nasdaq didn't reflate. There are stocks from the dot-com daze that are far from their old highs, and we will likely never see those highs again. And some—Pets.com comes to mind—disappear forever.

Reason #6: The Fraudulent Good-Time Charlie Gravy Train Ain't Comin' Back

Low interest rates were only one factor in the housing bubble; the other was loose lending standards. Heck, they weren't just loose; there was wholesale fraud going on. Now, with regulators and Congress breathing down their necks, mortgage lenders are likely to button up their standards tighter than a nun's pajamas.

That's a bit like closing the barn door after the horse is out, but it means the ingredients for a housing bubble just aren't there any more.

Reason #7: The United States Is Getting Older

A great wall of baby boomers, born between 1946 and 1964, are approaching retirement age. The oldest baby boomers turned 63 in 2009, and when the trend peaks in 2030, the number of people over age 65 will zoom to 71.5 million—one in every five Americans. Old people don't need huge homes.

How Long Could Home Prices Stay Depressed?

Maybe home prices will turn around in 2010, but I wouldn't bet the farm on it. Maybe we'll see home prices recover in 2012. Or maybe it will take a *lot* longer. Studies show that of the last three up-waves in housing prices, 1942 to 1956, 1975 to 1979, and 1985 to 1989, it took the run-up time plus 30% before housing prices started to move up again.

Since this last housing bull market went from (roughly) 1997 to 2007, then housing prices won't start a significant run-up until 2020.

And what will inflation do to the value of your home by then?

Now for the Good News

If you can free yourself from the my-home-is-an-investment mind-set, then you can approach your house from a fresh angle:

- Your house is your home, first and foremost.
- Your house will likely be a refuge in a crisis. The grounds around it can provide a food supply. And there are things—primarily water and power—that make your home more livable than not.
- If you adjust to this concept, then any improvements you make to your house can be judged on the following criteria:

- Will the improvement improve the livability of my home, or is it just an aesthetic change?
- Is the cost of the improvement going to be worth it in how much it improves my home's comfort, security, and survivability?
- Am I actively making the changes my home needs to be a safe house in a crisis?

Using these standards, it's pretty easy to decide between remodeling the kitchen and a solar-power electrical system. That doesn't mean you can never redo your countertops. A new kitchen is *fabulous* (be sure to flip your hand in the air when you say that).

If you don't have the money to make big changes to your house, don't sweat it too much. Just make sure you have the basics—water (covered in Chapter 3), food (covered in Chapter 4), gear like electric lamps and batteries, and an evacuation plan in case you need to leave.

On the other hand, if you have the money, time, and inclination, you can make your home into a fortress that can ride out almost any crisis.

Intruder Alert! Protecting Your Home

Along with being a shelter, a home is your refuge from the turbulent world outside. And as times get tougher, it's likely there will be more people trying to break into your home and steal your stuff, or worse. In this section, I'll cover several ways to protect your home.

The first rule: Don't make it easy for intruders to enter your home, whether they're intent on burglary or something else. Intruders can access your house when:

- Your door is unlocked.
- The doors can simply be kicked in.
- The door lock can be hammered until it simply falls off.
- Your lock can be drilled out using a power drill.
- The locks can be easily pried off with pliers or wrenches.
- The doorframes can be spread apart using a spreader bar.
- There are panes of glass in the door itself or beside the door. The panes can simply be broken before the intruder unlocks or destroys the lock.

Many of these problems can be fixed by installing a good lock with a deadbolt in your front door. And make sure that door is solid wood or metal, and the frame the deadbolt goes into is also solid and has metal strike plates.

For extra security on the cheap, you can install a bar brace. It isn't pretty, but it will let you sleep well at night. A bar brace is basically a heavy, adjustable steel bar that wedges against your door at an angle so that it can't be opened. These usually cost less than $25 and are easy to install.

Electronic Home Security Systems

The FBI estimates that a break-in occurs around every 16 seconds.[5] You only have to be burgled once to decide you need a home security system. It's best to get one *before* your heirlooms, electronics, gold, and guns are stolen. If we are in a worsening economic crisis, it's likely there will be more burglaries. And a study in Britain shows that electronic alarms really work. Only 1.6% of households with good home security systems were victims of burglary. But 22.5% of households with little or no home security measures were burglarized.[6]

The home alarms most people are familiar with are perimeter systems—detectors or sensors placed on and around main entry locations such as windows and doors. These usually work using magnetic detectors, switch detectors, and glass break detectors for windows. The alarm will be triggered if any of the sensors detect a foreign presence.

Most home security systems are comprised of a control unit, detectors, or *switches* built into door and window frames that sense when the door or window is opened. These then trigger a siren or bell. Most sirens sound for 20 minutes and then shut off. Some alarms are connected to a monitoring service via phone line.

Wired electric alarms have their good points and bad points. The pros:

- They're inexpensive.
- They're easy to operate.
- They will alert the police.

They also have cons:

- Most require a functioning electric grid.
- While they sound loud, they don't do anything to discourage a determined burglar.

- The time between alarm and police response is fairly long—long enough for a burglar to get inside, grab your most expensive stuff, and split.

Wireless home security systems have important differences. First, they're battery powered and they transmit a radio signal to the control unit in order to trigger the alarm—no wiring is involved, so the wire can't be cut, and these systems won't fail if the electric grid goes down. Second, most wireless systems I've seen are do-it-yourself systems and are not connected to a security company. So there won't be anyone picking up a phone.

Doing it yourself is cheaper over the long run (no monitoring fee), but you have a bigger investment up front. Going with a corporate provider is usually cheaper up front (they may even throw the system in for free), but it involves a recurring charge.

If you choose to go with an electric alarm, you'll want to make sure the alarm you choose is loud enough. Anything less than 95 decibels can't be heard from a distance.

Choose a big name for your monitoring (ADT, Brinks, APX).[7] ADT is the leader in the industry and they have five interconnected monitoring centers throughout the United States.

If you want a better price, go with an ADT Authorized Dealer. They own their own equipment, so you'll probably pay less at the time of installation.

An independent dealer (as opposed to a corporate representative) may also throw in extras to get your business—a free panic button, motion sensor, smoke detector, or an additional door sensor—along with the main home security package. But you'll never know unless you ask.

A good site for reading about home security systems is www .homesecurityguru.com. Another is www.securehomeadvice.com.

A Home Security System with Four Legs

There is a home security system that can be cheaper than an electronic alarm (not always) and is certainly more cuddly—a dog. Many burglars will ignore a ringing alarm during a quick smash and grab; they will not ignore a dog, and they usually won't take their chances on one, either. For home security, you want a dog that sounds big and vicious. Teacup poodles and other tiny dogs are not effective home security systems.[8]

Other cheap home security systems:

Lock the doors: Yeah, it sounds simple, but you'd be amazed how many burglary victims don't lock their doors.

Seal your windows with paint: Paint over your window seals on the ground floor. A thick coat of paint will make your windows much harder for burglars to open, and most burglars, being lazy good-for-nothings, are easily deterred by any unanticipated difficulty. Sealing your windows will also make your heating and cooling bills lower.

A neighborhood watch: Neighbors watching out for each other is one of the best deterrents against crime. And if you see suspicious behavior around the neighborhood, don't keep it to yourself. Saving someone from being burgled is a great way to be a hero. The safer your neighbors are, the safer *you* are.

When Things Get Really Bad—Guard Your Windows

I grew up in a house in Maine that was so old that it dated to the French and Indian Wars. One of the windows still had *Indian Shutters*—an interior piece of wood with a built-in gun slit. In good times, the Indian Shutter was recessed into the wall. In the bad times, you pulled that shutter tight and started shooting out the gun slit. Securing the windows (and doors) against attack saved lives more than once.

We can hope that things don't get that bad for our kids and us. But too many U.S. homes are designed with little thought for safety; there are windows directly beside the front door or close enough that a thief could just smash it and unlock the door. Sliding glass doors that open to patios and backyards are big enough to literally drive a truck through.

So how are you going to secure your windows? Newer homes in hurricane-prone areas are already equipped with nice steel hurricane shutters. You can put them up in a matter of hours—much more quickly than a breakdown in society will take.

If you're going to turn your home into a refuge, seriously consider steel shutters, roll-up shutters, or retractable shutters for your first-floor windows. Alternately, you can get impact resistant windows, a security grille, or retractable security grates.

Once you have your outside secure, it's time to think about the inside.

Hiding Valuables in Your Home—The Pharoah's Treasure

For a second layer of security, make the valuables in your home tough to find, even if someone does manage to get inside. Cash, important papers, gold, and guns—these are all things you want to hide as effectively as possible.

This reminds me of a story that illustrates the difficulty of home security. If you own gold and silver, you'll be able to sympathize with one of the most famous pharaohs in Egyptian history, Ramses III.

Ramses III was a noted collector of treasure. In fact, he may have ended up with the Lost Ark of the Covenant after sacking Jerusalem—Stephen Spielberg borrowed heavily from this legend for the movie *Raiders of the Lost Ark*.

According to the ancient Greek historian Herodotus, Ramses' vast and valuable hoard of gold dwarfed all others. Consequently, he faced a problem that has bothered gold owners to this very day—a problem that may be bothering you: *How do I keep my gold safe?*

Ramses thought he had the answer. He hired two of the most famous architects in the then-known world: the Greek brothers Agamedes and Trophonious.

They'd made quite a name for themselves designing temples and palaces—the kind of places that have a lot of gold to keep safe. And sure enough, the brothers designed an impregnable treasury for Ramses.

When it was done, the treasury was a huge stone building built next door to Ramses' palace (all the better for him to keep his watchful eye on it), and it was considered to be burglarproof.

The walls were thick stone, there were no windows, the door was sealed by the pharaoh's personal seal, *and* the door was manned around the clock by armed guards. Ramses made sure he was there in person every time the seal was broken and the building entered.

So it was especially disturbing for the watchful pharaoh when his treasure started disappearing.

The pharaoh was determined to solve this mystery. He had his personal guard set deadly traps throughout the treasury—traps that were kept secret from everyone else.

The Pharaoh Takes a Head Count

On his next visit, the pharaoh found that, indeed, one of the traps had worked and killed a would-be thief. However, the mystery deepened, as the thief's head was missing! And along with the missing head, the biggest share yet of the pharaoh's treasure had been pilfered.

The thieving stopped, but with no head, the thief couldn't be identified. It took some time for the persistent pharaoh to figure out the truth, but he eventually realized that his two architects had also disappeared.

The body was the corpse of Trophonious. He and Agamedes had designed the treasury walls with one outer stone that could be moved away easily, making a secret entrance. Thus, while guards stood dutifully at the front door, the unscrupulous Agamedes and Trophonius constantly snuck around the back and robbed the *impregnable* treasury.

When the trap caught and killed Trophonius, Agamedes didn't panic. Keeping a cool head (sorry, I couldn't resist the pun), he beheaded his dead brother and took as much gold as he could carry. He then high-tailed it out of Egypt.

Agamedes vanished into legend; he was supposedly swallowed by Earth. Maybe the pharaoh's treasure still remains to be discovered.

Though Ramses solved the mystery, things didn't go well for the pharaoh, either. Soon afterward, Egypt was beset by invaders. With one calamity after another, Ramses found himself chronically short of funds.

Eventually, he couldn't pay his workers, and he got hit with the first known labor strike in recorded history. Oh, if only he'd been able to efficiently safeguard his gold.

And that brings us to the question: What is the best way to store your valuables at home?

Expert Tips to Keep Your Treasure Safe

Let's say there's a crisis that triggers social collapse. Bad guys break into your home and threaten your family in front of you. The cops won't be showing up because they're too busy and overwhelmed, or they've run off. Of course you're going to give the bad guys your valuables. But you don't have to give them *everything*.

The first rule of keeping your treasure safe is *not* to store it all in one place (Ramses really had that one wrong). And there *are* other options . . .

Home safe. Make sure the safe is bolted to the floor, or otherwise secured, and it's much better if it's concealed. If you store valuables in your safe, just remember that it will be the first thing bad guys want to open. There had better be something in the safe, but that something doesn't have to be everything.

Gun safe. For that matter, if you have a gun safe, you can also use it to store other valuables. If big trouble arrives on your doorstep, you might be going for both your guns and your gold at the same time. A concealed or non-obvious gun safe, separate from your regular safe, is best—if bad guys get your guns, your situation goes from bad to worse.

Underneath the silverware. An alternate place to store gold and silver coins is taped or glued to the bottom (or top) of the drawer that holds the silverware. If thieves are using a metal detector, they'll assume that the silverware set it off and not look any further. For the same reason, the back of your tool cabinet can also be a good place to hide your valuables.

Hidden in your car. You might want to keep some precious metals in your car. If you do this, make it a place that you need at least a screwdriver to access. The advantage is that if you're racing to get out of town, you already have some gold in the car.

The disadvantage is that if you're in a car accident severe enough to rip up your car, you might lose your gold, too. Also, remove the gold before you have any work done on the car, or your mechanic could end up with one heck of a tip!

In the insulation of your attic. Most thieves are (1) not looking in the attic, and (2) lazy SOBs who aren't going to go crawling around in fiberglass insulation. If you have a hanging ceiling with removable panels, you can also tape valuables to the opposite (hidden) side of the panels. Just be sure not to put so much weight up there that it comes crashing down.

Secret cache. This is a concealed hiding spot in an ordinary wall, which anyone with even the most rudimentary skills (yes, even you) can construct. It works in typical wood-frame houses with sheetrock walls. Pick a section of wall in an interior bedroom where a mirror wouldn't look out of place. Locate the wiring in the wall. It typically runs through the wall about one foot up from the floor. Do not choose a section of wall with vertical wiring in it.

Use a magnetic stud finder or otherwise locate the studs in the wall. Make small holes to confirm the location of the studs. You also want to avoid sections of walls that contain fire stops, or building materials installed to slow the free passage of flame through concealed spaces.

Buy a vertical mirror that is at least 16 inches wide and three or four feet tall. It works best if you can find a mirror the same width as the distance between the studs in your wall. These mirrors usually come with a set of L-shaped mounting clips that attach to the wall with screws.

Cut a hole in the wall between two to four studs. This hole is your cache. Don't rest anything heavy directly on the wiring. Mount the mirror over the hole. You can access it by twisting the L-mountings, or if you're in a hurry to get out, by smashing the mirror.

What's the point of all this work? A determined burglar will sometimes steal a safe even if it's secured to the floor (hello, Mister Sledgehammer). You not only lose your safe;

The Most Important Rule of Hiding Valuables

There are pros and cons to all of these hiding places. For one thing, the safest way to hide anything valuable is to *not tell anyone where it is.*

As Confucius said: "Three men can keep a secret . . . if two of them are dead."

And yet, supposing you croak next week; after all, along with taxes, death is unavoidable. If you hide your valuables too well, your family may not be able to find them. So be sure to write down the location of your valuables in your will.

your floor is busted up, too. But most thieves who find a mirror attached to a wall won't bother investigating further—they're in too much of a hurry to stick around.

Do You Need a Gun?

You can turn your home into a secure fortress. But if there is a real social breakdown, you also need to think about defending that home.

A wired burglar alarm will summon the police, but in real chaos, the police won't be coming. In this case, you might want to consider arming yourself with one or more guns.

Some people hate guns. Having a gun will increase the chance that someone in your house will get shot through accidental discharge. That said, I sincerely believe in the right of individuals to own reasonable firearms, and I'd recommend a gun for every adult in the house.

Here are some things to consider . . .

You don't need a butt-load of guns. You may want to stock up on ammo if you plan on hunting. Otherwise, you just need enough for hunting and the very brief firefight in which you're (possibly) going to be engaged. The money you *don't* spend on a lot of guns and ammo is money you can spend on other gear and grub.

The time to buy guns and ammo is long past WTSHTF. You have to pass a background check, and ammunition is probably going to become nonexistent when a real crisis hits.

If you buy a gun, I hope you have someone to help you, as I did. Take safety and concealed weapons classes. You'll need ear protectors, safety glasses, a cleaning kit, and *a safe place to store your gun.* A gun is not something you load, stick in your desk drawer, and forget about—especially if you have children in the house.

If you have children in the house, you need some sort of trigger lock. A basic trigger lock came with each of my guns. If you don't like the one that comes with the gun, buy a better one, and use it.

Learn how to clean a gun from the manual or from a friend. You'll have to do that because you're going to be shooting your gun a lot, in practice. Hitting a human-sized target in a vital spot at even a few yards, distance with a handgun is much harder than you think. That goes double when you're in a stressful situation and low light. It takes a lot of practice. If you aren't going to put the time in at the range, then the odds are that you'll be wasting your money by buying a handgun.

For home defense, a shotgun is the better choice. The sound of a shotgun being cocked is one of the most distinctive sounds in the world. And it will scare the pants off of anyone trying to come into your house.

Consider getting a gun safe, even just a small one, for your handguns. Secure the gun safe to the wall or the floor (concealed is even better). I've known people who have been burgled, had their guns *stolen*, and then had those guns used in a crime. That sort of thing weighs on your conscience.

Along with all these factors, here are five things to consider when selecting a handgun:

1. Grip
2. Ease of loading
3. Ease of use (this includes reliability, as well as disassembling for cleaning)
4. Safety
5. Cost of ammo

Hold several guns before buying one. If the grip is metallic, sweat can build up on it as you hold it in a crisis situation. A sweaty gun can slip in your grip when you fire it. However, you can replace a grip easily, so don't let that be a deal breaker.

Try not to think about the gun's color. You *are* thinking about the gun's color, aren't you? Sigh. Really, it doesn't matter. You're not a frickin' commando. A nickel-plated or stainless-steel finish rusts less and is easier to maintain.

Avoid guns with unusual calibers. The ammo will be expensive and perhaps hard to get in a crisis situation. Stick to your run-of-the-mill .38, .357 magnum, 9-millimeter, and even the .45 for you cowboys out there. The less expensive your ammo, the more likely you are to go target shooting and therefore be able to hit your target when it counts. Some people will tell you that a 9-millimeter bullet won't stop a bad guy. It would stop me, that's for damned sure. Another good choice is the .40 S&W (Smith & Wesson), a good compromise for power and accuracy.

Glock pistols have a huge fan base. They have a three-safety internal safety system, hold a high-capacity magazine, and are made of mainly high-grade plastic, which translates into less maintenance.

Another good pistol is the Ruger P90. The difference is that the P90 has both a safety lever and an actual hammer. The Glock has a firing pin and no de-cocker or visible safety lever aside from the trigger catch. In a panic, people have been known to accidentally fire Glocks when their finger slides into the trigger guard. Other pistols with safety levers do not suffer from this problem. And when you chamber a round in a pistol with a de-cocker, you can always uncock the gun for additional safety.

Both guns have advantages. If you're thinking of buying a handgun, you should try one out first. You can often rent a gun at your local shooting range, and I'd recommend that to anyone before buying one. Yes, renting first costs more money than just buying right away, but a gun isn't about saving money—it's about staying safe in a very bad situation.

And if you want a handgun designed for people who occasionally do something really stupid, you can't get more stupid-proof than a double-action revolver. I write this as a satisfied Ruger .357 Magnum revolver owner. I haven't done anything stupid with it yet, and it's a very well-made gun.

Don't fixate on handguns. You may not need one—a .22 rifle will take care of your small-game hunting needs, if you're into that sort of thing. And when it comes to home protection, don't sell your basic 12-gauge pump shotgun short. Nothing says *leave me the hell alone* quite like the *cla-clack* of a round chambering into one of those bad boys. Mossberg and Winchester both make excellent 12-gauge pump-action shotguns, which are relatively inexpensive, especially if purchased used. They are easy to use and hard to screw up. The Remington 870 is also a nice choice, though one dealer told me that Remingtons need more maintenance.

I'm not writing about high-caliber rifles, because this is a book for suburban survivalists. If you miss with a high-caliber rifle, the bullet will potentially continue on to your neighbor's house, punch through his walls, and hit his kids. I would prefer that you stick to a shotgun for use in suburban settings, as shotguns have a shorter range than most rifle cartridges. But you should be aware that even a smoothbore shotgun has a maximum effective range of 100 yards, and a shotgun on full choke can do damage at greater distances.

There is also a misconception about *non-lethal* loads for shotguns, also known as rubber slugs or beanbags. Reality: There is *no* non-lethal load for a shotgun. A rubber slug is *less lethal.*

Guns have their place in the prepared home. That said, your first line of defense should really be the friendships you build with your neighbors. A neighborhood that stands together can ride out any crisis. A neighborhood where it's every man for himself can dissolve into chaos at the first wave of trouble.

Start or Join a Neighborhood Watch

A Neighborhood Watch is good to have anyway, and it will be a real lifesaver if society breaks down. Neighborhood watch members are extra eyes and ears for the police when law enforcement is functioning. If and when a crisis overwhelms the police, a neighborhood watch can channel information between neighbors to keep the bad guys out and the good guys safe.

The police probably will help you set up a neighborhood watch. Be the first on your block to get the ball rolling.

Establish the borders of the watch area at your first meeting. It must be an area that can be effectively watched and maintained. Set guidelines on what to report to the police and others. The police will tell you how best to use 911, and discuss crime trends in your town or city. Some police departments will discuss home security measures and make recommendations. A police officer will probably attend the first few meetings.

Any neighborhood watch needs block captains, so be one. A chairperson will give the program some direction and a rotating chairperson will prevent anyone from letting the power get to his or her head.

The National Sherriff's Association has a Neighborhood Watch manual that you can download at their web site: www.usaonwatch .org/pdfs/WatchManual.pdf.

A Watch Can Become Neighborhood Survival

A neighborhood watch can be one of the first steps to building a survival group out of your family, friends, and neighbors. In fact, your neighbors will probably make the difference between you riding out a crisis at home and you turning into a refugee.

Even the most prepared individual cannot defend his or her home 24 hours a day, seven days a week. Your home is your fortress in a crisis. And you'll make it as strong and survivable as you can. But you may not even need a fortress if your entire street or neighborhood is working together. You are going to need your neighbors, and they are going to need you.

Use the neighborhood watch as an opportunity to put together a list of all residents with their home and e-mail addresses, phone numbers, and *list of skills.* Be sure to note skills that would be useful in a real crisis or even a collapse (doctor, carpenter, plumber, etc.).

You can also do this with an informal meet and greet. I work a lot, so I was terrible about meeting the neighbors, beyond the usual friendly *hellos.* So, my wife and I organized a couple of barbecues—first for our Latino neighbors to the south of our house, and then for the neighbors on the north side of the street. In the first batch, we wound up with a bunch of people from Uruguay and Argentina, their amazing cooking, a pool guy who later saved us hundreds of dollars on fixing our swimming pool, a couple of accountants, and—special bonus—a Homeland Security agent.

In the second batch, we got a sheriff's deputy, a pharmacist, some Haitian immigrants (now *there* are some people with survival skills), a car salesman, his insurance-agent wife, and a programmer for Cisco systems.

These are friendships that will help us find out what's going on in an emergency on the local (sheriff) and national (Homeland Security) levels, advice on medicine in a post-crash situation, and how to survive if things get really bad (Haitians).

You can do the same thing in your neighborhood. Be the leader. Take the initiative to educate your friends on the kind of rough times that we will probably face, and how they can prepare for them. The more your neighbors are prepared, the easier it is for your *lifeboat* to float.

Along with the neighborhood watch, potluck, and barbecue dinners, here are some other activities you can do to educate, prep, and organize your neighbors:

- Start a garden club and get your neighbors going on their gardens. A couple of our neighbors have been inspired by our gardens.
- Learn as much as you can about their skills, backgrounds, and interests.
- Buy useful tools that you can share.
- Organize a neighborhood fishing contest at a local lake or stream.

- If you have a firearm, and some of your neighbors do, too, go to the shooting range together.
- Build a survival library of books and lend them to your neighbors. See what books they have that they would be willing to lend to others in the neighborhood.
- Get them started on food storage. If you have a coupon-obsessed wife who stuns store clerks with her shopping savvy, have her educate the neighbors on how to save money. Everyone wants to save money.

The Volunteer Center of Marin County, California, has a Guide to Organizing Neighborhoods for Preparedness, Response, and Recovery, which you can get FREE on their web site at http://www.preparenow.org/marin-g.html.

And supposing there is no disaster or crisis. Let's say nothing bad happens *ever* and you all live incredibly mundane lives. At the very least, you'll form lasting friendships with your neighbors and

Want to Know How Intruders Will Break Into Your Home? Ask a Fireman!

Firemen are the real experts at breaking and entering—they do it all the time to rescue people who are trapped in burning buildings. Here's an excerpt from *Fire Nuggets* by Eric Guida:

> Forcible entry is an art. On an engine company the art is in accomplishing the job with the tools that are ordinarily carried on an engine. Anybody can grab a circular saw and cut their way into a structure. The true art comes in doing it with just a Halligan and 8-pound flat-head axe.[9]

A *Halligan bar* is like a pry bar on steroids. It's a multipurpose tool for prying, twisting, punching, or striking a way into a door or wall.

Mr. Guida's article is an eye-popping introduction to the forcible breaking and entering that fire departments do all the time when they rescue people from burning homes. You can find his article by pointing your Web browser here: http://tinyurl.com/a2v6ym. You should go see it just for the photos.

So if you're not reinforcing your home because you worry that the fire department won't be able to get you out in an emergency, stop worrying—these guys could bust open Al Capone's vault in a New-York minute.

rebuild the sense of community that so often seems missing from modern American life.

The Next Step—A Water Supply

So far, if you followed the advice in this chapter, you've decided to secure your home and your valuables, and make friendly relations with your neighbors your first line of defense. But turning your home into a fortress won't do you any good if you are forced to leave it.

One of your biggest vulnerabilities will probably be water. Let's say you've already done the smart thing and stored potable water for your family, as well as purchased a water purification system as a backup. You may also want to consider a rainwater catchment system for your roof. Runoff water is saved in barrels, and can be used for irrigation in dry periods (for that spiffy garden you're growing).

My wife got a nifty rain barrel for the cost of a class at the local horticulture society. A hacksaw was all we needed to shorten one of the house gutters to feed into the barrel, and it has a strainer to keep out the large debris and/or lizards. It's just a form of extra protection in case TSHTF.

Now, on to Sanitation

You're drinking all that water, right? And you're eating your stockpile of food? Now, what are you going to do if the plumbing stops working, which is a real possibility in a power-down situation?

If you lose the water supply to your toilet, you can use your wastewater (from cooking or bathing) to flush the toilet once or twice a day (only as needed). Keeping the lid closed between each flush will help avoid odors and germs.

Alternately, in a short-term situation, you can poop and pee into plastic bags. You'd better double-bag to make sure there's no leakage. But that's short-term and it's not comfortable.

A better solution is to designate a five-gallon bucket as a toilet—even better, get a toilet seat that snaps on to a five-gallon bucket. You can buy those for under $20 on the Web (for examples, go to www.survivormall.com, www.cabelas.com, and www.quakekare.com). Acquiring one of these will make your life so much easier in the event of a crisis.

If you don't want to spend money for a specially designed toilet seat, happen to have a spare toilet seat hanging around, and are handy with simple tools, you can build your own composting toilet. You can find an example with excellent instructions at the Appropedia web site.[10] Point your Web browser to http://tinyurl .com/mty3gd.

However you get one, just do it! You'll also need a second five-gallon bucket. This will hold whatever you're going to sprinkle over the waste in the toilet after you use it; sawdust is a good choice. Lime or powdered bleach are other alternatives. If you don't mind spending a little money and you care about the planet, you can use RV-Trine Bacterial Formula (look for it at www.campingworld.com), which eliminates odor and digests waste and paper with good bacteria, and is all natural and biodegradable to boot!

When the sawdust bucket is empty, it's time to empty the waste bucket. You can bury its contents (at least four inches underground) as long as you keep it far enough away from your water source. Or, you can compost it. If sewers aren't working throughout the neighborhood, you'll have to organize the neighbors to compost it (hopefully, you've already talked them into buying bucket toilets). There's a good book that explains how to compost human waste called *The Humanure Handbook*, by John Jenkins. You can find out more about that at www.weblife.org/humanure/default.html or www.jenkinspublishing.com/humanure.html.

Meanwhile, snap the seat onto your second bucket, start using that, and after you have the first one cleaned out, it becomes the sawdust bucket.

If you're a gardening type, you can also collect urine in a separate bottle to use on your plants. I'd recommend using a funnel unless you have dead-shot accuracy. Dilute the urine with 5 to 10 parts water, depending on how concentrated it is, and put it directly on the plants; it's a good source of nitrogen. If you're paranoid or think peeing on your garden is icky, you can put off harvesting from the plants for a week (or until after a rainstorm), but that's probably paranoia. Some darned cat is probably peeing in your garden anyway.

Make sure you have hand-washing facilities in an emergency. Hand sanitizer is okay if water is restricted, but what you want is water and soap. Store soap (if you learn how to make soap, that's a possible post-crash occupation), and teach your family to wash their hands properly every single time.

I think the early chaos waves won't last long enough for you to run out of toilet paper, at least if you store as much of it as we do at our house. If you run out, you can decide which of your books you'll sacrifice to wipe your butt—yet another good reason to have a library. An alternative is reusable (washable) cloth, which may gross you out if you haven't already done the same thing with cloth diapers.

Washing your body is easy enough with water heated over a fire, and you can buy a solar shower at any camping store if you're so inclined. You might want to consider how you would wash laundry by hand. You'll probably wash clothes less if the washing machine isn't working. Consider buying a drying rack for laundry now, because they may be unavailable post-crash.

Electricity: The Real Refuge

So now your home should be secure, and livable because you've taken care of sanitation. You should already have plenty of water and food stored, and you might even have a backup water supply in the works. The next thing you might want to work on is electricity. Electricity is what can turn your home into a real refuge.

And I have news for you: You are probably going to see extended failures of the national grid system.

Since 1990, demand on the nation's electric system has increased by about 25%, according to the U.S. Department of Energy. The nation operates about 10,000 power plants. However, construction of the transmission infrastructure that distributes this electricity has decreased about 30% since 1990.[11]

"Unless substantial amounts of capital are invested over the next several decades . . . service quality will degrade and costs will go up," the Department of Energy says on its web site.

I live in the South; I like solar power. If you live on the wind-swept plains of Oklahoma, you might want to look into wind power. As with most other things in this book, there is no perfect answer. You need to find the answer that works best for you.

Just remember that both solar and wind are intermittent power sources; you might want to consider a backup battery system.

A typical U.S. home uses approximately 13,000 kilowatt hours per year. That can be handled by a five-kilowatt peak (kWp) solar system. This kind of system can run a homeowner $20,000 to $40,000.[12] There are federal tax credits that can help alleviate some of the expense, and check for state solar credits in your area. Solar power systems have a large upfront cost, but they last 30 years or more and pay for themselves in about eight years.

Because it is structured to wean the solar sector off subsidies, rebates are highest in the early years of the plan—in other words, *now*.

When you install solar panels on your home, you're not taking your own home off the electrical grid. On cloudy or overcast days, when your panels aren't generating optimum electricity, you don't have to worry about your lights going dark. Instead, you're converting your home into a hybrid-powered home—one that uses solar energy and then supplements the excess with traditional electricity.

On days you actually overproduce solar electricity, your home becomes a mini power plant, putting electricity back into the grid. That generates a credit on your utility bill. This is why it's important to cut your energy use as much as possible. For more ideas, see the section in this chapter entitled *Cut Home Energy Costs* Before *Crisis Strikes*.

The U.S. Department of Energy (DOE) put out a good introductory guide to solar power for consumers in 2003. It's called

Table 11.1 Wattages of Typical Household Electronics

Device	Typical Wattage	Surge Wattage
Standard light bulb	60	60
Fan	75	150
Small TV	300	400
Washing machine	375	400
Freezer	500	1,000
Electric blanket	400	400
Microwave oven	800	800
Furnace fan	750	1,500
Refrigerator	1,200	2,400
Home computer/monitor/printer	1,500	1,500
Well pump	2,400	3,600
Electric water heater	4,000	4,000
Heat pump	4,700	12,000
Central A/C	6,000	24,000

A Consumer's Guide: Get Your Power from the Sun. It's on the DOE web site at http://tinyurl.com/dfcnd7.

You can also find the DOE's guide to solar hot-water systems, *A Consumer's Guide: Heat Your Water with the Sun,* at http://tinyurl .com/yrjql3.

But you may not want to invest in a five-kWp system if all you plan to do is keep your refrigerator and water heater running and a few lights on, especially if you think your crisis will be short term.

In order to choose the right emergency power source and to size it properly, you need to understand something about the power requirements of the devices you plan to operate.

A normal 60-watt incandescent light bulb is required both for running it and turning it on. But a furnace requires twice its normal wattage to turn on—that's what is called its surge wattage.

If you plan to operate sensitive equipment like TVs and computers from an emergency power supply, you will want to have surge protection equipment in place, or you may blow out the circuits of whatever you're running. For computers, use an uninterruptible power supply (UPS). When a large device like a refrigerator turns on, an ordinary generator will not be able to keep power stable during the surge.

Portable Generators

Generators tend to get very expensive as you move above 5,000 watts.[13] A simple gasoline-powered generator will consume about a gallon of gas every two hours or so at 1,000-watt output. All generator manufacturers rate their generators' fuel consumption based on running with a load that is half the rated capacity. It's a bit misleading, but they all do it. So remember when you're generator shopping that the fuel usage numbers shown below are for half the rated continuous load! You can also purchase generators that run off of diesel fuel or propane.

But there are disadvantages to generators:

1. Maintenance. Generators need to be maintained throughout the year, and if you don't maintain them, they will not work when you need them.
2. Fuel storage. You'll have to keep enough gasoline to see you through (figure 85 to 90 gallons for two weeks).
3. Noise. The cheaper models can be noisy.

Flashlight Tip

Don't just have a flashlight—have multiple flashlights, including one in your bedroom and one in each car. At least one of your flashlights should be waterproof.

More importantly, get rechargeable batteries and a solar battery charger. They cost extra, but they'll be worth their weight in gold if a crisis drags on for a while.

Consider getting a hand-cranked radio that is also a flashlight. Also, if you can get a hand-cranked radio that can recharge a cell phone, even better.

4. Carbon-monoxide danger. Every hurricane season, there are stories of families that ran generators without proper ventilation and the entire family was killed.
5. Storage. Along with storing the fuel, you'll have to store the generator itself.

Another Solution—An Inverter and Deep-Cycle Batteries

An inverter converts 12-volt power (like that found in a car battery) into 120-volt power. Typically, you run an inverter off of your car's battery, and it can produce 200 watts. You can also buy what is called a *deep-cycle* battery.

An inverter is a very easy and inexpensive solution if you can keep your power demands in the 200-watt range. That's enough to run several light bulbs, a radio, and a small TV.

But what about running your refrigerator? Or a space heater? Inverters can run up to 2,500 watts, but the higher you go, the more expensive they get.

Of course, inverters are limited by your car's battery, too. Each battery has a reserve capacity rating. A typical rating is 80 minutes, which means the battery can supply 25 amps at 12 volts for 80 minutes. If you consume 120 watts continuously, that means you are draining about 10 amps from your car's battery continuously. A typical car battery can supply power at that level for perhaps three hours. That's not going to get you very far. You can keep running the car to recharge the battery, though. And you can do that with stored gasoline, just like you would a generator, as long as your gasoline supply lasts.

On the other hand, a deep-cycle battery can supply power at that level for six to eight hours. Then you will need to recharge the battery.

Inverters can be a good option up to about 2,500 watts, although again, they tend to get expensive at that point (a 2,500-watt inverter might cost $600 to $1,000; and then you still need to buy a number of deep-cycle batteries and a charging system).

The Pros of Inverters

- They are silent.
- They are maintenance-free (when you operate them from your car's battery).

The Cons of Inverters

- If you build your own deep-cycle battery bank, then you will have to maintain the batteries.

So, let's say you decide to go with the inverter and the deep-cycle battery. How do you recharge it? Well, you can charge your deep-cycle batteries off of a solar power system, either stationary

---

What You Need to Know About Deep-Cycle Batteries

Deep-cycle batteries are commonly used in golf carts, boats, and recreational vehicles. They're also used in large solar power systems.

Their similarity to car batteries is that both are lead-acid batteries and both operate on the same chemistry principles. However, a car battery is designed to provide a large amount of electrical current over a short period of time. The reason is that it's meant to turn on the car engine during the starting process. A deep-cycle battery is designed to provide a steady amount of current over a long period of time. It's also designed to discharge all its juice over and over again—a deep-cycle battery can withstand several hundred total discharge/recharge cycles. That would ruin a car battery, which isn't designed to discharge completely.

Source: How Stuff Works, What Is The Difference Between a Normal Lead-Acid Car Battery and a Deep Cycle Battery?

or portable. The number of batteries and size of the solar system will depend on your power needs. I think you should plan on reducing your energy footprint right now and even more so during a crisis. How much power will you need? You can find that out with a product called an electricity usage monitor. These are sold on Amazon.com and by some brick-and-mortar retailers.

Use the electricity usage monitor to measure the power requirements of everything you absolutely *must* run. This includes your refrigerator, some lights, and your water heater (unless you already have solar water heating), and maybe a TV or radio, and so on. Add it up and you'll know the size of the system you have to get.

But what if all you want to do is run portable electronics—your electric lamps, flashlights, and so on?

In that case, just consider a solar battery charger. You can buy universal solar battery chargers or even 15–50- and 60-watt solar charging kits on Amazon.com and at some major camping stores. You may also want to buy an amp charge controller (also for sale on Amazon.com).

One thing to remember with any solar power system: The cost of these items means it will be years (maybe more than a decade) before they pay for themselves.

Using the Sun to Stay Warm

For people in northern climes, staying warm in the winter is just as important as keeping the lights on. Woodstoves and pellet stoves are very popular, and I'll get to those in a minute. Solar power can also keep you warm in the winter. There are two basic types of active solar heating systems.[14] They are both based on the type of fluid—either liquid or air—that is heated in the solar energy collectors. (The collector is the device in which a fluid is heated by the sun.) Air-based systems heat air in an *air collector*; liquid-based systems heat water or an antifreeze solution in a *hydronic collector*. Solar liquid collectors are best for homes with central heating. Air-based systems are best for heating individual rooms.

The costs of these solar heating systems can vary wildly, and some states offer sales tax exemptions, income tax credits or deductions, as well as property tax exemptions or deductions for installing solar energy systems.

Heating with Wood

Wood heat, via a wood-burning stove, is another great alternative, especially if you're trying to survive up north in the winter. The choice many people face is whether to get a woodstove or a pellet stove.

I grew up in Maine, back in the day when we didn't have these fancy pellet stoves. Luckily, we could buy cords of wood (from the wood cutters) for cheap, but it still had to be cut to size to use in the house fireplace and woodstoves. So, winter involved a lot of chopping and cutting, and swearing under the breath as we trudged off to the barn through a blizzard (uphill both ways!) for yet another load of wood.

All that chopping and cutting and lugging is why a lot of people switched to pellet stoves—a stove that burns compressed wood or biomass pellets. However, most modern pellet stoves need electricity to feed the hopper; if the power goes out, there's no fire. Oops!

Luckily, you can get a battery backup system for a pellet stove. If you're going to go the pellet stove route, I highly recommend a battery backup. Your local pellet stove supplier should have information on it.

If you live up north, I strongly suggest you install some kind of alternative heating system before the next winter if you don't have one already. If you don't have the money for a woodstove or pellet stove, at least get a portable emergency camp stove. You must keep these properly ventilated, but they're better than nothing and can keep you warm if the lights go off for days on end. Camp stoves usually burn stove Hexamine, Trioxane, or some other solid fuel tablets.

In a severe societal breakdown, you may find it difficult to find material to feed the ever-hungry woodstove or pellet stove. But I'd count on being able to find scrap-wood for a stove long after wood pellets have disappeared, which is another point in favor of woodstoves. You'll need your own ax and access to a wooded lot if and when things get so bad that the woodsman stops making deliveries.

Cut Home Energy Costs *Before* Crisis Strikes

Here are some other ideas on ways you can cut electricity usage in different areas of your home.[15] Every penny you save is more you can put toward buying your survival gear.

Living Room

- One compact fluorescent light bulb (CFL) uses 20% of the energy of an incandescent bulb of similar brightness and can last up to eight times longer.[16] CFLs contain small amounts of mercury (an average four milligrams per each bulb; more in the long fluorescent tubes), so proper disposal is a must. On the plus side, your risk of exposure from a light bulb is minuscule compared to the amount you probably get through eating fish, especially tuna (about one milligram per pound).
- Also, the amount of energy saved by a CFL, thus reducing the amount of coal burned for its use, results in a *negative* mercury value for the environment (there's plenty of mercury in coal, too)—far beyond the four milligrams in the lamp. See also: http://www.energystar.gov/index.cfm?c=cfls .pr_cfls_mercury.
- Another alternative is a light-emitting diode (LED) bulb. LED bulbs can last 100,000 hours—10 times longer than CFLs, and 50 times longer than ordinary bulbs. And LED bulbs don't contain mercury. Good luck finding LED lights at your local hardware store, but you can buy them online at http://www.ledlight.com or similar web sites.
- Many electronics—DVD players, VCRs, TVs, stereos—draw as much as 100 watts an hour even when turned off. Avoid the drain and plug them into a power strip that you turn of when not watching TV.
- Plasma TVs use almost four times the energy of standard TVs. LCD flat panels use somewhat less than plasmas.

Kitchen

- Run the dishwasher only when it is full. You'll save an average of 20 gallons of water per day.
- Grill outside on hot summer days. You'll avoid heating up the house with oven and stovetop cooking.
- Refrigerators account for 14% of electricity bills. Replace any ill-fitting door seals, and don't stand in front of a fridge, with the door open, looking for something to eat.

Laundry Room

- Wash in cold water. 90% of the energy used to wash clothes is used to make hot water. Almost all but the filthiest clothes will be washed equally well in cold water with a cold-water detergent—really.
- Avoid dry cleaners. Try cleaning fragile garments at home with cold-water hand washing.
- Hang clothes outside to dry. Not only will you save roughly 6.5 pounds of greenhouse gases with every load; you're not adding heat to your house in summer.

Bedroom

- Use fans in summer to make the air feel cooler if you set the thermostat higher.
- Close window curtains while you're at work to keep the heat out in the summer or to be a better insulator and keep heat in during the winter.

Bathroom

- Take shorter showers. Every minute you spend in the shower uses four to six gallons of water. So get clean and get out. Try a *Navy Shower*:
  - Turn on the water.
  - Immediately wet the body.
  - Turn off the water.
  - Soap up and scrub.
  - Turn the water back on and rinse off the soap.

    The total time for the water being on is typically under two minutes. A 10-minute shower takes as much as 230 L (60 U.S. gallons) of water, while a Navy shower usually takes as little as three U.S. gallons; one person can save 56,000 L (15,000 U.S. gallons) per year.[17]

    Alternately, use a low-flow showerhead. Normal showerheads use four to six gallons of water per minute. A low-flow showerhead can cut that to less than two.
- A leaky toilet will waste 200 gallons of water every day. And yet it takes only a few minutes to replace a toilet's inner parts.

Toilets account for 40% of a home's water use, or about 9,000 gallons of water per person per year. Cut that by 60% by switching to a high-efficiency toilet.

And if disaster never comes, then at this point, you'll have gotten to know your neighbors, saved some money on electricity, and made your house safer and more energy efficient.

Tools You Should Have (or Have Access to)

If and when TSHTF, the plumber may not answer the phone. Or if your job disappears, you may not be able to afford a plumber. So what tools should you add to your home workshop and/or tool closet?

Let's start with the 12 basic tools that you should already own:

1. **A claw hammer.** Few problems exist that I can't pound into submission. A 16-ounce claw hammer is heavy enough to do the trick, but not so heavy that you'll break something without trying. One choice you'll have to make is whether you prefer a wood or synthetic handle. Wooden handles will break eventually; synthetic handles will last longer, but I've had them bend and then break when I least expected it.
2. **Adjustable pliers.** Problems that can't be beaten into submission can usually be twisted into acquiescence.
3. **Plumber's (pipe) wrench.** That goes double for plumbing problems. Hey, drippy faucet—I've got my eye on you!
4. **Adjustable (crescent) wrench.** When you get sick of stripping nuts and bolts with adjustable pliers, you'll buy a crescent wrench—a wrench with a jaw that moves when you rotate a screw mechanism.
5. **Assorted flat-head and Phillips screwdrivers.** The Phillips screwdriver was invented by a rogue Nazi scientist who wanted to take out his revenge on the world by having us all strip our screws. (Not really—Henry F. Phillips invented the Phillips-head screw in 1936. He was not a Nazi.) Nonetheless, you need Phillips screwdrivers in varying sizes; use the wrong size and you'll—you guessed it—strip the screwhead. Flat-head screwdrivers were good enough for my granddad and they're good enough for me. You'll need an assortment of flat-heads, as well.

6. **Leatherman-type multi-tool.** A collection of tools that is the half-assed solution to any problem under the sun. A multi-tool usually includes needle-nose pliers, which you also might want to buy separately.

7. **Tape measure.** You can get them short or long, but a 25-foot tape measure covers just about any project.

8. **Vise grips/locking pliers.** When you need an extra hand (or want to accidentally pinch your finger for painfully comic effect), vise grips will do the trick.

9. **Utility knife.** Useful on just about every project I've ever done.

10. **Cordless drill.** As long as you have power, you'll find this useful for drilling and screwing.

11. **Handsaw.** A good crosscut saw will probably fill 90% of your needs.

12. **A level.** A good tool to get things hanging straight the first time.

You probably have all of these. Heck, you probably inherited some of these from your dad. But if you're getting prepared for TEOTWAWKI, you might need more. You also might consider buying spares now while they're available—either for your own use later or for trade.

Popular Mechanics came out with a list of "50 Tools Everyone Should Own" in its May 2009 issue. You can read it online at http://www.popularmechanics.com/home_journal/tools/4314786.html.

In addition to the 12 tools I just mentioned here, *Popular Mechanics'* list includes the following:[18]

- Sledgehammer
- Center punch
- Putty knife
- Safety glasses
- Socket wrench set
- Metal file
- Combination square
- Combination wrench
- Bow saw
- Jig saw
- Coping saw
- Hacksaw

- Side-cutting pliers
- Snips (a.k.a. tin snips)
- Round-nose shovel
- Needle-nose pliers
- Drill bits
- Circular saw
- Spray lube (WD-40)
- Dust mask
- Nail set
- Machinist vise
- Allen wrench
- Wood chisel
- Chalk line
- Earmuffs
- Flashlight
- Bow rake
- Volt/ohmmeter
- Cold chisel
- Ball-peen hammer
- Multi-bit screwdriver
- Extension cord
- Gooseneck bar
- Pry bar (flatter and shorter than a gooseneck bar, and often used to remove trim and paneling)
- Square-nosed shovel
- Tongue-and-groove pliers
- Extension ladder
- Pick
- Stepladder
- Rope

Popular Mechanics has a pretty good list. I'll never have the need for both a gooseneck bar and a pry bar, but I guess that's just me. One tool they don't have on their list that I consider an absolute necessity is a rubber mallet. And I'd also make room for an ax.

More Tools You Can Consider

While doing research, I came across a fascinating book called *Handy Farm Devices and How to Make Them* by Rolfe Cobleigh. This is a reprint of a 1909 book, written in a day when farmers expected to work without electricity, which may be eerily similar to the times we'll experience in the semi-near future. The book is full of useful information; old-time farmers invented simple machines that were downright ingenious.

Let me quote from the book's introduction, in a section called "The Farmer's Workshop":[19]

> Some of the tools that will be found useful are the following:
> A rip saw, a crosscut saw, a back saw, and a compass saw; a jack plane, a fore plane and a smoothing plane; a shave or drawing knife; two or three chisels of different sizes for wood-working and a cold chisel for metal; a gouge or two; a good hatchet; two or three hammers, including a tack hammer and a bell-faced claw hammer; a brace or bit stock with a set of a half dozen or more bits of different sizes; one or more gimlets; a mallet; a nail set, a large screw driver and a small one; a gauge; a spirit level, a miter box, a good carpenter's square—No. 100 is a good standard size; compasses or dividers; cut nippers, a pair of small pincers and a pair of large ones; a rasp; a large, flat file; at least one medium sized three-corned file and a half-round file.

While some of the tools mentioned in *Handy Farm Devices* are still common, others are unknown to me. I wonder how many have disappeared into the mists of history and are only sold now as curiosities in antique shops and barn sales. And yet the writers of this book back in 1909 expected any self-respecting farmer to have these tools and more in his workshop. This crystallizes a problem that will likely bedevil the United States in any powered-down future—we don't even have the tools to make what we'll need, never mind the materials.

Here's one more passage from *Handy Farm Devices*:

> It is poor economy to buy cheap tools. Of course extravagance is to be avoided, but be sure that you get first-class material in every tool you buy.

That hardly describes the made-in-China junk we're all buying now, does it? How long will that stuff last, anyway?

Bottom line: In a serious economic crisis, good, high-quality tools may become less available and more expensive. You might want to stock up on them, and start scouting around for tools that will do the job just as well if and when there is no electricity.

The Least You Can Do

- Stop thinking about your home as an investment. Think of it more as a shelter and a refuge from the world.
- Get a strong lock on your front door. Try to make other entrances less accessible to burglars.
- Make sure you have a week's worth of water, and you might want to get extra buckets for sanitation.
- Stock up on:
  - Flashlight with extra batteries
  - Candles and matches
  - Manual can opener
  - Battery-powered radio—even better, get one of those emergency radios that you can recharge by winding
  - Wind-up or battery-powered clock

CHAPTER 12

Education and Entertainment

I have never let my schooling interfere with my education.
—Mark Twain

There are some upsides to a power-down, civilization-changing event. One is that, if you've prepped properly, you're going to have some spare time on your hands. That means you'll have more time for education and entertainment. In this chapter, we'll cover entertainment solutions for your family when there is no more boob tube, as well as how to prepare by incorporating education as entertainment, building a survival library, and using resources on the Web—and why you should access them before the Web goes dark!

Rethinking Home Entertainment

When you say the words *home entertainment,* most people think: television. Personally, I think that come hell or high water, TV is one of the things the government will work hardest to make sure Americans have access to. Why? Because TV is the drug of choice in the United States. The fact that we can watch 200 channels of *American Idol, Sports Center,* sitcoms, and cartoons is what keeps us from getting Hulk-Smash angry over what the villains in Washington and on Wall Street are doing with our money. In a long-term crisis, TV could be an effective way for the government to control an otherwise restless population.

The next time your family sits down to watch TV, pay attention to how you watch it. It's not called the idiot box or boob tube for nothing. A TV set demands we face it and not the others in our family. You may not be aware when people enter or leave the room. Children who talk over the TV are considered annoying and are shushed.

I sometimes think that future archaeologists will be convinced that Americans worshipped at their TVs. After all, TVs are in every house and they usually dominate the prime real estate in the room where the family gathers. TVs are the household gods of the telecommunications age. According to the Nielsen ratings agency, the average American watches over four hours of TV every day. If that person lives to 65 years old, he or she will have spent nine solid years staring at the TV.[1] Few of us are that dedicated in our religious worship.

And since there's more than one American per household, TVs are on *a lot.* Kids watch a large amount of TV. The average child in the United States spends 900 hours a year in school, and 1,023 hours a year watching TV.

The average U.S. household watched TV for eight hours and 18 minutes a day from September 2007 to September 2008.[2] That's a record high since the days Nielsen Co. started measuring television in the 1950s. Heck, that's probably as much or more than most potheads spend stoned every day. So you can see why I call TV the drug of choice for Americans.

And an economic downturn makes us watch more TV. Watching TV is cheap—a lot cheaper than going out and buying more stuff.

If and when TSHTF, especially if it's the end of the world as we know it, you might end up with a lot of time on your hands. If the cable TV goes out, you and your family might have to start talking to each other. For some people, that's going to be terrifying. They don't want to talk to their families; they can barely stand each other as it is.

So you might want to use your time wisely *now* to consider your options. What would you do if you didn't have TV? The broader question: How will your family entertain themselves if our society undergoes serious stress and TV goes buh-bye? After all, if you've followed the recommendations in this book, you've already built up your food stockpile, made your home more secure, arranged for alternative power, and more. You're going to need something to do with your free time.

And you're going to need entertainment. In a real crisis, you don't want to end up pacing your barricaded house like a caged tiger and lashing out angrily at the other people trapped in the house with you.

Here are some ideas to consider:

For Kids

Sports. Break that boob-tube habit now and get yourself off the couch to take the kids outside to toss a ball around. It'll keep everyone in the family healthier and give you something fun to do together. And if you want to prepare for being trapped inside the house, buy some Nerf balls. They won't destroy the furniture (too much), and they're loads of fun.

Reading. I know people who don't have a single book in their homes. The only books their kids read are the ones they must read for school. I think they're going to have bored kids on their hands when the TV goes out.

Even if your kids are already avid readers, you can work on your children's reading skills, add to their library, and you can always trade with neighbors if a crisis keeps you homebound. Used bookstores and library clearance sales are great sources of reading material. Start encouraging more reading now, before the cable TV goes out. Make it a regular habit.

Artwork. It's messy, but our back porch is our kids' art studio. And if the mess of paint freaks you out, colored pencils or crayons and reams of cheap paper are the way to go.

Make Your Own Cheap-Ass Games

Cheap-Ass Games is the name of a real gaming manufacturer, but it's also a description of the kind of games our grandparents used to make back in the days when no one had any money. People on a budget can still play games. Here are two examples:

Game #1: Liar's Dice. The only items you need are five six-sided dice for each player and plastic cups to use as dice tumblers.

(Continued)

(Continued)

The game is simple: Five six-sided dice with traditional dot faces are generally needed per player, with dice cups used for concealment. Poker dice can also be used, but some systems for bidding become difficult or impossible to use.

Each round, the players roll their dice while keeping them concealed from the other players. One player begins bidding, picking a quantity of a face value of two through six. The quantity states the player's opinion on how many of the chosen face have been rolled in total on the table. A *one* (ace) is often wild and counts as the stated face of the current bid; however the game can also be played without wilds. In a five-dice, three-player game with wilds, the lowest bid is *one two* and the highest bid is *fifteen sixes*. In turn, each player has two choices; believe the previous bid is true and make a higher bid, or challenge the previous bid as being wrong. Raising the bid means either increasing the quantity, or the face value, or both, according to the specific bidding rules used. Different bidding rule sets are described below.

If the current player thinks the previous player's bid is wrong, he challenges it, and then all dice are revealed to determine whether the bid was valid. Revealing the same number or more of the relevant face than was bid is a successful bid, in which case the bidder wins. Otherwise, the challenger wins. Simply revealing one's dice generally indicates a challenge, though it is customary to verbally make the challenge, by saying *I call you up, I call, You're a liar,* or simply, *Liar.*

Example: If a bid of *six fives* is challenged, the bid is successful (and the player who made it wins); if there are six or more fives, or less than six fives but enough wild aces (ones) to total six or more fives and aces (four fives and two aces, or five fives and one ace). The bid fails (the bidder is a Liar and the challenger wins) if there are fewer than six total fives and aces combined.

Game #2: The Dictionary Game. This is a game that was played in the Great Depression, and has since turned into a board game called Balderdash. All you need is at least four players, a big, unabridged dictionary, some scraps of paper, and pens.

Everyone sits at a table. You pass the dictionary around. When it's your turn, you look up the most obscure word you can find (a time limit helps here—five minutes, tops). You announce the word to the group and spell it, but *don't* tell them the definition.

Everyone writes down his or her best guess as to what the word means. If you picked the word from the dictionary, you write down the first definition from the dictionary.

Everyone turns in the scraps of paper. You shuffle them with your definition, and then read all the definitions aloud.

For example: Come up with a definition for *Pickelhaube*.

Players then vote on the definition they think is correct. If they guess correctly, they get a point. If no one guesses the correct answer, you get a point for every person in the game.

The correct definition for *Pickelhaube*, by the way, is a spiked helmet worn in the nineteenth and twentieth centuries, initially by the Prussian army and later, by the German military, firefighters, and police force.

This is a game that's more fun the more people you have playing, *and* it's educational.

For the Family

Fishing. You should be practicing your fishing anyway, in case you have to start supplementing your food supply with fish. And kids *love* it!

Orienteering. It's fun for families to find their way through the woods together, and a kid who can read a map and navigate with a compass has a leg up in a post-apocalyptic world. If you're looking for hiking trails near your home, check out http://gorp.away.com/gorp/trailfinder/index.html.

Cooking. Again, if you get the kids involved in this, you'd be amazed how much fun they'll have. Baking is a special kids' favorite, especially if they get to decorate what they make—sugar cookies, for example. Get your kids started cooking with the beans and canned goods you've got in your food stockpile. Then, when a crisis comes, your children will already be more self-sufficient.

And for adults, cooking is a great opportunity to explore some new recipes.

Board games. I should mention that I come from a very competitive family. My wife just thought I was a sometimes-sore loser until she met my parents—my father is a bad loser and worse winner, and the extended family is a rogue's gallery of poor losers. But they still love to play games. We all do—it's just that in my family, there is a lot of yelling, snarling, and gloating to spice up the fun. It's a great way to spend inexpensive time with the children.

If you have some bad sports in your family, consider noncompetitive kids' games like charades or *Apples-to-Apples*. But the real fun is in competitive games, like *Chutes & Ladders* and *Payday* for the younger kids; and *Uno, Yahtzee, Life,* and *Sorry* for the older kids. Many of these can be picked up for cheap when stores have sales on games, usually around the Christmas holiday.

You can find perfectly good games in thrift stores. If you want to know more about a game before buying it, you can find detailed reviews, pictures, and game-session descriptions at www.boardgamegeek.com.

You can also have your kids exercise their artistic talents by making their own board games. There are about a dozen versions of the *Game of Life* and at least four versions of *Risk* that come to mind—there's no reason your kids can't create their own. You can even create your own *Mad Libs* for your kids to fill in, which is bound to provide some amusement.

Music. In Charles Dickens' day, if a family could afford it, every member would learn a musical instrument. Start your kids early and they may even have a marketable skill they can call on later in life. At the very least, they'll learn the benefits of practice and the payoff that comes from sticking with something, and you'll have some music to enjoy when the power is out.

Get Your Neighbors Involved. A couple years ago, feeling culturally isolated, we started poetry readings at our house; we encouraged the kids to write their own poetry and we read them classics. We invited friends, but worried that not many people would show up. It turned out to be hugely popular. Pretty much everyone has some poetry to share. Now, we hold our *Poetry Jams* twice a year.

So remember those neighbors you're making alliances with for your neighborhood watch? In a dragged-out crisis, they're going to be bored silly, too. Invite them over for poetry, or music, or game nights, or something. It will strengthen neighborhood cohesion and deepen your friendships, and replace those nights you now spend watching *American Idol.*

Learn a New Skill. Who says learning has to be boring? We should always be open to learning new skills, and it's so much easier now, when we have the Internet, money, and more travel options than might be available after a social or economic crash.

The entire family can learn skills. *Popular Mechanics* has a great list of "100 Skills Every Man Should Know." You can find it at http://www.popularmechanics.com/home_journal/how_to/4281414.html.

They're all great skills for women to know as well. Carpentry, plumbing, and gardening skills will never go out of style. And if you already know everything, teach your kids how to do stuff. It's some of the best quality time they'll ever spend with you.

There are skills that are going to become more important in any crisis, and especially if it's an energy crisis that leads to a power-down. Growing food, which I've covered a bit in this book, will be very important in any case.

And then there are sewing skills. I'm old enough to remember a grandmother (by marriage) who made her boys' shirts from scratch, and she made them to last. Her sons and grandsons used those shirts more than 20 years later. Most people nowadays, including me, can't even hem pants. That's a skill we're going to have to relearn.

The list of useful skills is very long and it doesn't have to be drudgery. Instead, it can be a craft well learned. An ongoing lifelong education for you and your kids is how people used to entertain themselves in the 1700s and 1800s. It should work in the 2000s and 2100s, as well.

More Education for Kids

As I mentioned earlier, I expect that disaster will come in *chaos waves*—things will be very bad for a while, but then we'll get back to the new normal, whatever that is. This would include schooling for kids. But what if the crisis is bad enough that public schooling stops or is severely restricted? In that case, you'll have to educate your kids on your own.

You're probably already helping your kids with their homework—this is just the next step.

- Concentrate on the Three Rs—Reading, wRiting, and aRithmetic.
- Know what your kids are studying now and pick up study aids and curriculum books for their current level and the *next* level.
- Let your kids pick out their workbooks if possible—they'll enjoy them more.
- Flash cards are a great way to teach basic facts and reinforce important points. Make your own flash cards at home.

There is a lot of information on books you can use at Homeschool Curriculum and Homeschooling Information (http://homeschooling .gomilpitas.com) and Learning Things (http://www.learning things.com).

If schools are closed or severely restricted, and you're looking for a new career in a post-peak world, consider opening up your own school for kids the same age as your kids. I'm talking about the kind of situation where the government has basically given up. That kind of vacuum is just asking for smart people to fill it, and you could be one of those people. You'd give your kids a peer group in tough times, bring in extra income (though what we'll be using for money is another question), and help out other parents who are looking to keep their child educated when things are falling apart.

And what if you pick up study aids and workbooks, and the world doesn't fall apart? You'll still end up with better-educated children and be more involved in their education.

You Can Learn Really Ancient Skills

While you are at it, you could even learn skills that would help you in the Middle Ages. I talked to Chance Lipscomb, an expert in primitive technology who is based in Virginia. He runs conferences where people learn to start fires without matches, how to make arrowheads and spear points, how to tan hides, and more.

"The primitive way is the best way," Chance says. Ancient peoples "spent 10,000 years perfecting their technology. We haven't been working on our technology for a fraction of that time."

Glues made from boiling down animal bones are just as good as anything we have today, Chance says. Obsidian cutting tools are as sharp as any metal knife ever made. And there are bows recovered from ancient sites that are designed just as well as compound bows used by modern man.

Chance doesn't think we'll ever see people go back to flint-making out of necessity again. He points out: "Why go back to flint-making when you have steel?" But he also says one skill from the ancient world that can help you in any rough times to come is that tribes had a strong sense of community. "People shared what they had and helped each other."

Chance recommended The Society of Primitive Technology, at www.primitive.org, for anyone interested in learning ancient skills. There are plenty of videos on YouTube that teach how to make a bow and other primitive skills. And he says that thanks to a surge in interest, conferences like the ones he runs are taking place all around the country. "Ten years ago, there were only a couple hundred people in the U.S. who could make a fire with their hands," Chance says. "Now, there are 20,000 or 30,000 who can do it."

You can find a list of survival and primitive technology schools and courses at einet.net. Point your Web browser to http://tinyurl.com/mt8txs.[3]

Bottom line: In a crisis that lasts more than a day or two, you may be surprised by how bored you get, especially if there's no TV. Plan ahead for activities for your kids and for the whole family. There are plenty of things you can do that are just as cheap as cable TV. Stock up on books and games and put some right in one of your survival pantries. You'll need entertainment as well as peanut butter and canned peaches. And make a commitment to relearning the skills we'll need in a powered-down society.

Trial Run for the End of the World Can Be Your Entertainment Now

Consider putting yourself and your family on a TEOTWAWKI weekend *retreat*. It's the only way you'll find the weaknesses in how prepared you really are. And heck, it can even be fun.

Here's what to do: When you come home from work on Friday evening, shut off your cell phones, unplug your land line, close your main water valve, and turn off your gas main or propane tank. Turn off the circuit breakers for everything but the refrigerator and seal the refrigerator with painter's tape (no cheating, kids!). If you have a backup power system, you can give that a workout and then use your fridge.

The *game* you'll be playing, as you can explain it to your kids, is to spend the weekend in primitive conditions. Practice using only your storage food, preparing it on a camping stove, solar oven, or open fire.

You have probably made some assumptions about how prepared you are, and those assumptions *will* be tested. There will be surprises along the way. Have prizes (awarded on Monday) for family members who come up with the best solutions. It's all the fun of camping *and* you get to sleep in your own bed.

You'll also gain the benefit of a weekend truly unplugged from the world. People pay good money for that,[4] and you get it for free. Your family will have to interact and will probably grow closer, or you will be at each other's throats, and you'll learn that you still have some relationship obstacles to conquer.

As a bonus, all that unplugging will probably save you money.

Making Beer—Real Cheap Home Entertainment for Real Men (and Women)

Making beer is #17 on *Popular Mechanics'* list of "100 Skills Every Man Should Know." If you're going to keep yourself entertained at home, one thing you can start now that's a lot of fun is making beer, or hard cider, or wine. Hard cider is super easy, and beer is easy. And if you are a beer drinker, and you start making your own beer now, you'll save money over what you'd pay for premium beer in the store.

You can buy home-brewing kits. They sell them on Amazon.com for $30 to $120 or more, depending on what you want to do. The kits cut some corners, reducing the time you have to spend in the brewing process. The reviews on Amazon.com are very good.

There probably is a brewing supply store in your local area. Many brewing supply stores sell starter kits for $75 or less. And you can buy books like *Homebrewing for Dummies*.

There are many, many variations on making your own beer. Here's one very simple way. You'll need:

- Five gallons of water.
- One two-and-a-half-pound canned malt extract. Use *pre-hopped* extract; otherwise you're going to have to add hops, too.
- One five-pound bag sugar.
- One package of brewer's yeast (maybe two).
- One large, clean bucket or other container. Cheap-ass brewers will use a large garbage can; I don't endorse that. Garbage-can plastic is light, inexpensive, and prone to scratches that will harbor bacteria that might ruin your beer. Experienced home brewers will use a large bottle-shaped glass container called a carboy. Glass is scratchproof but has an uncanny tendency to slip from your hands and shatter. I recommend food-grade plastic.
- One winemaker's hydrometer for measuring the sugar content of the fermenting beer.
- One plastic siphon hose, about six feet long, about three-eighths of an inch in diameter.
- One bottle capper. If you use twist-offs, you won't need a bottle capper.
- At least 70 bottles and caps to hold the beer. Alternately, you can use two-liter plastic soda pop bottles, as long as they add up to the same volume.
- A bottle filler (optional, but a good idea).

That's all the supplies and ingredients you'll need. Water purity counts for a lot, so use purified (or at least filtered) water. You can purchase hop-flavored malt extract at the supermarket or at any wine- or beer-making supply outlet. Important: You don't want malt; you want malt extract. Likewise, you want brewer's yeast, not baker's yeast.

Cleanliness is incredibly important. You must clean and sanitize all of your equipment right before you start brewing, and keep everything clean throughout the process. Bacteria and fungi are everywhere and if enough of them get into your beer, they will completely ruin it.

Clean all equipment with warm, semi-soapy water. Rinse well to remove soap residue. Then sanitize using household bleach at a quantity of one tablespoon per gallon of water. Or, you can purchase a no-rinse acid sanitizer such as StarSan, which is effective and leaves no aftertaste.

(Continued)

(Continued)
DIRECTIONS

Step 1

- Open the can of malt extract and set it in a saucepan of hot water. This will soften up the extract.
- Heat three gallons of water to boiling. Use a stainless steel or enamel-coated metal pot for this part. Don't use aluminum; it will make the beer taste funny.
- When the malt is nice and warm, pour the syrup into the hot water and mix thoroughly. Cook and stir for 20 minutes. If you don't used pre-hopped malt extract, you'll want to add a handful of hops in a cheesecloth bag at this time and extend your cooking time by another hour.
- Dissolve the sugar in the hot water.
- During the boiling process, a good deal of foam will rise to the surface of your brew pot. This is natural. The key for you is to make sure that the pot doesn't boil over, sending the foam all over your stove. Monitor your heat levels closely and lower them if it begins to boil over.
- As soon as the sugar is dissolved, pour contents into the bucket or container. Pour, or *splash*, the contents quickly, which adds air to the mixture. The more air the yeast gets initially, the better. It allows yeast to rapidly grow and get things going.
- Add the remaining water.
- At this point, you have created *wort*, or malt solution.

Step 2

- Let the wort cool until it's lukewarm. The quicker you can cool it, the better.
- Add the yeast. When the side of your fermentor feels cool to the touch, it is safe to add your yeast. If you're a screw-up like me—the kind of guy who will accidentally kill the yeast—add two packages. That way, the worst thing that will happen is you'll get a nice, vigorous fermentation.
- Cover the container/bucket with a lid or a sheet of plastic, set it in a cool spot where it won't be disturbed, and wait. Don't seal the top too tightly—the container could explode.

Step 3

- Lift the lid once a day and check to see that the wort is actually fermenting—you'll know because there is froth on the top. At the same time, use the hydrometer to check to see that the sugar content is dropping.

Step 4

- When the sugar content of the brew has dropped from 6% to 1% (this can take 4 to 10 days), and there's little to no bubbling action, it's time to bottle your beer. Almost all the original sugar has been converted into alcohol and CO_2. The small bit remaining will allow fermentation to take place inside the bottle.
- Gather your 70 bottles. Wash them well and then sterilize them with heat. Sterilize the caps, too.
- Siphon your brew into the bottles. Be careful not to transfer sediment from the fermentation vessel in the process. Line up all your bottles on the floor underneath it and stick the hose into one of the bottles. Then you're ready to open up the spigot on the bottling bucket and let the beer flow. Stick the hose in all the way to the bottom, and when the beer gets really near the top, yank the hose out and stick it in the next bottle. The level in the bottle drops when you take the tube out, and you want to leave about one inch of airspace at the top of the bottle. Put a little sugar in each bottle; this is for the final carbonation process.
- Cap the bottles, and set them in a dark, cool place for about a week. The longer you let it ferment in the bottle, the better it will probably taste. It's best not to drink your homebrew out of the bottle, because doing so will probably result in you consuming sediment and leftover yeast.

It's my experience that *some* of the bottles will explode. So make sure the place where you put the bottles has a tiled or linoleum floor, or they're all sitting in a big plastic tub. Your refrigerator is too cold—the yeast won't be able to do its work.

Some resources for home brewers include the following web sites: www.byo.com, www.mrgoodbeer.com, and http://brewwiki.com.

Building a Survival Library

When TEOTWAWKI finally hits, you may have a lot of time on your hands. Our forefathers worked hard, long hours, but they still had plenty of time to read, write long letters, argue about politics, learn to play the fiddle, and so on. You don't know how much time TV steals from you every day. But you may get the chance to find out when the boob tube goes buh-bye.

Before that happens, I recommend you start stocking up your personal library. We have a designated library room in our house, but yours doesn't have to be that big. It's just a place or even a space where you put the books you're going to read when you have time.

Popular novels are always good (I'm a huge Stephen King fan). But you should also build a library of useful books that will help you survive in crisis situations or in a powered-down world. It's important to realize that we may be going into a situation where the Internet won't work for weeks, or ever again. You'll need hard copy, paper books. If there are interesting articles you've found on the Web, consider printing them out. They may not always be available to you.

Books

I don't know if we're facing a worst-case scenario societal collapse in our lifetimes. But I think you should build a library as if that is the case. You'll need books that are useful to you now, to your kids 10 to 20 years from now, and for their children and their children's children.

You might start by stockpiling old textbooks, which can be found dirt-cheap at used bookstores, on useful subjects like chemistry and math. Beyond that, here are some other *get-you-started* ideas:

- *The New Way Things Work* by David Macaulay. This brilliantly conceived guide to the principles and workings of hundreds of machines takes you from levers to lasers and does it all in a fascinating way. It's great for kids and the young at heart.
- *Collapse: How Societies Choose to Fail or Survive* by Jared Diamond. This covers how societies have fallen prey to pollution, drought, famine, social collapse, war, and disease over hundreds and thousands of years of human history.

- *Life After Doomsday* by Bruce Clayton. This book shows you how to survive a post-nuclear scenario. It offers a thorough investigation of survival strategies and of the problems that will face those who survive. The author outlines step-by-step procedures for preparing and defending shelters, storing food, and treating illnesses and injuries. It has a great *flow chart* where you can answer questions depending on what you're most concerned about, and it then tells you how to best prepare.

- *Tappan On Survival* by Mel Tappan. The Amazon.com write-up explains this book pretty well: "Mel Tappan was the godfather of the modern preparedness movement, and this classic collection of his writings is an indispensable resource for information on how to develop a survival mind-set, identify the best survival locations, store food, maintain communications, select firearms, and much more."

- *U.S. Air Force Survival Handbook.* This one is so good, it's recommended by members of other services. Basically, the book details everything you need to know to survive under any conditions.

- *The Merck Manual 19th Edition* (or any edition) by Mark H. Beers. Affectionately known as *the hypochondriac's bible*, this is the single-volume how-to manual for doctors. In fact, it's written for doctors, so you need a fair knowledge of medical terminology, and experience/training in medicine, veterinary medicine, or nursing to fully comprehend its contents. The book mainly tells you how to diagnose and what to prescribe for most conditions.

- *Advanced First Aid Afloat* by Peter F. Eastman, M.D. This book tells you how to handle emergency medical care at sea, and it covers much more serious crises than typical first-aid books.

- *How To Be Your Own Doctor* by Carl Shrader. This book offers excellent advice for injuries and illness that will allow individuals to self-triage their problems (that is, figure out if they need to go to the hospital or not). It also offers pointers on how to save money on prescriptions.

- *Field Guide of Appropriate Technology* by Barrett Hazeltine. A handbook for non-technical people on how to provide water systems, food sources, medical supplies, and more in third-world countries (in other words, where the United States may be heading). The book includes step-by-step instructions and illustrations showing how to build and maintain a vast array of appropriate technology systems and devices.

- *The Encyclopedia of Country Living: An Old Fashioned Recipe Book* by Carla Emery. This is the classic for learning a self-sufficient lifestyle. Tips, recipes, folk wisdom, and plenty of hard facts are provided.
- *Forgotten Arts and Crafts* by John Seymour. I hope we don't have to reinvent the wheel after TEOTWAWKI, but if we do, I want this book at my side. Mr. Seymour has rediscovered natural ways of making tools, shoes, furniture, and many other items. He doesn't go into detail but rather gives the basic facts. It's a good place to start if you're doing research for what you might do in a post-everything world.
- *Hand Dug Wells and Their Construction* by Simon Watt and W.E. Wood. Do you have a big rainwater tank? If not, you might need a well. And if you need a well, this book could be the difference between life and death.
- *Gaia's Garden: A Guide to Home-Scale Permaculture* by Toby Hemenway. A good start for anyone thinking of using a sustainable way of landscaping inspired by natural ecosystems. Hemenway seems to have experience with semi-arid and shady gardens; you'll need more advice if your problems are too much water and too much sun. But still, it's a good read, and it will start you asking the right questions.
- *The Backyard Homestead* by Carleen Madigan. This covers everything you need to put your backyard to work growing vegetables and fruits, and it even covers animal husbandry—chickens, goats, pigs and cows.
- *The Urban Homestead: Your Guide to Self-Sufficient Living in the Heart of the City* by Kelly Coyne and Erik Knutzen. This covers everything from growing food on your patio to diverting grey water to your garden.
- *Seed to Seed: Seed Saving and Growing Techniques for Vegetable Gardeners* by Suzanne Ashworth and Ken Whealy. This is a detailed, complete seed-saving guide that describes specific techniques for saving the seeds of 160 different vegetables, as well as when and how you should plant them depending on what region you live in.

- *The New Seed Starter's Handbook* by Nancy Bubel. A great book for learning how to grow plants from seed, including proper seed-starting mediums, lighting, fertilizing, transplanting, and more.
- *Root Cellaring: Natural Cold Storage of Fruits & Vegetables* by Mike Bubel and Nancy Bubel. This is a practical guide to using the earth's naturally cool, stable temperature to store perishable fruits and vegetables.
- *Gardening When It Counts: Growing Food in Hard Times* by Steve Solomon. This book is a good, solid introduction to vegetable gardening. It lays it out for you and tells you how to grow enough food on the cheap to cut your food bill in half.
- *The Drinking Water Book: How to Eliminate Harmful Toxins from Your Water* by Colin Ingram. Ideas for reducing pollutants in the home water supply without spending a lot of money. The author discusses virtually all the possible alternatives, from purchasing bottled water to using a home treatment system. Ingram outlines various water purification systems with details of how each one works and the advantages and disadvantages of each.
- *Basic Butchering of Livestock & Game* by John J. Mettler. This is a very detailed how-to book, written by a veterinarian, on how to butcher animals, as well as some ideas for preserving meats. Butchering is not a pleasant business, but it may be one that's in demand in a powered-down future.
- *The Self-Sufficient Life and How to Live It* by John Seymour. This book covers skills useful in an unplugged world, such as raising crops, keeping livestock, preserving foodstuffs, making beer and wine, basketry, carpentry, weaving, and more.
- *Old-Time Farm and Garden Devices and How to Make Them* by Rolfe Cobleigh. This book includes handy tips for building everything from a cheese press to a hog house, and even a bicycle-powered washing machine.
- *The Humanure Handbook: A Guide to Composting Human Manure* by Joseph Jenkins. If the plumbing goes out, are you going to let your town drown in its own excrement, or are you going to step up and propose a solution? This book tells you how to go about it.

Resources on the Web

There is enough useful information about preparation, self-sufficiency, and survivalism on the Web to fill several libraries. You might want to check out the following sites before they're gone:

- **e-Commerce for the Third World:** You can find the mother lode of self-sufficiency and sustainability at http://www .cd3wd.com/CD3WD_40/CD3WD/index.htm or http://www .cd3wd.com/INDEX.HTM.
- **National Center for Home Food Preservation:** The USDA has a great free guide to canning that you can find online at http:// www.uga.edu/nchfp/publications/publications_usda.html.
- **USDA National Agricultural Library:** Along with that, you can check out the National Agricultural Library at http://www .ars.usda.gov/services/docs.htm?docid=1423.
- **USDA Cooperative Extension Systems Offices:** One more USDA site—The Cooperative Extension Service, with state-by-state listings, with invaluable information on animals, crops, construction, food preparation, and much more for free download. You can find it at http://www.csrees.usda.gov/ Extension/index.html.
- **A Guide to Organizing Neighborhoods for Preparedness, Response, and Recovery:** The Volunteer Center of Marin County, California, offers this guide free on their web site. Visit http://www.preparenow.org/marin-g.html.
- **Hesperian:** The entire text of *Where There Is No Doctor* and *Where There Is No Dentist* are both available for free online. They're part of Hesperian.org's free online library (I don't know how they worked out the copyright) at http://www .hesperian.org/publications_download.php.
- **First Aid in Armed Conflicts and Other Situations of Violence:** The International Red Cross offers this free download at http://www.icrc.org/Web/Eng/siteeng0.nsf/htmlall/p0870.
- **GlobalSecurity.org:** This web site offers many free download-able documents regarding security—from the U.S. Army, Navy, Marine Corps, Air Force, and international bodies. Check out their *White Papers* section, plus a lot more. Go to http://www.globalsecurity.org/index.html.

- **The Oil Drum: Campfire:** This site was spun off the peak oil web site, The Oil Drum, and is for people concerned with surviving what comes next after TEOTWAWKI. Check it out at http://campfire.theoildrum.com.
- **Journey to Forever:** Lots of free information for those who want a more self-sustained lifestyle is available at http://journeytoforever.org/index.html.
- **HowStuffWorks:** This site is so much fun, and so educational. Made for boys from 8 to 80. Go to http://www.howstuffworks .com.
- **Paladin Press:** Supplier of books that are of interest to survivalists. They also have books on surviving a street fight, throwing knife techniques, and more military knowledge than Uncle Sam is probably comfortable with you knowing. Be careful what you order from them, as it's likely that the National Security Agency is watching these guys like hawks. Check it out at http://www.paladin-press.com.
- **Thedisease.net:** This site provides free downloadable documents on combat, medicine, survival training, ammunition, explosives (including improvised explosives), and more. The same warning goes here—start downloading documents on how to blow things up and it's likely you'll be scrutinized by Uncle Sam. If you're up for taking the risk, go to http://thedisease.net.

There are also some great libraries of books on the Web, and most of them are—you guessed it—free.

- **Project Gutenberg:** This is a good place to download eBooks before the Web goes away. Go to http://www.gutenberg.org/wiki/Main_Page.
- **Smithsonian Institution Libraries:** The Smithsonian digitized many older books, maps, and documents in their collection. Check it out at http://www.sil.si.edu.
- **Digital Book Index:** This is more direct than a Google search. It accesses more than 100,000 free books, indexes collections specifically, and won't throw out red herrings. The index is available at http://www.digitalbookindex.org/search001a.htm.

- **2020ok:** This is another directory of free online books and free eBooks, found at http://2020ok.com.
- **LearnOutLoud.com:** A great free resource for home schoolers—this is the Internet's largest directory of free audio and video learning resources. It is maintained by LearnOutLoud .com, and can be accessed at http://www.learnoutloud .com/Free-Audio-Video.

These sites are great to visit, but what if a crisis happens? What if the Web isn't always there?

Get Your Downloads Before the Internet Goes Dark

There are three solid reasons why Internet usage will probably be spotty at best in years to come, and that's before we get to extraordinary events.

1. **The Internet uses an insane amount of power.** If we're headed into a global, long-term energy crisis, the Internet could run into an energy crisis of its own. The power plants that keep the server farms of the Internet alive don't run on gasoline, but they do use a lot of power.[5]

    For example, the two big server farms that keep Yahoo!'s group of Web services online use more electricity between them than all the televisions on Earth put together. Some estimates put Internet electricity demand at 9.4% of U.S. energy usage and 5.3% of global electricity usage.

    And then there's the coal, which generates 49% of electricity used in the United States. If we start to experience severe consequences of global warming, we'll probably see stronger opposition to new coal-fired power plants, even as the nation's energy demands go higher. That will make existing coal-fired electrical power more expensive.

    The Internet exists because of cheap, easily available energy. When energy becomes scarce and expensive, big parts of the Internet may become unaffordable, and could go dark.

2. **Another problem, which may happen concurrently with parts of the Internet going dark, is that other parts of the Internet will likely no longer be free.** If providers have to choose between providing free content with an advertising model

that works only for the largest, most popular sites and a small base of paying subscribers who will help them keep the lights on, more and more web sites will probably become subscription-access only.

3. **We may see the actual physical connections of the Internet disappear.** The metal wires that carry the Internet are going to become very valuable and probably prohibitively expensive to replace if thieving becomes rampant. In other countries that have collapsed—parts of Africa come to mind—thieves have stolen literally every piece of copper wiring they can get their hands on, to be melted down and sold for scrap. If the United States goes into a severe Depression, copper thieving could become rampant. Satellite links will keep things functioning for a while, but they won't be cheap to maintain.

These are just a few common problems that could darken vast swaths of the Internet. Then we have the uncommon problems. I can think of several scenarios—a terrorist Electro-Magnetic pulse bomb, destruction of orbital satellites, or a power-down scenario that would either block your access to the Internet or destroy the World Wide Web itself.

On the plus side, we could see a concerted effort to stop computer spam. According to Microsoft, 97% of all e-mail sent on the Internet is spam.[6] If governments and gatekeepers made a serious effort to stop spam, that would lighten the electricity load for the Internet and the planet.

What to Do? Download Your Information While It's Available and Free

You can download information to your computer, and in effect build your own electronic library. Tons of information can be stored, digitally, on your computer, and I suggest you do so quickly. But even then it isn't safe—the computer could crash or otherwise be destroyed. So you have three other options:

1. **Store information on a DVD.** This is the super-cheap option. You can burn multiple copies of information on a DVD, and build swap libraries of information with friends.
2. **Store information on a memory stick, or USB flash drive, also known as a** *travel drive* **or** *thumb drive.* The price of

memory sticks has plummeted in the past couple of years. They're generally sturdier than DVDs, and when you plug them in to your computer, they function like any hard drive. This book you're holding was written on a 4-GB memory stick I swapped between my work and home computers. The cheapest memory sticks hold 2 GB of information, but watch for sales on 4- and 8-GB flash drives.

3. **Store information on a portable hard drive.** This is like a memory stick, but it is larger and stores a lot more information (ours holds 500 GB).

You should already be backing up your important computer information *at least* monthly. Having that information on a memory stick in your bug-out bag is a smart move; you'll have access to your electronic info as soon as you can find a working computer.

The Least You Can Do

- Gather some books you want to read and games you want to play.
- If you have kids, especially, get some things to entertain them, including art materials.
- Back up important files on your computer using DVDs, a memory stick, or a portable hard drive.

PART

V

TRANSPORTATION AND EVACUATION

CHAPTER 13

Transportation

When hope hardly seems worth having, just mount a bicycle and go out for a spin down the road, without thought on anything but the ride you are taking.

—Arthur Conan Doyle

Imagine dealing with getting to work, buying groceries, and getting the kids to school if there's no gasoline or severe rationing. This chapter will explain what you can do to prepare.

The topics we'll cover include five ways to ease your dependence on oil; whether a motorcycle is right for you; how to get around without gasoline; how to find the right bicycle for you; seven tips for staying alive on a bicycle; and how to safely store gasoline for emergencies.

How Vulnerable Are You?

According to recent Energy Information Administration Data,[1] Americans each use around 1.2 gallons of gasoline per person per day, or 441 gallons per year.

So what would you do if your 441 gallons was cut by a third, or cut in half, or cut off? How about if there was a shortage of heating oil, jet fuel, or the diesel that powers the truck that brings food to your local grocer?

The smart thing to do is to get ahead of the curve by making changes in your lifestyle to use less gasoline now. If there is rationing, or just intermittent shortages, you'll have an advantage if you already are used to using less gasoline than other people.

One of the first promises that any U.S. presidential candidate trots out is to make the United States energy independent. This is a promise that will never be kept in a nation that functions as it does today. The United States imports 65% of the oil we use, up from 37% at the start of the Arab Oil Embargo in the 1970s.[2] The United States is becoming *more* dependent on foreign oil, not less.

Any number of crises—war in the Middle East, an embargo by oil-rich nations, pirate attacks on tankers, international terrorism— can interrupt that supply. Some potential sparks for an energy spike include the following:

- Mexico is our number-two supplier of imported oil.[3] Mexico seems to be teetering dangerously on the edge of chaos. Worsening Mexico's problems, its oil production is falling off a cliff—down 7.8% in the first quarter of 2009 (to 2.67 million barrels per day).[4]
- A disruption at a refinery, transmission hub, or pipeline could break the flow of oil and gasoline to millions of Americans, sending prices at the pump spiking.
- A bad hurricane could take out much of the United States' refining capacity in one swoop. In 2005, Hurricane Katrina slammed into the oil facilities along the Gulf of Mexico. As a result, 11 petroleum refineries were shut down, representing 2.5 million barrels per day or 15% of U.S. refining capacity.
- Severe winter storms are enough to disrupt the *just-in-time* flow of gasoline and heating oil across the country. Add in other natural disasters, the disruption we could see from a pandemic or economic meltdown, and you can see that there are plenty of things that could put your gas gauge on *E*.

I expect most fuel interruptions in the near future to be short term. The deeper threat is a long-term fuel disruption, due to a currency collapse, global financial collapse, or problem with our foreign oil suppliers.

A deeper emergency will probably be dealt with using rationing. Or we could have a cascade of long-and-short-term emergencies—for example, a currency collapse compounded by a pandemic spiked with an oil embargo—which could frazzle and snap the thinly stretched oil and gas supply lines that stretch across the country. These crises could leave you without gasoline for days or weeks, only to see it come back again when a semblance of normalcy is restored.

So I think you should expect that you'll be unable to buy gasoline for at least some short periods in the years ahead, and maybe sooner than you think. The question you should ask yourself is: "How stranded are you going to be?"

How well could you get by without a car? A web site called WalkScore (www.walkscore.com) is a great place to get a sense of how car-dependent you are now. Just type in your home address, and it will give you a map showing distances to grocery stores, restaurants, schools, libraries, drug stores, hardware stores, and more.

If you're a renter, you can use this kind of map to find a home in a place that will allow you to be less car-dependent. If you own your home, and you aren't moving anytime soon, you can use it to plan how you might get around in an oil-starved future.

One thing you might not be able to change easily is your job. And yet for most Americans, we spend more gasoline getting back and forth to work than any other kind of activity.

Five Ways to Ease Your Dependence on Oil

Here are five things you can do *right now* that will lessen your dependence on gasoline. The best part is that any one of these ideas will also save you money.

1. **Telecommute.** These are the facts: Nearly half of all commuters travel more than 20 miles round-trip to and from work; 22% travel more than 40 miles; and 10% travel more than 60 miles.

   According to a report by the American Electronics Association, an estimated 1.35 billion gallons of gasoline could be conserved annually if every U.S. worker with the ability to telecommute did so 1.6 days per week (in other words, some people work at home one day a week; some work in their bathrobes two days per week).

   Your boss may not agree to let you telecommute. In that case, see if he or she will let you adjust your hours to come in and leave 30 minutes later or earlier, so you can avoid rush hour. Traffic congestion cuts your fuel efficiency by 10% to 15%. According to the U.S. Department of Transportation, in 2003, drivers in the 85 most congested urban areas in the United States experienced 3.7 billion hours of travel delay, and as a result, they burned 2.3 billion gallons of wasted fuel.

The U.S. Department of Energy projects that the number of telecommuters will reach 29.1 million by 2010, or about 27.4% of the U.S. workforce. That alone should help save over 79 million gallons of gasoline. And if your job is something you could do from home, at least some of the time, there's no reason you shouldn't be one of the telecommuters. It makes you more efficient, it gives you an automatic raise, and the less we drive, the less of a stranglehold the Saudis have over us.

So if your boss is the flag-waving sort, it won't hurt to mention that it's our patriotic duty to make the United States as energy independent *as possible*. As I said, complete energy independence is not possible in a United States that you would recognize.

The disadvantage to telecommuting is that if you can work from home, it's hard to separate work time and home time. Work can bleed into and take over your off-hours.

2. **Use a remote office center.** Your boss might not want everyone in the company to telecommute for a good reason: You work with a bunch of goof-offs who'll spend their days surfing YouTube and Facebook and not getting the job done if they are home alone.

But you can still save a drive to work if a bunch of your coworkers live in the same area. You can all go to a satellite office or remote office center. These are usually cheap offices in an industrial location—maybe not the prettiest place to work, but it beats the heck out of an hour-long commute.

A remote office can also be a safeguard for important company data if it is combined with a backup computer network.

3. **Move closer to work.** This can be worth it for people who live far from the office. You save so much time on the commute that it's like you get a whole new life. But is it worth it for you?

The excellent web site Political Calculations has an online calculator that makes the decision easier. It takes into account variables including the amount of your current rent or mortgage versus your new rent or mortgage, vehicle mileage, distance of your commute, and more. You can find this calculator at http://tinyurl.com/3jgnod.

4. **Buy a more fuel-efficient car.** This can be another expensive decision, though not as expensive as moving. Luckily, there's a Political Calculations calculator for this, too, at http://tinyurl .com/2gweq9.

5. **Slow down!** Most gasoline-powered vehicles in the United States are operated at speeds that aren't at their peak level of fuel efficiency. At highway speeds, for instance, the forces of aerodynamic drag can substantially increase the amount of fuel an automobile engine burns. (See Figure 13.1.)

   If you're a habitual speeder, slowing down to 55 miles per hour (mph) could increase your fuel efficiency anywhere from 7% to 21%. For every mile per hour faster than 55 mph you go, fuel economy drops by about 1%.

   Fueleconomy.gov reports that you can assume each five mph you drive over 60 mph is like paying an additional 24 cents per gallon for gas.[5]

   According to PoliticalCalculations.com, a quick back-of-the-envelope calculation reveals that the amount of drag force seen by a car being driven at 75 mph is some 33% higher than that of the same car being driven at 65 mph.

   Find out how much you can save by slowing down—use the online calculator at http://tinyurl.com/6m7qb6. Other simple

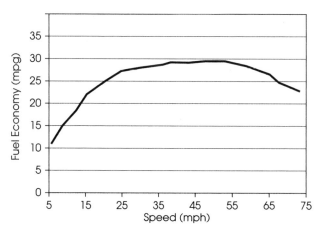

Figure 13.1 Slow Down to Save Gas
Source: Fueleconomy.gov.

ways to save gas include using cruise control on the highway, removing excess weight from your car, and fully inflating your tires (this can boost your mileage by up to 3.3%). And when it comes time to buy new tires, try low-rolling resistance tires like those used on the Toyota Prius. An individual vehicle could save up to 6% of its gasoline use if it were fitted with very efficient tires, paying for the additional cost in about one year.[6]

Here is a link to 11 ways to improve your gas mileage in your car at Bankrate.com: http://tinyurl.com/35np86. Along with these tips, you can also check gas prices at sites like GasPriceWatch.com (http://tinyurl.com/33mqx6). Just enter your zip code and compare. However, don't drive out of your way to get cheap gas—you'll burn more gas on the detour than you'll save at the pump.

Plan on Alternate Transportation

If there is an energy crisis, you're more than likely going to have to change how you get around. If you start now, you'll be way ahead of the game, and certainly far ahead of the *sheeple* who are driving around, oblivious to how thin a thread their current lifestyle depends on.

Use Public Transportation

This is a winner in many ways—cost, convenience (leave the driving to someone else), and environmental impact. The downsides are time (having to wait for a bus) and the fact that public transport is becoming more popular. Subways, trains, and buses are becoming very crowded in some urban areas, even as budgets are being cut due to falling state and municipal revenues.

If public transport isn't conveniently located for you, consider car-pooling or van pooling with coworkers who live in the same area. This also gives you an excuse to leave work when the boss wants you to work late. ("Sorry, boss, my ride is waiting—hey, wouldn't telecommuting solve this problem?")

Downsize to a Motorcycle, Scooter, or Moped

It used to be that only kids and crazies would ride a moped around town. But an increasing number of people are using scooters and small-cc motorcycles to zip back and forth to work.

The difference between motorcycles, scooters, and mopeds is engine size. Mopeds are typically restricted to an engine displacement of 50 cc, though there are a few variations. Scooters are all over the map. Engine displacements range from under 50 cc to over 800 cc. Basically, scooters are a mid-size between mopeds and motorcycles. And motorcycles generally have engines of 250 cc or more—sometimes much more.

Most states set the maximum attainable speed for scooters used by riders *without motorcycle licenses* at 30 mph. In a post-crash future, those laws will probably go away or be widely ignored, but in such a future, scooters and motorcycles could also become much harder to get.

One thing to consider: The smaller your ride, the harder it is for automobile and truck drivers to see you. Be prepared to drive defensively.

Now for the big plus—the gas savings can be *huge!* But only if your motorcycle is a small-engined, miserly gas sipper. On the other hand, some owners of large, fast motorcycles say they don't save a whole lot of money over a car, thanks to big expenses on tires and engine maintenance like valve adjustments.

Keep Your Motorcycle a Cheap Ride.   People who ride 'em tell me that a Japanese bike in the 500- to 750-cc range is the best combination of speed, comfort, and being easy on the wallet. Not only are these bikes cheap, but they also tend to be dependable, and easy to maintain.

Here are a few tips that will keep a motorcycle as cheap as possible:

- Don't buy a big motorcycle for commuting. Unless you're doing high speeds on the Interstate, you don't need a big bike. A big motorcycle won't get much better mileage than an economical car.
- Buy a used motorcycle. People who own motorcycles are often trading up—that means a lot of used, well-loved motorcycles are on the second-hand market. You'll have to add in the cost of having the bike checked out and tuned up by a mechanic, but it will probably still be a lot cheaper.
- Don't buy a motorcycle with lots of plastic bodywork. It's very expensive to replace.
- Learn to do routine maintenance like oil changes yourself.

You might not need a motorcycle at all; a scooter might fill your needs. A growing section of Americans agree with this. In fact, 78,000 scooters were sold in 2008, up from 13,000 sold in 2000.

Large European motorcycles tend to require more maintenance (ka-ching!). If you do it right, the priciest regular expense on a motorcycle should be your tires. They wear out quickly, and you'll be surprised how much the good ones cost.

If you're worried about stability, you might consider the Piaggio MP3—a tilting three-wheel scooter that can be brought to a stop and parked like a car. I don't know what the repair bills on a fancy import would be, though.

Anyone riding a motorcycle, scooter, or moped should take a safety course and wear a helmet.

Storing Gasoline

Hopefully, gasoline shortages will be temporary and some semblance of normality will return. Still, if we start to experience on-and-off fuel shortages, you may be tempted to store gasoline at home.

If you're *not* the kind of complete idiot who could accidentally blow him- or herself up with a can of gasoline, get some jerry cans— cans specifically designed to store gasoline. You could fill them up right away, but I'm of the mind that you shouldn't fill them up yet. After all, a real fuel crisis could be years away. Instead, I would recommend only filling them when you hear about local fuel shortages or a worsening crisis. When shortages start, there should still be time for you to get out and fill up.

Storage could be a problem. You can't put jerry cans of gasoline in a storage facility, or an apartment, or any space without ventilation. You can't store them in your car, unless you have a death wish. Cans full of gasoline are portable bombs, for Pete's sake. Keep that in mind.

Gasoline does degrade with time; it won't last longer than a season unless you're using a *fuel stabilizer* like STA-BIL, which is another reason not to buy gasoline until you hear a shortage is starting. When gasoline goes bad it has a very distinctive *skunky* odor. Skunky gas can gum up your car's fuel system. So if a shortage has been resolved quickly or didn't get too serious, use up that gas soon. You can always refill your reserve with fresh gas.

Gasoline stabilizers can preserve gasoline for up to a couple of years. You should only add stabilizer to an empty jerry can. Measure out enough to treat a can of gas; pour it in the can; and then fill the can with gas to about 95% capacity. That minimizes the possibility of condensation and still leaves a bit of room for expansion and contraction.

Important: Liquid fuels should *never* be stored in a typical attached garage. Along with the usual danger of evaporated fuel hanging around in an enclosed space, many suburban garages also have a natural gas-fired or propane-fired hot water heater with a continuous pilot flame. That is a very dangerous combination of a vapor source and vapor ignition.

If you fill the cans when a fuel crisis starts, and store them safely, you'll have the option of leaving when other people in town are stuck *and* hungry.

Getting Around without Gasoline

All the transportation tips so far still center around the internal combustion engine. That's good as far as it goes, but there are other options. The world is undergoing a transportation revolution with electric vehicles, and a low-tech solution—the bicycle—is an excellent choice for many people.

Electric Cars

I think the days of powering passenger cars with gasoline are in their twilight stage. That doesn't mean they're going away this year, or next year, or even in 10 years. However, while you may not drive an electric car, your kids probably will.

Toyota is now testing an electric car that plugs into an ordinary home outlet. GM is working on its Volt concept car for 2010, and Nissan plans to introduce an all-electric vehicle for fleet customers in 2010. A company you may not have heard of, called Think, will bring its electric vehicle to the United States by 2010. A Think model called *City* reaches a top speed of 65 miles per hour and can drive up to 110 miles on a single charge. Think has a strategic partnership with energy giant General Electric, who is also an investor in Think, and the company has established partnerships in the United States with battery suppliers A123 and EnerDel.

These are just some examples of how automakers around the world are turning to electric cars in a hurry.

It makes sense. After all . . .

- There are electric/gas hybrid cars in development right now that get over 100 miles per gallon.
- Recharging your car at home would cost you the equivalent of 50 cents per gallon at today's prices.
- Our national electricity grid, as decrepit as it is, could probably power about 180 million electric cars plugged in overnight.

Electric cars could be a long-term solution to the oil/gas crunch along with electrified rail transport. However, it will take a commitment of many years of time, *trillions* of dollars, and political will—all three of which are in short supply.

And I think we're rapidly running out of time; you might say the United States is running on fumes. We won't have enough electric cars before the next oil shock hits. Luckily, you have more, less-expensive options.

Electric Scooters

Electric scooters can zip around town quietly and some have ranges of up to 100 miles. They are particularly well suited to single working adults who live less than 20 miles from the office. Electric scooters run on batteries that can be recharged from a domestic socket. Some of the more popular brands include X-Treme Scooters (www.x-treme scooters.com), eGo (www.egovehicles.com), and Vectrix (www.vectrix .com). A high-end electric scooter could cost you $3,000 or more, but you can buy them for a lot less.

The web site MetaEfficient (http://www.metaefficient.com) has a good review of different electric scooters at http://tinyurl .com/5qv9m7.

Electric Bicycles

Electric bicycles are just what they sound like—bicycles with an electric battery assist for climbing hills (or just hauling your lazy ass around town without pedaling). Electric bicycles, or e-bikes, bridge the gap between bicycles and scooters by giving you a vehicle that is both human- and electric-powered. Most e-bikes come with one battery that will get you about 10 miles if you don't like to pedal; if you feel the need, you can buy a second battery and extend your range to 20 miles. The models I've seen have detachable batteries so that you can charge up at a cafe or an office.

You can spend as little as $1,500, or you can get a high-end e-bike for $2,000 to $3,000 and solar panels to charge it for less than $500. An example of a solar charger would be something like the Sunforce 50044 60-Watt Solar Charging Kit (http://tinyurl.com/dlxjwz).

An appropriately sized solar charging system is a good idea for *any* electric vehicle if you want to go off the grid or are worried that the grid could go down a lot.

One of the better-known electric bicycle brands is the Currie IZip (www.Currietech.com). It's run by Dr. Malcolm Currie, the former chairman of Hughes Aircraft and Delco Electronics. Dr. Currie founded Currie Technologies, Inc., in 1997 based on his conviction that hybrid and electric vehicles would become increasingly important for fundamental economic and environmental reasons.

Other well-liked manufacturers include Ohm Cycles (http://www.ohmcycles.com), Schwinn (yes, Schwinn makes an electric bike—check it out at http://tinyurl.com/d8hnph) and Electric Motion Systems (http://www.epluselectricbike.com). If you're cramped for space, consider the eZee Quando, a folding bike with a lithium battery. It's not too expensive, either.

Electric bikes can be *heavy* when the batteries are on them, but they're easy to ride.

You'll find a good review of some electric bikes at Zimbio (http://tinyurl.com/d7a4pc). An electric bike usually requires assembly with manuals translated from the original Martian lingo; if you get stumped, bring the mess o' parts to your local bicycle shop and they'll probably assemble it for a fee.

Seven Tips for Staying Alive on a Bicycle

The biggest threat faced by any bicyclist (or moped rider, for that matter) is traffic. Here are seven tips to staying safer when you ride.

1. **Don't weave between cars.** This is especially tempting when traffic slows to a crawl right before a traffic light—you see kids doing it all the time. (By the way, kids—you see that angry old man who's shouting at you out of his car window? That's me!).

(Continued)

(Continued)

Just because you're hyper-alert to the cars around you doesn't mean they see you. Heck, they might be having a fight with their significant other on a cell phone, and they'll accidentally squish you like a bug.

2. **Keep both hands on the brakes.** When I was a boy, I used to ride around with my hands off the handlebars all the time. What an idiot—I'm lucky I survived high school. Certainly you should keep your hands on the bars, but also keep your hands on the brakes—the split-second of time you save could save your life.

3. **Learn how to look behind you.** It's natural to turn your head to look behind you, but on a bike, this can throw you off balance. Instead, lower your chin to your left collarbone to look left, and to your right collarbone to look right. That way, you won't shift your center of gravity.

4. **Be extra careful at intersections.** Odds are, if you get nailed by a car when you're riding a bike, it's going to be at an intersection. Cars that are pulling right may be about to turn left. Use pedestrians at intersections for clues. Even though the *walk* sign is on, have they suddenly stopped? Then you should, too.

5. **Be extra, extra careful of trucks.** Never put yourself between a big truck and a curb. Too many people get seriously injured or killed when trucks swerve or turn suddenly. And the rule of thumb is, the bigger the vehicle, the less likely they are to see you.

6. **Don't hug the curb.** It's too easy to slide off into a soft shoulder or bump a mailbox and go sprawling. Plus, if automobile drivers think they can slip by you, they'll try. If you ride further out into the road, they might honk, but it's better than getting accidentally bumped.

7. **If you ride at night, slow down!** In the dark, you can't see as well, which means you're slower to react to danger. Also, automobile drivers can't see as well, either, and a bike can be invisible to them until it's too late.

You can also try to use hand signals to alert motorists to what you're doing, but I can tell you that, in Florida, anyway, (1) most car drivers don't know hand signals; (2) they'll probably think you're waving at somebody; and (3) the most common hand signal on Florida roads requires just one finger. Is it just Florida? You tell me.

I'm not putting wear a helmet on this list, because you should be doing that anyway. If you're not, all the common sense advice in the world won't save you.

Getting Around on the Standard Bicycle

I hate to use the word *standard* because there is so much diversity within bicycles. But by *standard bicycle*, I mean human-powered bicycles. If there is a real fuel crisis, a lot of people are going to become much better acquainted with the good ol' fashioned bicycle. As long as you can keep your tires inflated, you can travel at least three times as fast on a bicycle than you can on foot.

There are bikes for all sorts of activities: Cruising around town, speed racing, dirt-biking. What I'm going to write about here is car replacement—a bicycle you intend to use as your main form of transportation, especially after society powers down or crashes.

To fit the bill, look for a bike with the following characteristics:

- **Durable.** It has to be capable of taking punishment.
- **Adaptable.** While a street bike will do the trick for probably 90% of riding, if you're going to do any traveling off-road or even on muddy or sandy roads, you'll want a bike that can handle all types of terrain.
- **Uncomplicated.** In a post-crash society, you won't be able to put your bike in your car and take it to the shop if something goes wrong. So, you want a bike you can keep in serviceable condition with basic tools.
- **Expandable**. In a post-crash society, you'll want to haul things around on your bicycle as they do now in third-world countries. Panniers (also known as side baskets) do the trick for me, but there are other ways to make your bike a cargo carrier.

If money is tight, consider a used bike. Older bikes can be an excellent fit for a post-apocalyptic world, especially if they have heavy steel frames. Many older bikes were overbuilt in that they were made for durability rather than speed. Heck, I've seen neighbors throw away old bikes with the trash. I rescued one from the trash pile, oiled it up, put some new tires on it, and gave it to a friend—she's still riding it today.

If you shop for a used bike, don't be turned off by cracked or flat tires. You can always replace those, and probably should. I recommend puncture-proof tires. I have Specialized brand Armadillo tires on my bike; they're made with Kevlar—yeah, that's right, my tires are bulletproof![7] There are even airless tire manufacturers (Green Tyre and Amerityre), but I haven't tried those out.

You can also fit tire liners (strips of puncture resistant material) on the inside of your tire of choice; these work well but don't stop sidewall punctures and they can move around in the tire if the pressure doesn't hold them in place. I used to use tire liners before I moved on to Armadillos.

One last note on tires: In a post-crash world, bicycles will probably become valuable and bicycle tires could become unavailable. You might want to stock up with a spare pair or two—they'll probably be very good for bartering.

Multispeed or Single Gear

You might think a single-speed bike is the right thing for a post-crash world. But you will wear out a lot faster with a single-speed bike, and your bike's drivetrain might wear out, too. A single-speed bike can burn through chains, wheels, cogs, brackets, and cranksets faster than a multispeed bike.

Road touring bikes—with 10, 12, 21, or more speeds—are what most adults who ride bikes in the United States are used to riding. A road bike is not technically a commuter bike, but is instead built to be lightweight and fast. And they're probably what you're looking for if you have to start riding a bike back and forth to work, because their skinny tires make for a faster ride. You can find good road bikes cheap on craigslist (www.craigslist.org). Just be sure that the frame isn't bent, the gears aren't stripped, and you can tinker-fix most everything else.

Mountain Bikes

Many mountain bikes have some sort of gearing system, and mountain bikes often have frames and tires that are designed for off-road use, which is good if you need that. Just be aware that mountain bikes, with their fat tires, are notoriously slow under normal riding conditions.

Comfort Bikes

If you're a fat-assed suburban daddy like me, you should look at a comfort or *hybrid* bike. They are designed so you don't have to crouch over the handlebars and often have shocks for a much nicer ride. A bicycle with a more upright riding position will keep pressure off your wrists and arms. Their tires are bigger than a road bike's but not cumbersome like those of a mountain bike.

Getting back to craigslist, you might find one of the old 1960s or 1970s era three-speed suburban cruisers for sale either on craigslist or at a garage sale. These bikes were built like tanks—they aren't indestructible, but properly maintained, they will last long enough to turn into family heirlooms, which is why you find them bargain-tagged at garage sales. If you're looking for a Doomer bike, find one of these babies.

Adult-Sized Tricycles

Generally associated with older folks who are having trouble with their sense of balance, adult-sized tricycles are excellent vehicles for the post-crash era, especially if you can find one with multiple speeds. These usually have a large basket positioned behind the seat, which is great for hauling stuff. Schwinn makes one that is generally praised but has cheap-ass tires. You can buy the bike, replace the tires right away and keep the old ones as spares.

And sure enough, there are now electric adult-sized tricycles. For example, Currie Technologies makes the iZip Tricruiser electric tricycle, which you can buy on Amazon.com. It has a range of 30 to 35 miles per charge, so you can make it back and forth to the grocery store several times without running low on power. The Tricruiser has a top speed of 15 miles per hour.

Bike Trailers and Cargo Bikes

In a post-crisis world, a guy who can move cargo around without gasoline might be very popular. So check out the cargo bikes at Xtracycle (http://www.xtracycle.com) and Yuba (http://www.yubaride.com). They can carry just about as much as you could fit in the trunk of a small car. In fact, when you check out these bikes, consider that you might be looking at the poor man's car of the future.

And bicycle trailers are another way to go. These are cheap, you can buy them at Walmart, and they hook on to any normal bicycle. The better ones can carry two kids, or a lot of cargo if gasoline goes to seven dollars a gallon.

Biking for the Family

When I was a kid, everyone got on a bike at age six or seven; a bike represented freedom. In today's overprotected, under-athletic world, I meet lots of kids who never learned to ride and don't plan on it. That's no way to head into a worst-case-scenario future.

If your kids are too young to ride, get a bike trailer. If you absolutely must evacuate your home during a fuel shortage, your family may be riding bikes to get the heck out of Dodge, or at least get out of immediate danger.

And if things don't come to worst, your whole family can still have fun riding bikes together. You'll get some exercise, be outdoors, and probably even lose a few pounds.

Learn to Repair Your Bicycle.   Actually, this goes for any of the alternate forms of transportation in a post-crisis future—whether you're driving a bicycle, scooter, motorcycle, or whatever. You may not be able to depend on your local mechanic. It would behoove you to learn how to fix simple machines, especially if you're looking for new job opportunities, and bicycles are simple machines to fix.

To fix a bike properly, you'll need tools and training. Amazon .com has a list of bicycle repair books, and naturally, you want to buy one now, because by the time you depend on a bicycle as your main form of transportation, mail delivery may be a little spotty. As for tools, I recommend checking out BicycleTutor .com (www.bicycletutor.com), which has instructional videos. I also recommend nosing around the *crank* and *wrench* sections at Jim Langley's web site (http://www.jimlangley.net). He also has a blog, Jim Langley's Bicycle Beat (http://www.jimlangley.blogspot.com).

However, nothing beats hands-on training. Many vocational and tech schools now teach bicycle repair, and you might be able to sign up for a weekend or extension course. And ask at your local bike shop if they need a free-but-untrained helping hand.

If you want to buy them new, you'll find the tools you need at Park Tools (www.parktool.com), or on eBay or craigslist if you don't mind used tools. Well-made bike tools should last a long time.

Every Day You Ride a Bike . . .

- Check the air pressure in the tires. Riding on tires that aren't fully inflated causes extra wear and tear on the tires and rims.
- Check the brakes—make sure they're in place, making proper connection with the rims, and not worn down. Don't let oil get on the brake pads.

- Make sure moving parts are free of dirt and debris.
- A monthly check-up would include checking to make sure that the tires have no bald spots; the wheel spokes are tight; the nuts on the handlebars, handlebar stem, axles, pedals, and cranks are secure; any quick-release levers are secure; and all the cables are secure and working properly.
- Every thousand miles or so, clean your chain. When the chain and sprockets on your bike get gummy with dirt and grit, it slows you down and they wear out faster. There's a good description of how to clean your chain at Quamut: http://tinyurl.com/cag49k.

What to Pack on a Bicycle

Bicycles are powered by your muscle, so you want to pack as little as possible. Still, you want to balance light loads with safety. Here are some things you might want to consider hauling around:

- **Patch kit.** A typical kit includes sandpaper for tire prep, glue, and patches to fix holes. Some patches are self-adhesive—no glue required. If you're using puncture-proof or airless tires, you can skip this.
- **Spare tube.** Unless you're using puncture-proof tires.
- **Tire lever.** One of the basic bike repair tools—a flat utensil with one tapered end that is slightly curved and a hook on one end; a tire lever is used for quick removal of a tire from a bike rim.[8] Again, this isn't necessary if you're using puncture-proof tires.
- **Portable bicycle pump.** Some people use CO_2 cartridges because they're easier, but a good, portable pump like the Lezyne Pressure Drive M Pump or Topeak Road Morph is nearly as easy and can be used over and over again.
- **Multi-tool.** There are variations on these, but I prefer one with all sorts of bike tools—hex wrenches, chain tool, screwdrivers, and so on—mounted on a Swiss-Army-knife-type platform.

You'll also need your ID and some money, if not a full wallet. If you have a cell phone, it's smart to bring that along as well. Just don't talk on your phone and ride at the same time (I've done that—oops!).

More Stuff to Pack on a Bicycle.   If you're going on a longer trip—just for fun or fleeing the ravenous zombie hordes—you might want to pack more stuff on your bicycle.

Some ideas . . .

- Needle-nose pliers.
- Adjustable wrench.
- Spoke wrench.
- Oil/lube.
- Swiss Army knife.
- Chain tool.
- Zip ties—for binding broken spokes, patching together broken chains, and so on.
- Duct tape or bungee cords.

And for even longer trips . . .

- Bike-mounted or handheld GPS device.
- Spare batteries—for headlights and tail lights.

You also might want to consider . . .

- Sunglasses/safety glasses. Sunglasses are good for riding in the day. If you're going to ride at night, safety glasses are a must to keep bugs, and so forth, out of your eyes.
- Reflective tape (for riding at night).
- Reading glasses if you need help seeing for up-close work they'll make fixing your bike easier.
- Bandana or small towel.
- Energy food bars.
- Bottle opener.
- Disposable poncho.
- First-aid kit.
- Sunscreen.
- Kleenex/toilet paper.
- Aspirin or non-aspirin substitute, and Aleve (for aching muscles).

The Least You Can Do

- Get in shape. You don't have to be an Olympic athlete, but get in good enough shape that you can walk for five miles with a loaded backpack, because you could be doing that a lot if your area runs out of gas.
- Keep your car's gas tank at least half full at all times.
- Buy a bicycle and equip it with a basket and/or panniers (baskets on each side of the rear wheel). If gasoline becomes extremely expensive, you're going to need it.
- Buy a big bike lock. In a real gasoline crunch, good bicycles will become *very* valuable.

CHAPTER

14

The Final Option—Evacuate

No problem is so big that it can't be run away from.
—Charles Schultz

You can turn your home into a fortress, but the ugly truth is that no matter how well you prepare, fate can still turn you into a refugee. And it's best to be prepared ahead of time. In this chapter, topics we cover include:

- What to put in your *bug-out* bag, and why you might want multiple bug-out bags
- Nine signs that you should *get out of Dodge*
- Things to figure out before you leave
- Where to go when you bug out
- How to use Google maps to help plan your escape
- What to do if you're the one taking in refugees
- What to tell your kids

Pack Like a (Smart) Refugee

If you *must* leave home in a crisis, you'll want to have what is called a *bug-out* bag or *GOOD* (Get Out Of Dodge) bag ready to go the minute you make the decision to leave. This will be packed with must-have supplies, and a change of clothing is recommended.

Why must it be ready immediately? Because just as you're deciding it's time to leave, half the people in town are making the same
decision. If your bag is already packed, when everyone else in town
is packing, you can hit the road—the road that is going to clog up
with refugees pretty quickly.

There's an old saying in the stock and commodity markets: "If
you're going to panic, panic early." In other words, when it comes
time to run, you don't want to be the last to leave.

You actually need at least two bug-out bags, and maybe more.
The big two are (1) a car bag, the one you want to have in your
vehicle all the time, and (2) the house bag, the one you want to
have in a specified place in your home (near the door is good),
which you can grab easily and run.

Other bug-out bags can include a medical bag and an important records bag. All of them should be ready to grab and go at a
minute's notice.

Why have a bug-out bag in your car? Well, there are the scary
reasons. For instance, let's say you're out at the mall when there is a
chemical spill in your neighborhood, and you can't go home until
it's cleaned up. You'd want to have a bag of supplies handy.

And then there are the mundane reasons—plenty of 'em.

For example, I once took the family on a trip to an outlet mall
that's over an hour away. Little did we know that our young son
was harboring a nasty virus in his intestines—a virus that made an
explosive exit from his body when we were halfway there. If we'd
had a bug-out bag at the time, we could have changed him into a
spare set of clothes and at least made him more comfortable for
the ride home, and spared the rest of us the smell of his messed
pants.

I can't count the number of times we've left the house for an
outside event under blue skies, only to have storm clouds roll in
later. That's Florida weather for you. A good bug-out bag includes
ponchos or other appropriate weather gear (for example, if you live
up north, you could include a sweatshirt or light jacket for every
member of the family).

And then there's the time I was running around with the kids at
the park and managed to slice my hand open. It wasn't bad enough
for a trip to the hospital, but it would have been nice not to bleed all
over the steering wheel. Every good car bag contains a first-aid kit.

A Bug-Out Bag for Your Car

A bug-out bag that rides around in a car should not take up too much space nor should it contain items that will be damaged by heat or cold when your car sits in the elements. You can customize your bag to suit your needs, of course.

Start with the basics . . .

- Jumper cables
- Can of Fix-a-Flat
- Air compressor that plugs into the cigarette lighter
- Lug wrench and car jack
- Assorted bungee cords
- Adjustable wrench
- Needle nose pliers
- Assorted screwdrivers
- Duct tape
- Box of tissues
- Portable flashlight/spotlight/emergency road flasher that runs on batteries *and* plugs into the lighter.

Those are the basics, and it's important that you know how to use everything you put in your kit.

You can build your car bug-out bag around that list. Here are some examples of other items for a car bug-out bag:

- First-aid kit
- Package of Wet Wipes
- One set plastic cutlery and cup per family member
- One poncho per family member
- One change of pants, shirt, and underwear for every family member
- Katadyn Exstream XR Water Purifier Bottle
- Three towels (one big, two small)
- Toothbrushes and toothpaste
- Leatherman-type multi-tool
- Fixed blade knife and sharpening stone
- Box matches/lighter/fire starters
- EverLife flashlight (the kind you shake—it doesn't need batteries)

- Hand-crank radio/emergency road hazard flasher/flashlight
- Roll of reflective tape
- Assorted packed peanut-butter crackers and cheese crackers
- Small bag of dog/cat food (if you have pets)

This is what our cars are stocked with, along with suntan lotion and bug spray, because we live in Florida. Also, our change-of-pants are shorts (again, Florida). Maybe you need different seasonal or emergency items, like snakebite venom, mittens, and a stocking cap, or if you live in a Lyme-disease-prone area, tick-proof undergarments like those from http://www.rynoskin.com. One of my friends hates cell phones, but he keeps a pay-as-you go cell phone and a portable power pack/instant cell-phone charger in his car—just in case.

And if your cell phone doesn't have a built-in camera, you should consider adding a disposable camera to your kit to document car accidents. We always have a car charger for our cell phones in each car.

Finally, if you habitually wear work or dress shoes you wouldn't want to walk a mile in, pack some comfortable shoes or sneakers.

The obvious weakness in our plan is that the Katadyn Exstream Water Purifier Bottle, which combines a purifier and water bottle into a single unit, only holds 28 ounces at a time. But I figure that's enough for a very short-term emergency. Any portable water purifier will do. Also, we pack little food to speak of—the peanut butter crackers are just to hold my kids over in an emergency. But even food bars won't last long sitting in a car in Florida's extreme heat. Also, I don't live in the desert—odds are we'll be able to find something to eat in a short-term, get-out-of-Dodge scenario.

You also might want to keep some cash in your car. If you do, don't store it in the same place as the rest of your kit—hide it well. You'll be able to stash most of your gear in different places in your car. Those things that are grouped together—clothes, for example—should be put in a bag that is just big enough to fit everything and also homely as hell. A bag that matches the interior color of your car, and therefore blends in, might be a good idea if you can manage it. The kind of thieves who break into parked cars are usually stupid or just kids (or stupid kids), and you don't need to give them incentive by having a spiffy-looking bag. Your bag should have a wide strap of some sort in case you are forced to carry it for a distance.

If you *really* want to be prepared, you can carry some other items around in your car. For example:

- Bottle of window washer/defroster
- Roll of paper towels
- Tow rope
- 100 feet of parachute cord
- Spare belts specific to your vehicle
- Assorted hoses and hose clamps
- Multiple flashlights
- Spare batteries for flashlights
- Tarp (at least 8 × 10) and nylon rope
- Wire cutters
- Small hammer
- Hatchet
- Folding shovel
- Plastic trash bags
- Multiple changes of clothes and foul weather gear
- One quart of engine oil
- One quart of transmission fluid
- One pint of power steering fluid
- One gallon of water per person
- One whistle (if you need help, you can blow a whistle for much longer than you can shout. Also, the sharp sound of a whistle travels over longer distances than the human voice, and provides a much more distinct sound.)
- Small bag of cat litter (if you live in snow country and can get stuck in the snow)

I know of people who carry all these things (and more) in their vehicles all the time. But there are downsides—for example, being a mobile packrat really uses up your available space and hurts your fuel economy.

I prefer to keep just the limited bug-out bag I listed earlier and keep a bunch of other stuff at home, ready to go at a minute's notice.

I am not in favor of loading the car to the gills, but the bug-out bag you keep in your house can be much bigger. You can include food and other perishable goodies, as long as you store it in a place where it won't be subject to extremes of heat or cold. When it comes to food and water, you should have three days' worth of supplies in your emergency bug-out bag at a *minimum*.

A Bigger Bug-Out Bag for Your Home

Since you already have a car bag, its contents can be incorporated into the bigger bug-out bag you keep at home. Additional materials for your big bag could include:

- Three days' worth of food/snacks per family member
- Paper plates, plastic cups and bowls, and more plastic cutlery
- Portable water purification system
- One gallon of water per family member per day (you can pack less if you carry a portable water purification system)
- One backpack per adult, in case you have to abandon the car
- Toilet paper
- Roll of paper towels
- Bottle of Windex-type cleaning product
- Sponges and rags
- Sewing kit
- Notebooks and pens (for messages)
- Larger medical kit, including extra gauze bandages and medicines you don't want to leave in the car
- Manual can opener
- More matches/lighters/fire starters
- More flashlights (one per family member)
- Extra change of clothes, including two pairs of socks and one pair of comfortable shoes, as well as hats and sweatshirts, if appropriate
- Survival Guide (Air Force or Special Forces recommended)
- Regional maps
- Compass
- Small mirror
- Plastic garbage bags
- Small hammer, pliers, screwdrivers
- Pointed shovel or garden trowel
- Gardening gloves
- Spare batteries (rechargeable) for electronics

- Solar battery charger
- Road flares
- Fishing poles and fishing tackle, including a fishing knife
- Small fire extinguisher
- Photocopies of credit and identification cards, as well as important records: insurance information, medical records, bank account numbers, Social Security cards, and so forth. These should be in a sealed, waterproof bag or container.

To this, you'll add your prepacked toiletry bag, and if you need a separate medicine bag, that too.

A lot of this stuff can be packed in the backpacks, which can be stored in a closet, hopefully near your door. Put the other items in the same closet in a plastic or steel garbage pail, so you can grab and go. The fishing poles can stay in your garage, of course, and are optional. But if you're going to end up in a campground waiting for the Red Cross to show up, fishing can be a good way to pass the time.

If you feel like cooking, you can bring a camp stove and some pots, but for short-term crises, most kids can survive and even thrive on foods like cold Chef Boyardee cheese ravioli out of a can. If I thought my family was going to be stranded somewhere for longer than three days, I might throw the portable mini-grill in the car, and add some folding lawn chairs.

The pointed shovel is for waste disposal. If all else fails, and restroom facilities are unavailable, you're going to bury your poop (that's also what the gardening gloves are for, as well as handling other disgusting materials). It's a lot better than leaving it around for others to step in.

Also, know what pillows and sleeping bags you're going to bring, have them in one place, and have easy access to them. Are you going to bring a tent? You can always sleep in the car, if it's comfortable enough. Have your toiletry bag(s) packed as if you're going on a trip, all the time—that way, you won't have to waste time packing them when it's GOOD time. If you have guns, plan on bringing at least one of them, as well as ammunition, and plan ahead of time how you're going to transport a gun in your vehicle. I think you can expect at least a cursory search at roadblocks—and depending on the situation, guns may be confiscated.

If you have kids, remember to pack books and/or favorite toys for them, to keep them occupied while their parents are quietly freaking out. It doesn't hurt to keep a favorite toy in the car anyway, and you can save a step that way. A portable DVD player—one you can remove from the car and run on rechargeable batteries or a wall plug—is a great distraction for kids.

As for the food you put in your bug-out bag, there are a few simple guidelines to follow:

- Pick foods your family will enjoy. Comfort foods are highly recommended for stressful situations.
- Ease of preparation is very important.
- Rotate the food in your bug-out bag. Check your bag monthly to stay on top of expiration dates and prevent food spoilage.
- Do it on the cheap. Peanut-butter crackers, fruit cups, and granola bars are all good choices for most people and a lot cheaper than specialized, prepackaged survival food.

Important: You need things ready for you to grab and be out of the house in *minutes*—time *will be* of the essence in a real evacuation.

If you're the type with more money than patience, you can buy a fully equipped bug-out bag at various places on the Web. However, I *don't* recommend buying one for three reasons:

1. You will pay through the nose.
2. You'll probably get a *lot* less than what you pay for. Pricing pressures apply to all merchants, and you know whoever is selling the bag is probably going to cut corners in order to cut prices or maximize profits.
3. You won't be as familiar with what's in the bag as you would be if you put it together yourself.

That said, if you *must* buy a bag, the Red Cross offers one-, two-, and four-person kits at its online store: http://www.redcrossshop .org/disaster/index.htm. You can find variations at Emergency Essentials (http://beprepared.com) and The 7 Store (http://www .areyouprepared.com).

Now that You're Packed, Should You Leave?

If you think you can hunker down and ride it out, fine. But like I said earlier, if you're going to panic, panic early—and get out.

Here are nine signs that you should maybe hit the road . . .

1. **Two full days without power.** We are all only nine meals (three full days) from anarchy. Studies have shown that's how long between a disaster that interrupts the food supply and the onset of widespread looting and rioting, as hungry people get proactive. You don't want to be too paranoid about this—heck, I've been through five hurricanes and every single time, the day after the hurricane, I saw people lined up at the stores to buy food. They must have made close to no preparations.

   But if the power goes out across the city, and doesn't come back for two days, the piles of spoiled food are growing and so is the hunger level. You're probably getting close to the looting stage.

2. **Fires spread unchecked.** When the fire department can't fight fires effectively, something is wrong. You'll stand a better chance somewhere else.

3. **Rising water.** Worse in some ways than a raging fire (because water is so damned deceptive), flooding from a hurricane or other heavy storm can turn your home into a deathtrap. Know the elevation and flood potential of your home. If there are warnings of a storm that could swamp your house, get out ahead of time.

4. **Epidemic.** The important question: Is the illness airborne or spread by some other method? With anything other than an airborne illness, your best bet is probably to stay home and button up. On the other hand, few homes are equipped to keep out airborne diseases, and the more heavily populated the area, the more risk you run.

5. **Distant popping or cracking sounds.** That could be the sound of small arms fire, as looters get bold and shop owners protect their stores. You'll have to drive *away* from the shooting, which is why you should have multiple escape routes planned.

6. **The government sets a curfew.** Things are getting worse, not better. Time to hit the road, Jack! The only thing worse is when the media broadcasts government directives to *stay indoors*. There's a definite red flag. Get the hell out, if you can. Have your alternate routes ready, because the main roads could be blocked.

7. **The sound of explosions in the distance.** This could be fires setting off fuel tanks or other problems, and those problems aren't being handled properly.

8. **Emergency public information broadcasts run on an endless loop on TV.** You're probably late, but that could be your last chance to Get Out of Dodge.

9. **If the TV starts showing video footage of clogged roads,** you're already too late. Stay home unless you absolutely must leave.

How to Get Out When the Gettin's Good—or Bad!

If you must leave, you should have (1) a definite destination in mind, and (2) a plan to get there. This means planning an escape route now. There are five important things to keep in mind.

1. **Who are you taking with you?** Is it just you and your immediate family, or your extended family, too? Are you taking pets, and if so, have you packed food, water, and poop bags for them? Are you taking more than one vehicle, and if so, do you have a rendezvous point? Do you have a travel plan, with agreed-upon stops where you'll meet up? Decide these things ahead of time—you don't want to leave anyone behind.

2. **Main roads could be packed.** Throw in desperation tinged with panic and a heavily armed population, and major routes out of the big cities could become dangerous places to be in the event of a massive involuntary urban evacuation.

   So, plan multiple routes using secondary roads, even country back roads, and side streets through neighborhoods.

3. **Don't plan on going any further than you can on one tank of gasoline.** If you're escaping, probably every Tom, Dick, and Harry is doing the same thing. Gasoline stations will run out of supplies fast, if they haven't already. Also, you might be stuck in traffic for hours or have to double back to use one of your alternate escape routes—your mileage is probably going to suck.

4. **Drive smart.** Driving at speeds over 60 miles per hour will eat up gas in a hurry. Slow-moving traffic is okay, but if you get into an actual traffic jam, one that stops for more than a minute, turn your engine off. You'll save gas, and can restart when it's time to move forward. You should let your engine run a minimum of three minutes after you start it up. You can

run the heater, but running the air conditioning will eat up your gasoline.

As you drive, listen to your car radio to see if there are traffic problems along your escape route. Be prepared to switch to an alternate route *before* the roads clog.

If you come to an official checkpoint, go out of your way to be polite, helpful, and friendly. If it's an unofficial checkpoint run by non-uniformed types, you're going to have some tough choices. If possible, let other cars pass you and see what happens to them.

5. **Think outside the box.** Thinking will get you out of more tight spots than muscle any day. For example, do you have to flee by car? Could you take the train? If you're childless, can you pack everything you need on a bicycle? What about water—do you live near a river that you could put a kayak on? If you have a safe place to go to further down river, you might want to keep that as an alternate plan.

How to Use Google Maps to Plan Your Escape

Google maps is far from perfect, but with options of map, satellite, and terrain mode, it allows you to explore your locality and make plans for escape routes. You can even store an escape route map online.

- Go to Google maps (maps.google.com). If you aren't a member already, become one. You'll just have to create an e-mail account.
- Now, click on the *My Maps* tab (under the Google logo).
- Click *Create new map*; title it *Escape Route* or something you'll remember. If you want this to be yours alone, keep it *Unlisted.* Otherwise, select the *Public* option so it can be easily accessed.
- Zoom in on your house, or where you expect to be when the invasion hits.
- Click the *Placemark* icon (it looks a bit like eyedropper) to make your first landmark (your house). After you write the title and description, you can click the icon in the window to select a more visually descriptive one. (I mark my house with a martini glass icon.)
- On the left side window, click the check mark next to *Places of Interest* under the Featured Content header. This will allow you to

(Continued)

(Continued)

help plan your route and find places you might want to go (gas stations, motels, pharmacies, etc.), as well as places to avoid.

- Check the traffic on roads you're considering. *Traffic* is one of the buttons at the top of the map. Of course, traffic will be different on the day of your escape than it is now, but click on *Traffic* and you'll get the option to pick a particular time and day. Afternoon rush hour on a Monday will give you an idea of which roads are heavily traveled.

Now it's time to figure out your route: Find your first stop, make a new placemark, and use the *Draw a line* icon to connect the two. Continue thusly until you reach your destination.

If you do make a map of your escape route ahead of time, you can also make a list of the phone numbers of motels and gas stations along your route. Keep that list in the car. When you evacuate, use your cell phone and start calling the list to find out who has gas and who has rooms available. Knowing these things, and potentially making a room reservation while you're on the road, could lower your frustration and anxiety factors.

Where to Go When You Bug Out

If you can get out of the immediate area of danger to a place where life is *normal* and roads aren't clogged with refugees, you're ahead of the game. Where do you go next? The hope is that you planned this next step far in advance.

The best choice is relatives, because they'll be most likely to put up with you for however long it takes. If you don't get along with family, then a close friend is an alternate choice.

In either case, check with them ahead of time. In fact, it's best to do it *now*—just put down the book, make a short list, and start making phone calls. Make each person you call the following offer: If they'll agree to put you up for a short period of time if you have to evacuate in an emergency, you'll do the same for them.

It's important to have more than one *safe house* in more than one direction. The direction that might be your first choice might be impassable, or your relative or friend might be affected by the same disaster that is forcing you from your home.

Once you have arrived at a friend or family member's house . . .

- Make immediate offers to pay for groceries and so forth. Even if your gracious host initially says "no," make the offer again if you're stuck there for three or more days.
- Ask them for a list of their house rules. While you are a guest, and they'll want to treat you like one initially, it's best to know what the rules are so you don't irritate them, leading to a blow-up down the road.
- Acknowledge that your life has been disrupted and you may be frustrated, impatient, and short-tempered. You don't want to appear ungrateful or demanding. See what you can do to make your host's life easier.

If a friend or relative's home is unavailable, you're on your own. Remember, in most emergencies it's best to choose rural, unpopulated areas over urban, heavily populated areas. You do have some options.

Hotel or motel. You might want to choose a hotel or motel outside the crisis area. Ahead of time, look for *extended-stay* motels along your escape routes—you can pay by the week or month and each room has appliances such as a refrigerator and a microwave; some even have dishes and cutlery. Before paying the rent, always politely ask to see the room you will be renting.

Forest campground or recreational vehicle (RV) park. If you have an RV or tent, this can be a good option. Many campgrounds have community shower areas, one for men and one for women, and drinking water available near the campsite. Alternately, you can camp for free in most National Forests. However, you will need to move your campsite at least once per week to a different area to comply with forest regulations. Also, your belongings will not be safe and you can bet that thieves will be running rampant after a disaster.

Church or community shelter. A church-operated temporary disaster shelter is usually less restrictive than other types of shelters, and generally friendlier. If you have to relocate due to the disaster, they may be able to help you find more permanent shelter and give you employment leads in the area.

Storage facility. A secret shared by many working poor is that some storage facilities will let you rent a storage space as a living space, even if it isn't technically legal (many municipalities outlaw it as part of their *screw the poor* initiatives, but many storage facility managers allow it anyway). A storage facility manager may bend the rules in a time of crisis. You may have to rent one storage bay to store your car in and one to live in. It would still probably be cheaper than a motel.

Government shelter. A government shelter is usually not a good choice, and only one step up from a refugee camp. Government shelter personnel will search you and confiscate any weapons, drugs (including prescription medicines), tools, children's toys, money, keys, and food you may be carrying with you. You may or may not get all of it back when you leave. Plus, it can be harder to leave a government shelter than it is to enter one.

Refugee camp. Get out as soon as you can—you might be better off living in the woods. If you don't feel like a prisoner in a refugee camp, you aren't paying attention. Gangs will probably rule a camp after any length of time and make the lives of non-gang members a living hell. Make alliances, protect each other, and get out as a group.

Communication Is as Important as Evacuation

Don't expect your cell phone to work during a disaster—everyone else will be trying to make phone calls at the same time, and whatever crisis is going on may have taken out cell towers to boot. The thing to do is to have an out-of-state friend as a family contact, so all your family members have a single point of contact. Everyone in your party should have that contact number on a laminated piece of paper in his or her bag. If you get separated, call your out-of-state contact on a landline (or whenever possible), and make arrangements to regroup.

Crossing the Border

Do you have a plan if things get so bad that you have to leave the country? My family has a plan. The first important step is to have passports for every member of your family.

You'll want to carry as much cash as possible, of course, as well as any valuables that can easily be converted to cash.

You'll also want to have a plan for what you're going to do once you get *over* the border. Again, making arrangements with a friend or relative on the other side is the best thing to do.

What if the border is closed? In that case, it's probably all the more urgent that you get across it. Despite efforts to close it, the U.S. border with Mexico is still pretty porous. Northern Mexico is already an often violent and dangerous place, and it will probably be more so during a crisis. On the other hand, Mexicans are less likely to turn you in to the police than Canadians. And if you can get out through Northern Mexico, Southern Mexico is peaceful, lush, and very warm.

The border with Canada is extremely porous, and stretches over 3,000 miles; it's nearly impossible to seal without tremendous effort and a lengthy investment of time. On the down side, Canada has its picture next to *cold as hell* in the dictionary. Winters in most of Canada are brutal.

What to Do If You Leave Your Home Permanently

Most survivalists expect that if TSHTF, they'll be able to button down and ride out the bad times. And that's a good plan. But what if you lose your home? What if you become a refugee? Or what if bank agents seize your home?

The bad news is you may not be able to count on social services, which are already overwhelmed by the economic downturn's victims. And you may not want to go to a shelter. The rule of thumb is that half the people in shelters are crazy, and the other half are thieves.

When you're homeless, you don't want just survival tactics. You want *thrival* tactics—you want to improve your situation and *thrive*. Here are some tips on *really* roughing it.

- Buy a tent and sleeping bags for people in your family ahead of time. Check out the local campgrounds and see what's available.

(Continued)

(Continued)

- If you can't camp, consider sleeping in your car. You can do that with a car cover. Park in an apartment complex. Put a car cover on your car, but leave enough room to get in the door. Close the door, and roll down the window. Pull down the rest of the car cover and roll up your window.
- If you can't afford rent, don't want to stay in a shelter or sleep in your car, and alternative housing isn't available, see if you can scrape together money to join a gym. A gym gives you a place to use the bathroom, shower, and freshen up. The better you look, the easier it is to improve your situation.
- If you lose your home, most people will think there's something wrong with you. Do not bring it up in conversation with potential employers or casual friends (though you can tell casual friends you're looking for a cheap place to crash because you don't like where you're staying now).
- Do not fixate on the loss of material things. Things can improve, but you have to keep a good attitude, even in the worst of times.

What If You're the One Taking in Refugees?

Remember all those reciprocal deals you made with your friends and family? Suppose your Uncle Clem, his loudmouth wife, and their five dysfunctional kids take you up on the offer. They tell you that the Apocalypse made its debut in their backyard, so they're going to stay a while.

After three days, you may get the urge to announce you're going out for a carton of milk, pick up your own bug-out bag on the way out the door, and not come back until you're sure they're gone. Fight that urge! If you've been acting on the recommendations in this book, you're better prepared than most to ride this out.

Here are some of the things you need to think about in advance . . .

Food. Feeding a family of flat-broke refugees can get expensive, but that year's worth of emergency food you've laid in is going to come in handy.

Sleeping arrangements. You keep your own bed—no giving it to the refugees. It will only make you resent them more. The kids can sleep on the couch, reclining lawn chairs, or even on the floor if they use your sleeping bags. Big pillows are all the bed a little kid needs in a pinch. In preparation, you might want to stock up on extra blankets, sheets, towels, and other bedding, which you can often find cheap at garage sales. Refugees can't be choosers.

Lay down your rules, but don't be a tyrant. Keep rules to a minimum, but if you get the ground rules out of the way, everyone's going to be happier. Post the rules you care about—keeping them to yourself and then shouting, "Because I say so!" makes you sound like a jerk.

Break out the entertainment. Now's the time to have fun with your stash of board games and playing cards. And if you've been making your own home-brewed beer or wine, so much the better.

If your reciprocal arrangements are with a family that has younger kids than your own, keep an eye out for garage sales where you can pick up a few toys for the younger ones. It's a good way to make them feel safe and welcome.

Be a gracious host. Offer to look after the kids while the adults try to salvage their lives long-distance. Buy them clothes if they need them, and introduce the kids to neighborhood children.

It is okay to keep a running tab of expenses. It would be pretty mean-spirited to keep track of every nickel and dime, but if you make big outlays on your guests' behalf, they'll want to pay you back down the road.

An important part of being a gracious host—*do not* use this as a time to re-open old feuds.

Medicines. If you have stashed medical supplies, you may get a chance to use them. If refugees show up on your doorstep needing medical attention, break out the supplies and do what you can to stabilize them. This is one reason why it's handy to know which of your neighbors are doctors, nurses, EMTs, or other health professionals.

Find work around the house. Giving your guests projects around the house and/or yard will not only lighten your load, it will also make them feel useful and take their minds off the apocalypse at hand (or whatever).

If it comes down to it, help them get established. Sometimes, *normal life* disappears with a roaring fire, raging river, or mushroom cloud over a city. In that case, your guests will need help starting a new life.

Your guests may need a gentle nudge to start re-establishing their lives, especially if they've been traumatized or are simply lazy couch potatoes. That means you may need to devote some time and energy to helping them find an apartment, apply for needed services, and look for a job. If yours is the only car, phone, and computer, you may need to share more than you'd like. Remember, it is for a good cause.

And when a gentle nudge doesn't work, you may need to be blunt and give them a deadline. Tell them gently but firmly, "We've been glad to host you while we could, but we simply can't anymore."

Above all, be grateful that you are the one who gets to help. It sucks to have to be on the receiving end of someone else's generosity.

Do You Want to Put Gas Masks in Your Bug-Out Bag?

When you bring up the question of gas masks, the response of many people is, "you're too paranoid." On the other hand, a friend of mine was murdered by deliberate anthrax poisoning, so my answer usually is, "you're not paranoid enough."

The main problems with gas masks are (1) the expense is high for something you'll probably never use, and (2) finding any that will fit kids can be a challenge (although medical tape will help that problem). But when you need gas masks, they're worth their weight in gold.

In 1978, in Youngstown, Florida, a freight train derailed in the middle of the night and a rail car containing chlorine gas split open. A cloud of deadly gas boiled out.[1] Chlorine gas turns to acid in the lungs and leaves victims bleeding from the nose and mouth.

Residents close to the derailment were alerted and the story goes that many tried to escape the harmful fumes by getting in their cars and driving off. Unfortunately, the chlorine gas saturation level in the area was so high that many vehicles would not start. Families were poisoned sitting in their cars, their lungs burning from the inside out. A total of eight people died and 138 were injured.

The same thing (railroad accident, chlorine gas spill) happened in Graniteville, South Carolina, in 2005. Nine people died and at least 250 were treated for chlorine exposure. Residents in the area were forced to evacuate for two weeks.[2]

Naturally, there is concern that rail-transported toxic gas could be used in a terror attack. According to a report in *USA Today*, Navy researchers say an attack on a chemical-carrying train could kill 100,000 people.[3]

Bottom line: Gas masks are a good idea for a bug-out bag if you can afford them. You can find child-sized gas masks at www.armynavydeals.com and http://approvedgasmasks.com.

What to Tell Your Kids

These preparations will not go unnoticed by your kids—neither will the extra bag you're carrying around in your car.

What you tell your kids depends on their ages and how comfortable you are being honest with them. You don't want to scare them, perhaps unnecessarily.

On the other hand, kids love being involved in projects. If your kids are anything like my youngest, they'd like a special job helping prepare for a super-secret spy mission that we can't talk much about. It requires him to choose clothes and toys to go in the *spy bag* on a monthly basis. He also enjoyed picking most of his foods for the three-day spy mission.

Now, he doesn't believe Daddy is really a spy. He just knows we're preparing for *something like* a spy mission. Pretty mysterious, eh? Pretty fun, too!

The Final Word

You've made it to the end of the book. I hope you found it informative, entertaining, and useful. If you haven't already, start preparing for the worst! I don't think you'll find it overwhelming or scary. In fact, I've found that it's empowering and liberating. It's better than sitting on the couch, doing nothing as you wait for the world to end.

The end of the world as we know it may come next week, or it may not come for decades. But by using the information in this book, you should be better prepared, you should be better positioned to profit in the bad times as well as the good times, and you should be able to save money in the process.

The Least You Can Do

- Get an old backpack. Pack at least some of the following items:
  - First-aid kit
  - Package of Wet Wipes
  - One set plastic cutlery and cup per family member
  - One poncho per family member
  - Flashlight, with batteries separate
  - Hand-crank radio/emergency road hazard flasher/flashlight
  - Assorted packed peanut-butter crackers and cheese crackers
- Put this bag by the door and keep some bottles of water in the refrigerator.
- Plan your basic escape routes ahead of time.

Notes

Introduction

1. Jim Jubak, "Higher Food Prices Are on the Way," MSN.com, March 17, 2009.
2. Lisa Friedman, "Coming Soon: Mass Migrations Spurred by Climate Change," *New York Times*, March 2, 2009.
3. Siobhan Gorman, "Electricity Grid in U.S. Penetrated by Spies," *Wall Street Journal*, April 8, 2009.
4. Jane Sutton, "Recession Fueling Right-Wing Extremism, U.S. says," *Reuters*, April 14, 2009.
5. Dimitry Orlov, "The Five Stages of Collapse," Cluborlov.com, http://cluborlov.blogspot.com/2008/02/five-stages-of-collapse.html.
6. Jared Diamond, *Collapse: How Societies Choose to Fail or Succeed* (New York: Penguin Books, 2005).
7. Joseph Tainter, *The Collapse of Complex Societies* (Cambridge, UK: Cambridge University Press, 1988).

Chapter 1: The Most Likely Disasters You'll Face

1. FEMA, "Floodsmart Consumer Campaign Highlights Risks, Consequences Of America's Most Common And Costly Natural Disaster," June 29, 2004, www.fema.gov/news/newsrelease.fema?id=12786.
2. FEMA, "Flooding Season Around the Corner: Are You Ready?," April 26, 2006, www.fema.gov/news/newsrelease.fema?id=25518.
3. Department of Defense, Joint Operating Environment, "Challenges and Implications for the Future Joint Force," 2008. www.jfcom.mil/newslink/storyarchive/2008/JOE2008.pdf.
4. Sean Brodrick, "Oil, Water and Wheat," *Money and Markets*, April 2, 2008, http://earthhopenetwork.net/forum/showthread.php?tid=532.
5. MSNBC, "Food Price Hikes Changing U.S. Eating Habits," April 1, 2008, http://www.msnbc.msn.com/id/23882299.
6. "Timeline of the Great Depression," PBS.org, www.pbs.org/wgbh/amex/rails/timeline/index.html.
7. Dale Allen Pfeiffer, "Eating Fossil Fuels," From the Wilderness, 2004, http://fromthewilderness.com/free/ww3/100303_eating_oil.html.
8. Robert Felix, "US Food Riots Much Closer Than You Think," www.rense.com/general78/riots.htm.

Chapter 2: The Quick and the Dead—and the Survivors

1. Michael Holman, "One of the Millions of Hurricane Katrina Stories," Sept. 5, 2005, http://michaelhoman.blogspot.com/2005/09/one-of-millions-of-hurricane-katrina.html.
2. AP/MSNBC "Looters Take Advantage of New Orleans Mess," Aug. 30, 2005, www.msnbc.msn.com/id/9131493.
3. CNN "Racism, Resources Blamed for Bridge Incident," CNN.com, Sept. 13, 2005, www.cnn.com/2005/US/09/13/katrina.bridge.
4. ABC News Online, "Law and Order 'Restored' in New Orleans," www.abc.net .au/news/newsitems/200509/s1452745.htm.
5. Halifax Live, "FEMA Corrects Error—2 Million People Displaced by Rita and Katrina," www.halifaxlive.com/content/view/410/2.
6. *The Economist*, "A Decline Without Parallel," Feb. 28, 2002, http://academic .reed.edu/economics/course_pages/201_f06/Cases/argentina_collapse.htm.
7. Ana Simo, "Dirty Money, Big Banks and the Mafia State," theGully.com, www .thegully.com/essays/argentina/010227corruption.html.
8. Ferfal, "Lessons from Argentina's Economic Collapse," thesilverbearcafe.com, Dec. 13, 2006, www.silverbearcafe.com/private/10.08/tshtf1.html.

Chapter 3: Personal Finance

1. Mark Pittman and Bob Ivry, "Financial Rescue Nears GDP as Pledges Top $12.8 Trillion," *Bloomberg News*, March 31, 2009.
2. Grandfather Economic Report Series, "America's Total Debt Report," http:// mwhodges.home.att.net/nat-debt/debt-nat.htm.
3. Martin Weiss, "New Treasury Plan: Dead on Arrival?" MoneyandMarkets.com, http://blogs.moneyandmarkets.com/martin-weiss/new-treasury-plan-dead-on -arrival.
4. Lisa Twaronite, "China Seeks Oversight of Reserve Currency Issuers," MarketWatch.com, April 19, 2009, www.marketwatch.com/news/story/china -seeks-oversight-reserve-currency/story.aspx?guid={7C4F805C-C5DC-4666-A1EA-565D8147261A}&dist=msr_1.
5. *China Post*, "Zimbabwe Stock Exchange Up by Over 300,000% in '07," January 2, 2008.
6. Weiss, "New Treasury Plan: Dead on Arrival?" MoneyandMarkets.com.
7. Linda J. Blimes and Joseph E Stiglitz, "The Iraq War Will Cost Us $3 Trillion, and Much More," *Washington Post*, March 9, 2008, www.washingtonpost.com/ wp-dyn/content/article/2008/03/07/AR2008030702846.html.
8. Line stolen from Stephen Colbert's Press Club dinner. I'll see you in court, Mr. Colbert!

Chapter 4: Gold, Hard Assets, and Alternative Currencies

1. *Science Daily*, "American Adults Flunk Basic Science," March 13, 2009, www .sciencedaily.com/releases/2009/03/090312115133.htm.
2. Mark Twain famously said: "The difference between the right word and a nearly-right word is the difference between lightning and a lightning bug."

3. Carol Brouillet, "Reinventing Money, Restoring the Earth, Reweaving the Web of Life," www.communitycurrency.org/reweaveWeb.html.

4. Jason Bradford, "Food-Backed Local Money," The Oil Drum Campfire, March 4, 2009, http://campfire.theoildrum.com/node/5158#more.

Chapter 5: Investing for the Five Emergencies

1. Energy Information Administration (EIA), "International Energy Outlook 2009," www.eia.doe.gov/oiaf/ieo/highlights.html.

2. Ismail Serageldin, World Bank Vice President for Environmental Affairs, quoted in Marq de Villiers' *Water*, 2000.

3. Food and Agriculture Organization of the United Nations, "Crop Prospects and Food Situation," April 2009.

4. Center for Urban Education about Sustainable Agriculture, "How Far Does Your Food Travel to Get to Your Plate?", 2006.

5. U.N. climate panel study on global warming, April 6, 2007.

6. The International Forum on Globalization, "The Rise and Predictable Fall of Globalized Industrial Agriculture." 2007, http://www.ifg.org/pdf/ag%20report.pdf.

7. Earth2tech.com, "FAQ: Smart Grid." January 26, 2009, http://earth2tech.com/2009/01/26/faq-smart-grid/

8. Michael D. Lemonick, "How to Send Energy Across a Continent,"*Newsweek*, May 30, 2009, www.newsweek.com/id/200068.

9. Alan Drake, "Stop Ignoring Rail America," EV World.

10. PowerShares DB Commodity Index Tracking Fund, www.dbfunds.db.com/dbc/index.aspx.

Chapter 6: Water

1. Watercrunch.blogspot.com, Interview with Must-Read Author Cynthia Barnett, http://watercrunch.blogspot.com/2007/09/part-i-interview-with-must-read-author.html.

2. Heartspring, A Guide to Water Filters and Water Treatment, http://heartspring.net/water_filters_guide.html.

Chapter 7: Food Storage for Couch Potatoes

1. Maryland Cooperative Extension, Fact Sheet 803, Root Cellars http://extension.umd.edu/publications/pdfs/fs803.pdf.

Chapter 8: Smart Shopping—How to Plan Ahead for Next Week's Meals (and Save Significant Money)

1. ConsumerReports.org, "Shopping Tips," May 2009.

Chapter 9: Gardening

1. "Rocket Fuel Contaminates Lettuce and Milk," Organic Consumers Association, Nov. 29, 2004, www.organicconsumers.org/foodsafety/lettuce120104.cfm.
2. Rory Harrington, "Toxic Chemical in Plastic Pallets Could Be Leaching into Food, Says Group." June 26, 2009, FoodProductionDaily.com, www .foodproductiondaily.com/Quality-Safety/Toxic-chemical-in-plastic-pallets -could-be-leaching-into-food-says-group.
3. Tom Philpott, "E. Coli O157 Comes Back With a Vengeance,"*Grist Magazine*, June 29, 2009, www.grist.org/article/2009-06-29-meat-wagon-O157.
4. Barbara Feiner, "Victory Garden Revival," OrganicAuthority.com, June 18, 2008, www.organicauthority.com/blog/organic/victory-garden-revival-green-living -green-savings/ and MasterGardening.com, http://mastergardening.com.
5. "Planning and Preparing Your Vegetable Garden Site," Oregon State University, October, 1999, http://extension.oregonstate.edu/catalog/html/ec/ec1228.
6. "Block Style Layout in Raised Bed Vegetable Gardens," Colorado State University, http://cmg.colostate.edu/gardennotes/713.pdf.
7. Vegetable Gardening Basics, University of California, http://camastergardeners .ucdavis.edu/files/63771.pdf.

Chapter 10: Health, Medicine, and Disease

1. *USA Today*/AP, "Study Shows More Americans Taking Prescription Drugs," May 14, 2009, www.usatoday.com/news/health/2008-05-14-medication-nation_N.htm.
2. Cresson Kearny, "Prevention of Thyroid Damage From Radioactive Iodines," Nuclear War Survival Skills, www.ki4u.com/free_book/s73p924 .htm#Message2476.
3. Public Health Reports, "Can the Health-Care System Meet the Challenge of Pandemic Flu? Planning, Ethical and Workforce Considerations," September –October 2007, www.publichealthreports.org/userfiles/122_5/4_PHR122-5_ 573-578.pdf.

Chapter 11: Your House, Home Security, and Power

1. Robert J. Shiller, *Irrational Exuberance*, 2nd Edition, www.irrationalexuberance .com/index.htm.
2. Bloomberg News, "Financial Rescue Nears GDP as Pledges Top $12.8 Trillion," www.bloomberg.com/apps/news?pid=20601087&sid=armOzfkwtCA4.
3. *USA Today*, "How Will the $787 Billion Stimulus Package Affect You?" www .usatoday.com/money/economy/2009-02-12-stimulus-package-effects_N.htm.
4. www.oftwominds.com/blogapr09/housing-not-coming-back04-09.html.
5. Levi Mortensen, Home Alarms Deconstructed, http://ezinearticles .com/?Home-Alarms-Deconstructed&id=2244478.
6. Annora Smith, "Preventing Burglary," http://www.articlesbase.com/ business-articles/preventing-burglary-through-quality-burglary-repairs -877371.html.

7. Michelle M. Kelly, "How to Select a Home Security System Provider," http:// ezinearticles.com/?How-to-Select-a-Home-Security-Systems-Provider—ADT, -Brinks,-Monotronics—So-Many-Options&id=1888812.
8. Nor are they effective dogs, for that matter.
9. Eric Guida, "Residential Forcible Entry," *Fire Nuggets*, January 2007.
10. "How to Make and Use a Sawdust Toilet," www.appropedia.org/ How_to_make_and_use_a_sawdust_toilet.
11. Brent Snavely, "Challenges to Grow with Electric Cars' Sales: Aging Grid Needs to Handle More Power." April 17, 2009
12. CBS News, "Solar Power for Your Home," Aug. 7, 2007, www.cbsnews.com/ stories/2007/08/06/earlyshow/contributors/dannyseo/main3138054.shtml.
13. How Stuff Works, "How Emergency Power Systems Work," http://home .howstuffworks.com/home-improvement/household-safety/security/emergency -power2.htm.
14. U.S. Department of Energy, "Active Solar Heating," www.energysavers.gov/ your_home/space_heating_cooling/index.cfm/mytopic=12490.
15. *National Geographic*, National Recycling Coalition, "True Green, 100 Everyday Ways You Can Contribute to a Healthier Planet," 2007.
16. *USA Today*, "Going Green," April 23, 2008.
17. University of Florida Institute of Food and Agriculture Services Electronic Data Information Source. "The Conservation Balancing Act: Part II, In the Bathroom," (PDF), 2001, http://edis.ifas.ufl.edu/pdffiles/FY/FY13800.pdf.
18. Logan Ward, "50 Tools Everyone Should Own (With Tips!)," *Popular Mechanics*, May 2009.
19. Rolfe Cobleigh, *Handy Farm Devices and How to Use Them*, New York: James R. Babb, 1996, 7–8.

Chapter 12: Education and Entertainment

1. California State University, Northridge, Television and Health.
2. *LA Times*, "Americans Now Watch More TV Than Ever," Nov. 24, 2008.
3. www.einet.net/directory/953801/Schools_and_Courses.htm.
4. *Forbes Traveler*, "10 Unplugged Vacations," June 26, 2008.
5. EIA, "US Electricity Generation Broke Down as 49% Coal, 22% Natural Gas, 19% Nuclear, 6% Hydropower, and 2.5% Renewables," 2007.
6. Jacqui Cheng, "Microsoft: 3% of E-Mail Is Stuff We Want; the Rest Is Spam," ars technical, April 8, 2009, http://arstechnica.com/security/news/2009/04/ microsoft-97-percent-of-all-e-mail-is-spam.ars.

Chapter 13: Transportation

1. Energy Information Adminstration Petroleum Navigator, February 2009, http://tonto.eia.doe.gov/dnav/pet/hist/mtpupus2m.htm.
2. Jay Inslee, *Apollo's Fire: Igniting America's Clean Energy Economy*. Washington, DC: Island Press, 2008, 14.

3. EIA, "Crude Oil and Total Petroleum Imports Top 15 Countries," May 28, 2009, www.eia.doe.gov/pub/oil_gas/petroleum/data_publications/company_level_imports/current/import.html.
4. *Reuters*, "Mexico Oil Output Falls," April 21, 2009.
5. www.fueleconomy.gov, "Driving More Efficiently," www.fueleconomy.gov/feg/driveHabits.shtml.
6. Treehugger.com, "Low Rolling Resistance Tires," www.treehugger.com/files/2005/05/low_rolling_res.php.
7. Not really true—there's Kevlar in the tires, but that doesn't mean they're bulletproof.
8. Wisegeek.com, "What is a Tire Lever?" www.wisegeek.com/what-is-a-tire-lever.htm.

Chapter 14: The Final Option—Evacuate

1. GenDisasters.com, "Youngstown, FL Train Derailment with Chlorine Gas Cloud," Feb. 1978.
2. CALEA, "The Graniteville Train Disaster," www.calea.org/online/newsletter/No88/graniteville.htm.
3. *USA Today*, "Rail Industry Petitions to Stop Moving Toxins," May 18, 2009, www.usatoday.com/news/nation/2009-05-19-chemrail_N.htm?csp=34.

About the Author

Sean Brodrick is a natural resources analyst for Weiss Research. He writes about gold, oil, and other natural resources, and travels far and wide searching for small-cap values. He is the editor of *Red-Hot Global Small-Caps* and a regular contributor to Uncommon Wisdom Daily (www.uncommonwisdomdaily.com).

Recognized for his expertise on natural resources and Canadian and Australian investment opportunities, Brodrick has been featured on many financial talk shows, including *CNBC Squawk Box, Fox Business, CNN, The Glenn Beck Show, Your World with Neil Cavuto,* and *Bloomberg Market Line.* He is a contributing columnist to MarketWatch.com, and a frequent commentator on one of Canada's premiere financial web sites, HoweStreet.com.

In his spare time, Brodrick rides his bike, works on his garden, and prepares for the end of civilization as we know it, and what comes next.

Index

From the Author

As my way of saying "thank you" for reading my book, I have a special report for you on the Web. You can find it by pointing your web browser to http://www.uncommonwisdom daily.com/bookoffer.

To read my daily web commentary on the markets, natural resources, and more that you'll need to know to survive the coming economic and societal upheavals, point your browser to my Red-Hot Energy and Gold blog at http://blogs.uncom monwisdomdaily.com.

Best,

Sean